A JOHN CONSTANTINE
GRAPHIC NOVEL

HELLBLAZER

PANDEMONIUM

WRITER
JAMIE DELANO

ARTIST
JOCK

LETTERER
CLEM ROBINS

Karen Berger SVP – Executive Editor
Pornsak Pichetshote and Casey Seijas Editors
Robbin Brosterman Design Director – Books
Louis Prandi Art Director

DC COMICS
Paul Levitz President & Publisher
Richard Bruning SVP – Creative Director
Patrick Caldon EVP – Finance & Operations
Amy Genkins SVP – Business & Legal Affairs
Jim Lee Editorial Director – WildStorm
Gregory Noveck SVP – Creative Affairs
Steve Rotterdam SVP – Sales & Marketing
Cheryl Rubin SVP – Brand Management

JOHN CONSTANTINE, HELLBLAZER: PANDEMONIUM
Published by DC Comics, 1700 Broadway, New York, NY 10019
Copyright © 2010 DC Comics. All Rights Reserved. All
characters featured in this publication, the distinctive
likenesses thereof and related elements are trademarks
of DC Comics. VERTIGO is a trademark of DC Comics.
HC ISBN: 978-1-4012-2035-8
SC ISBN: 978-1-4012-2039-6

SUSTAINABLE
FORESTRY
INITIATIVE
Certified Chain of Custody
Promoting Sustainable
Forest Management

Fiber used in this product line meets the
sourcing requirements of the SFI program.
www.sfiprogram.org NFS-SPICOC-C0001801

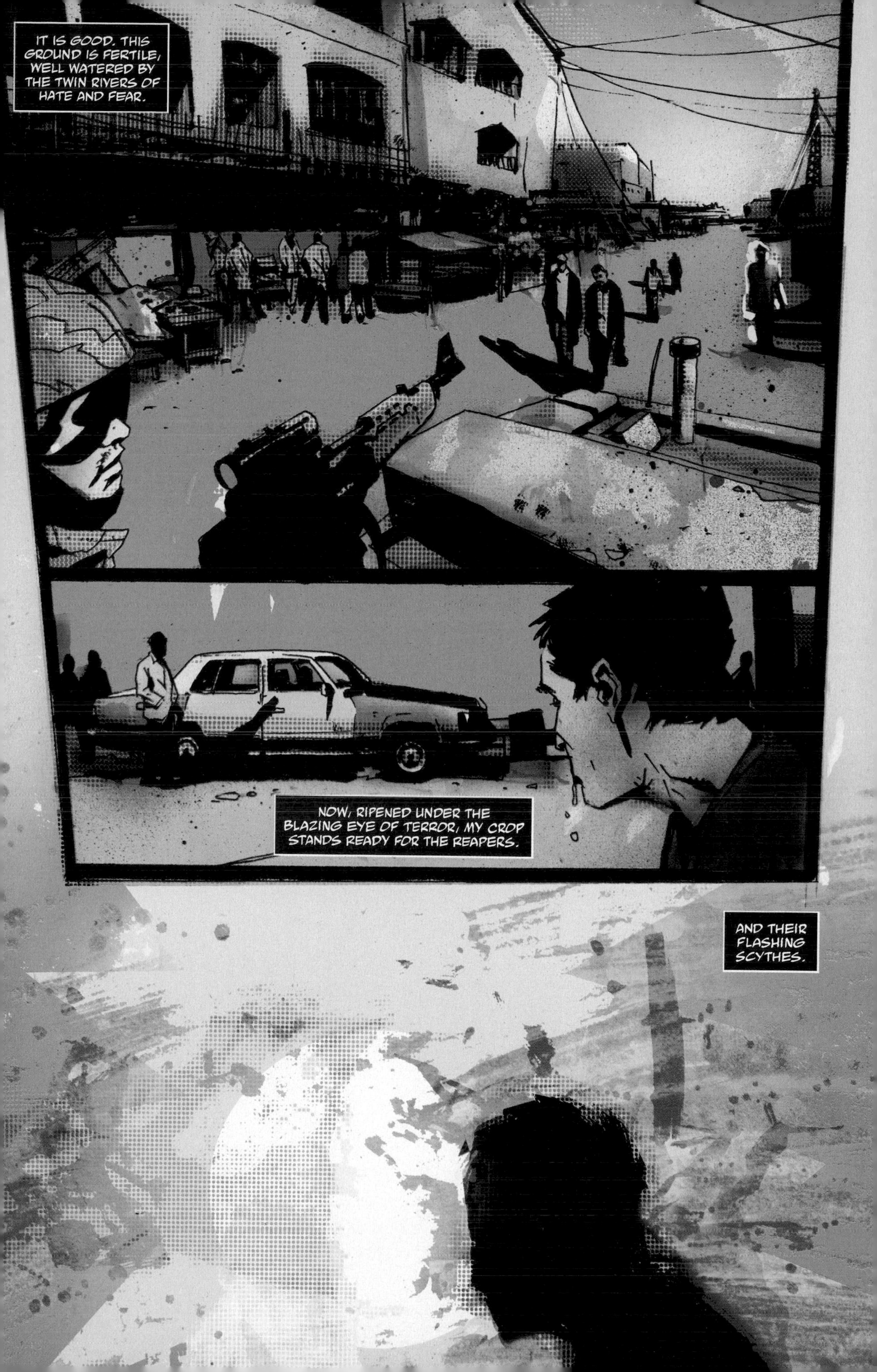
IT IS GOOD. THIS GROUND IS FERTILE, WELL WATERED BY THE TWIN RIVERS OF HATE AND FEAR.
NOW, RIPENED UNDER THE BLAZING EYE OF TERROR, MY CROP STANDS READY FOR THE REAPERS.
AND THEIR FLASHING SCYTHES.

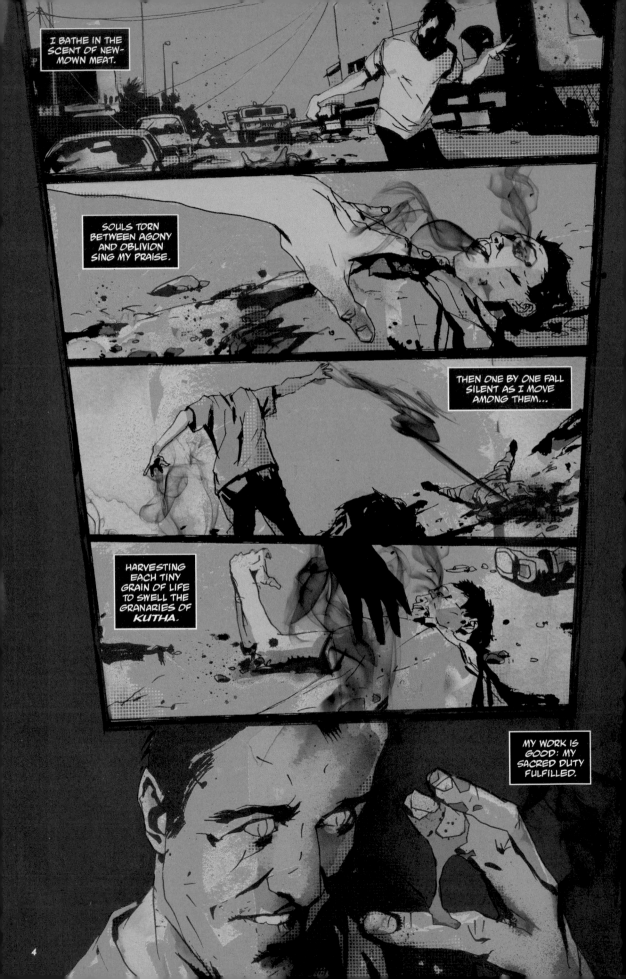

I BATHE IN THE SCENT OF NEW-MOWN MEAT.

SOULS TORN BETWEEN AGONY AND OBLIVION SING MY PRAISE.

THEN ONE BY ONE FALL SILENT AS I MOVE AMONG THEM...

HARVESTING EACH TINY GRAIN OF LIFE TO SWELL THE GRANARIES OF *KUTHA*.

MY WORK IS GOOD: MY SACRED DUTY FULFILLED.

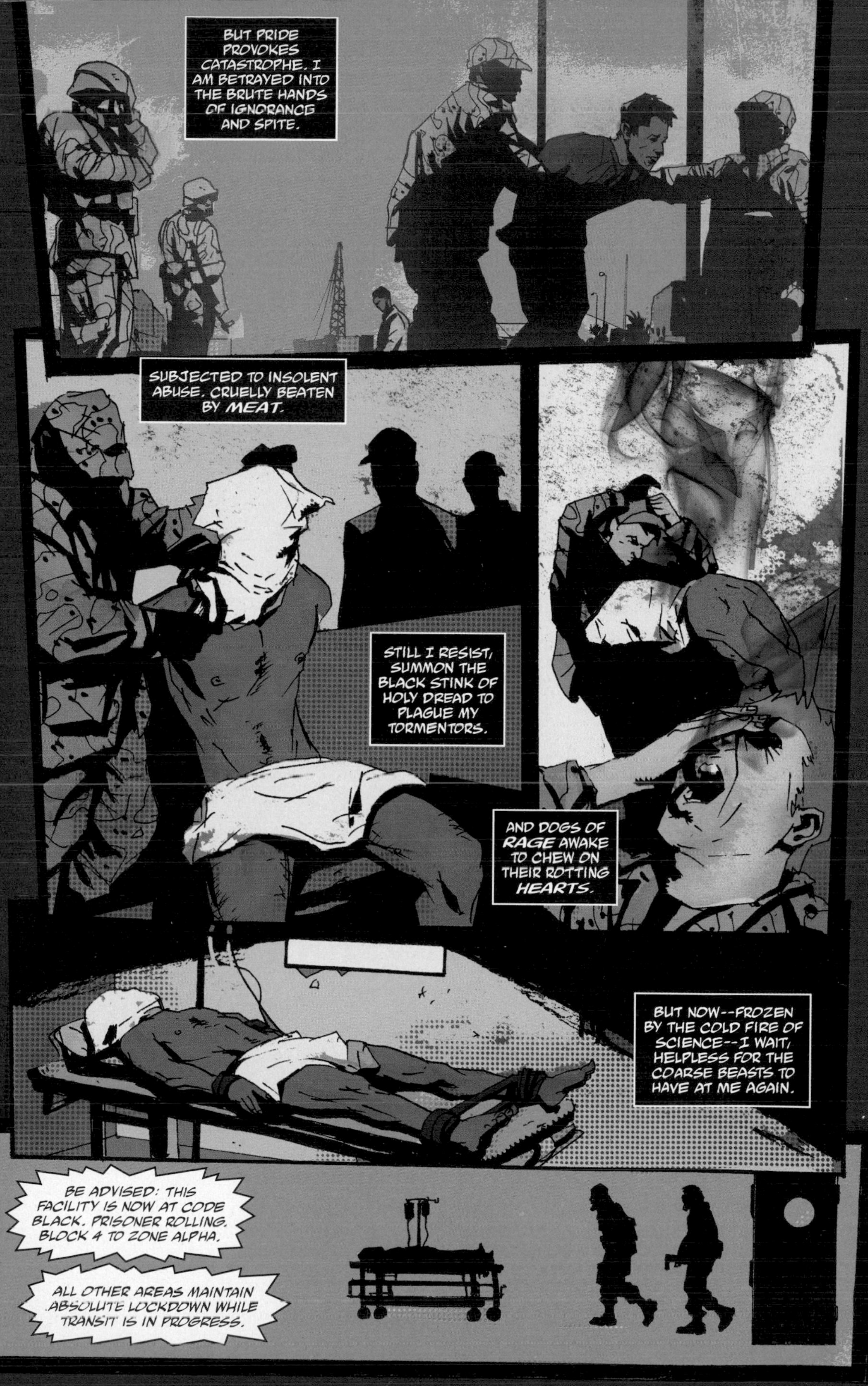
BUT PRIDE PROVOKES CATASTROPHE. I AM BETRAYED INTO THE BRUTE HANDS OF IGNORANCE AND SPITE.
SUBJECTED TO INSOLENT ABUSE. CRUELLY BEATEN BY MEAT.
STILL I RESIST, SUMMON THE BLACK STINK OF HOLY DREAD TO PLAGUE MY TORMENTORS.
AND DOGS OF RAGE AWAKE TO CHEW ON THEIR ROTTING HEARTS.
BUT NOW--FROZEN BY THE COLD FIRE OF SCIENCE--I WAIT, HELPLESS FOR THE COARSE BEASTS TO HAVE AT ME AGAIN.
BE ADVISED: THIS FACILITY IS NOW AT CODE BLACK. PRISONER ROLLING. BLOCK 4 TO ZONE ALPHA.
ALL OTHER AREAS MAINTAIN ABSOLUTE LOCKDOWN WHILE TRANSIT IS IN PROGRESS.

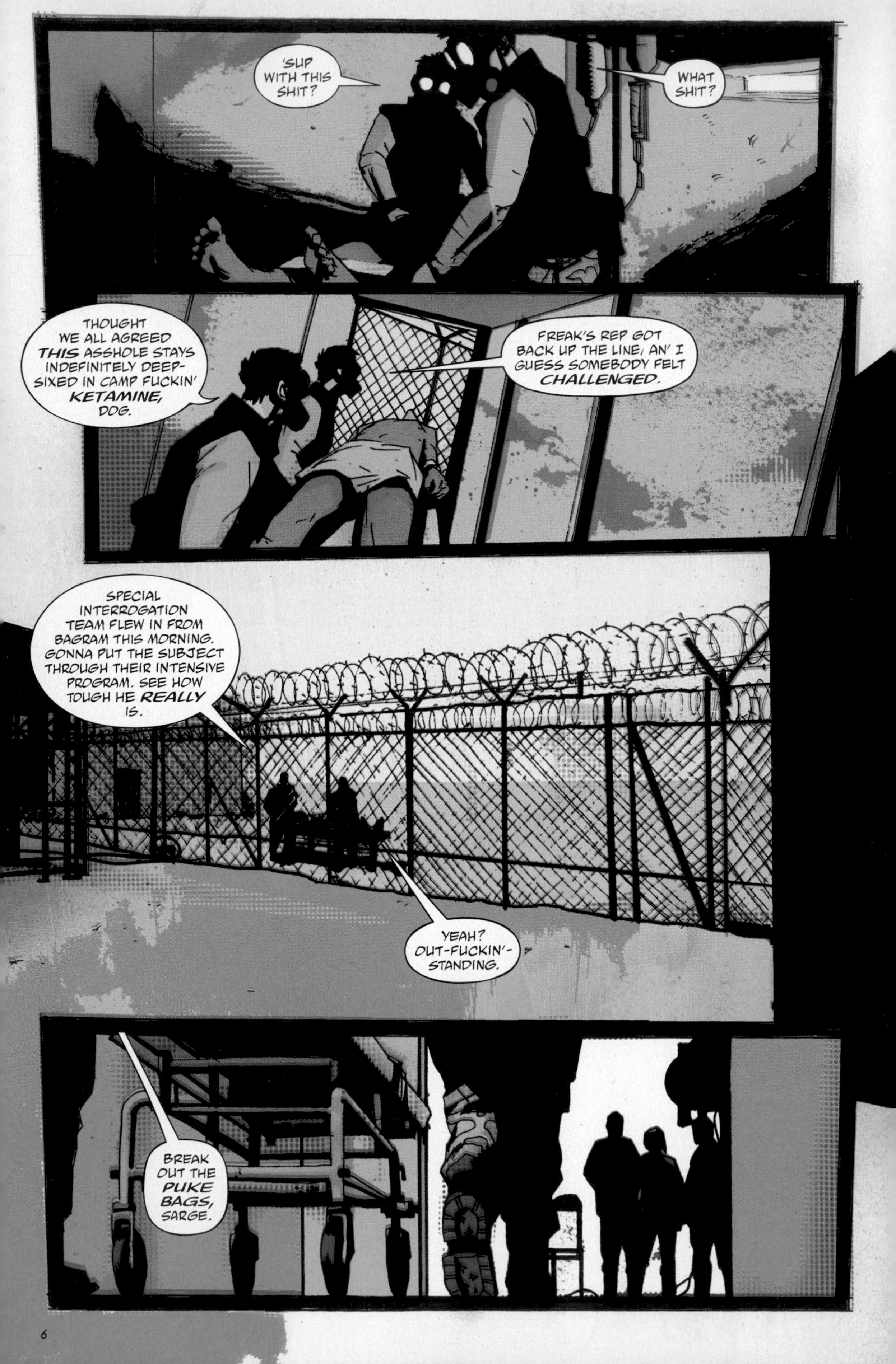
'SUP WITH THIS SHIT?
WHAT SHIT?
THOUGHT WE ALL AGREED THIS ASSHOLE STAYS INDEFINITELY DEEP-SIXED IN CAMP FUCKIN' KETAMINE, DOG.
FREAK'S REP GOT BACK UP THE LINE, AN' I GUESS SOMEBODY FELT CHALLENGED.
SPECIAL INTERROGATION TEAM FLEW IN FROM BAGRAM THIS MORNING. GONNA PUT THE SUBJECT THROUGH THEIR INTENSIVE PROGRAM. SEE HOW TOUGH HE REALLY IS.
YEAH? OUT-FUCKIN'-STANDING.
BREAK OUT THE PUKE BAGS, SARGE.

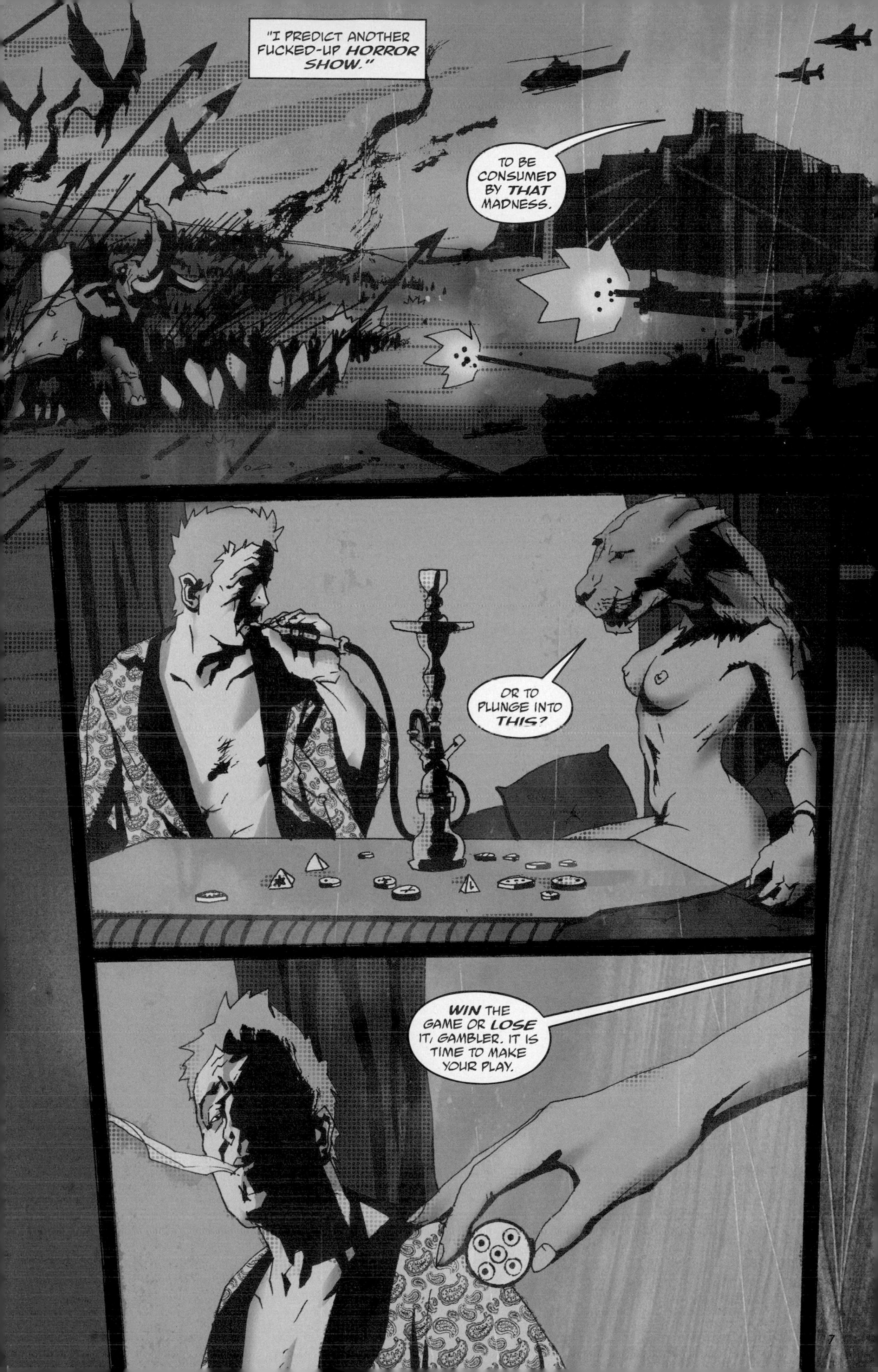
"I PREDICT ANOTHER FUCKED-UP HORROR SHOW."
TO BE CONSUMED BY THAT MADNESS.
OR TO PLUNGE INTO THIS?
WIN THE GAME OR LOSE IT, GAMBLER. IT IS TIME TO MAKE YOUR PLAY.

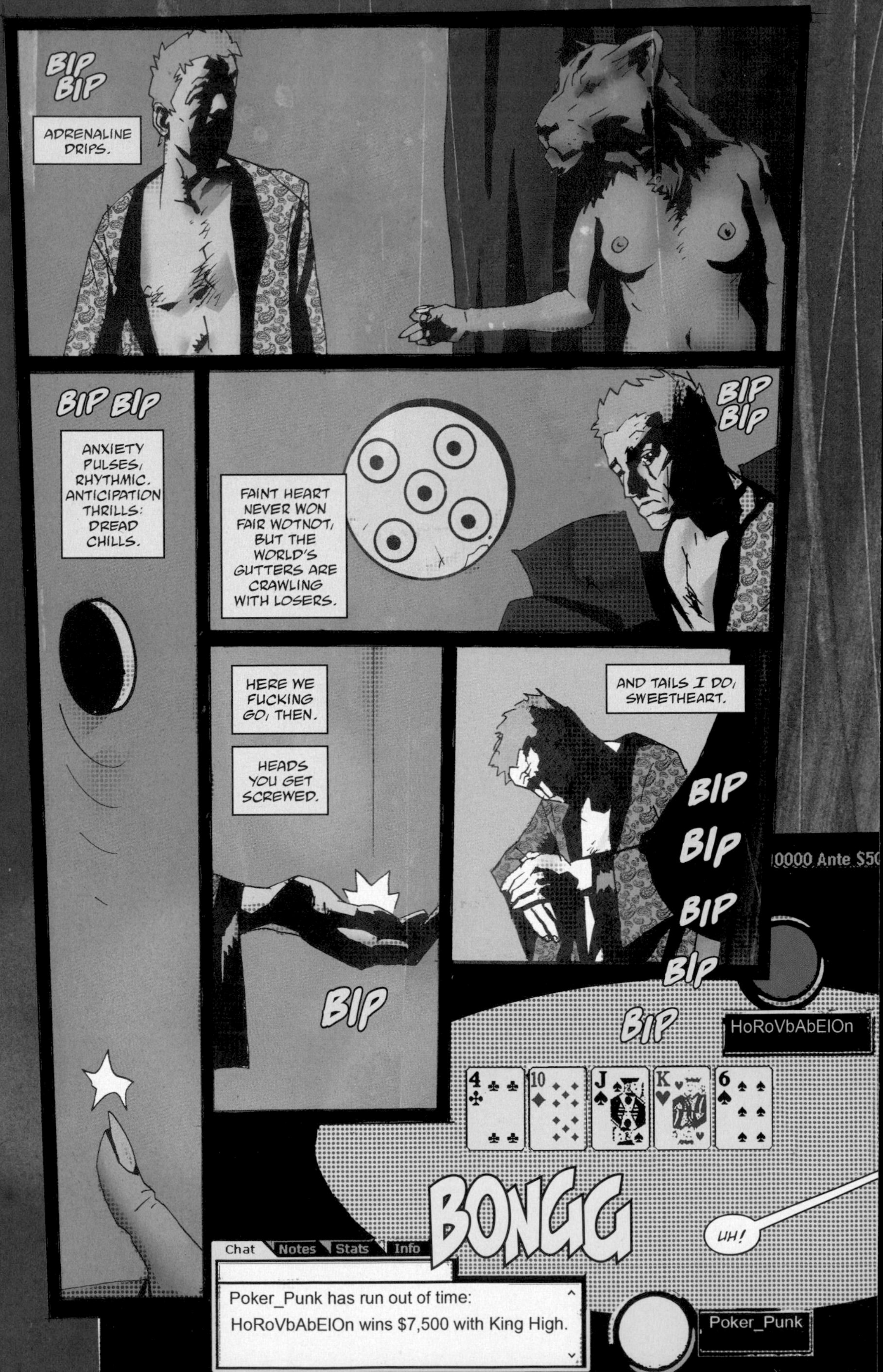
BIP BIP
ADRENALINE DRIPS.
BIP BIP
ANXIETY PULSES, RHYTHMIC. ANTICIPATION THRILLS: DREAD CHILLS.
FAINT HEART NEVER WON FAIR WOTNOT, BUT THE WORLD'S GUTTERS ARE CRAWLING WITH LOSERS.
BIP BIP
HERE WE FUCKING GO, THEN.
HEADS YOU GET SCREWED.
AND TAILS I DO, SWEETHEART.
BIP
BIP
BIP
BIP
BIP
BIP
0000 Ante $50
HoRoVbAbElOn
BONGG
UH!
Chat
Notes
Stats
Info
Poker_Punk has run out of time:
HoRoVbAbElOn wins $7,500 with King High.
Poker_Punk

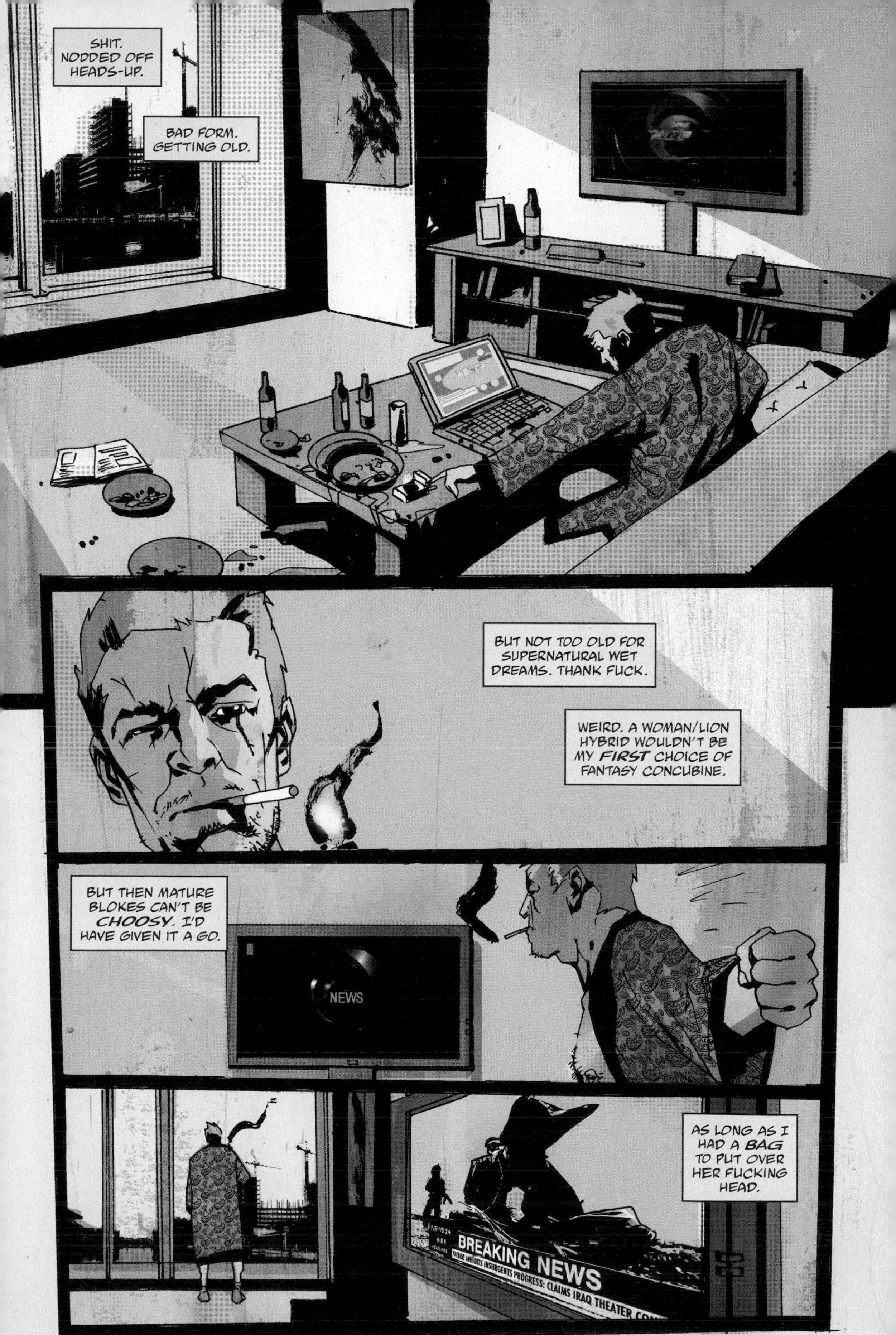
SHIT. NODDED OFF HEADS-UP.
BAD FORM. GETTING OLD.
BUT NOT TOO OLD FOR SUPERNATURAL WET DREAMS. THANK FUCK.
WEIRD. A WOMAN/LION HYBRID WOULDN'T BE MY FIRST CHOICE OF FANTASY CONCUBINE.
BUT THEN MATURE BLOKES CAN'T BE CHOOSY. I'D HAVE GIVEN IT A GO.
NEWS
AS LONG AS I HAD A BAG TO PUT OVER HER FUCKING HEAD.
BREAKING NEWS

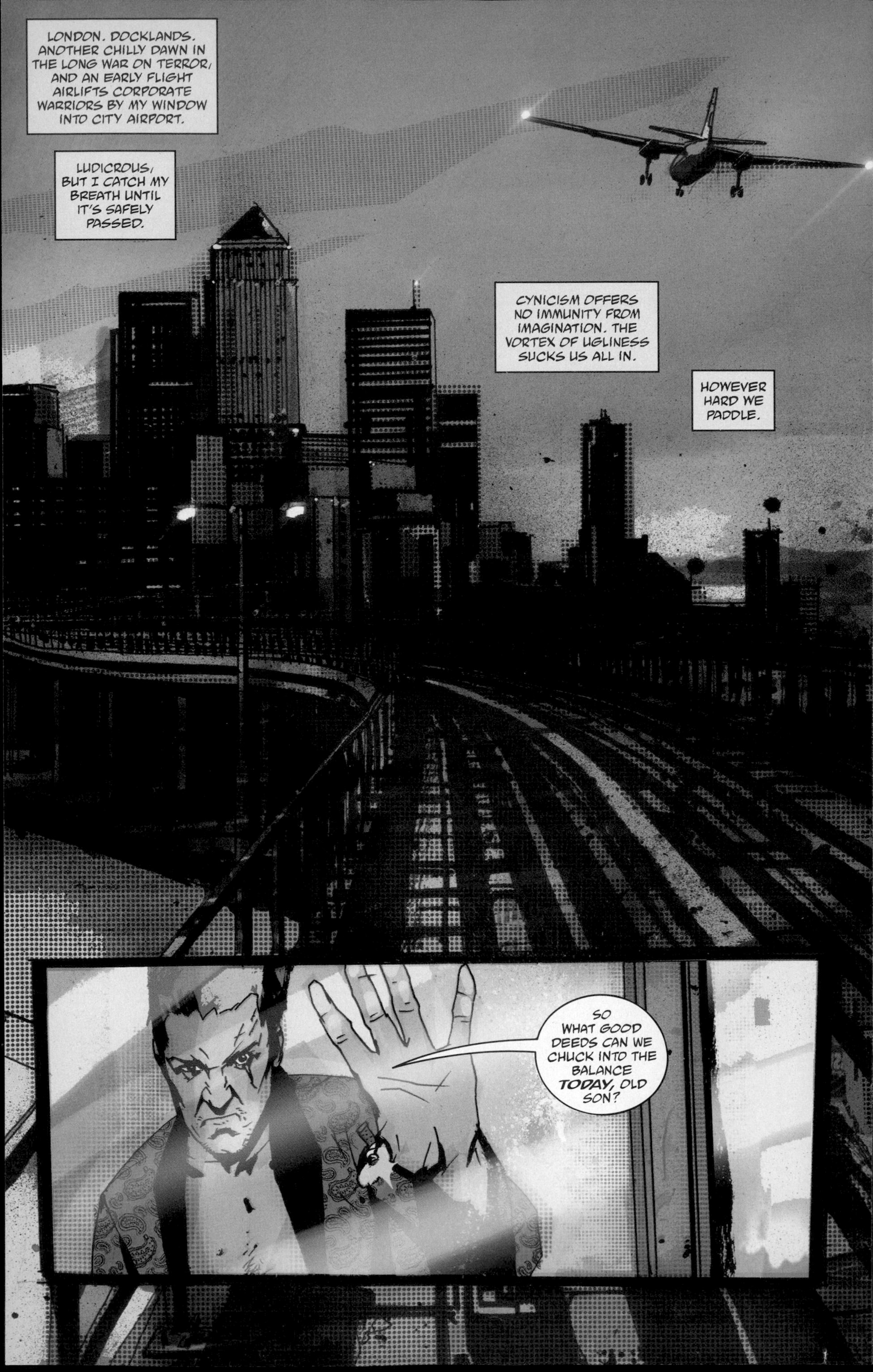
LONDON. DOCKLANDS. ANOTHER CHILLY DAWN IN THE LONG WAR ON TERROR, AND AN EARLY FLIGHT AIRLIFTS CORPORATE WARRIORS BY MY WINDOW INTO CITY AIRPORT.
LUDICROUS, BUT I CATCH MY BREATH UNTIL IT'S SAFELY PASSED.
CYNICISM OFFERS NO IMMUNITY FROM IMAGINATION. THE VORTEX OF UGLINESS SUCKS US ALL IN.
HOWEVER HARD WE PADDLE.
SO WHAT GOOD DEEDS CAN WE CHUCK INTO THE BALANCE *TODAY*, OLD SON?

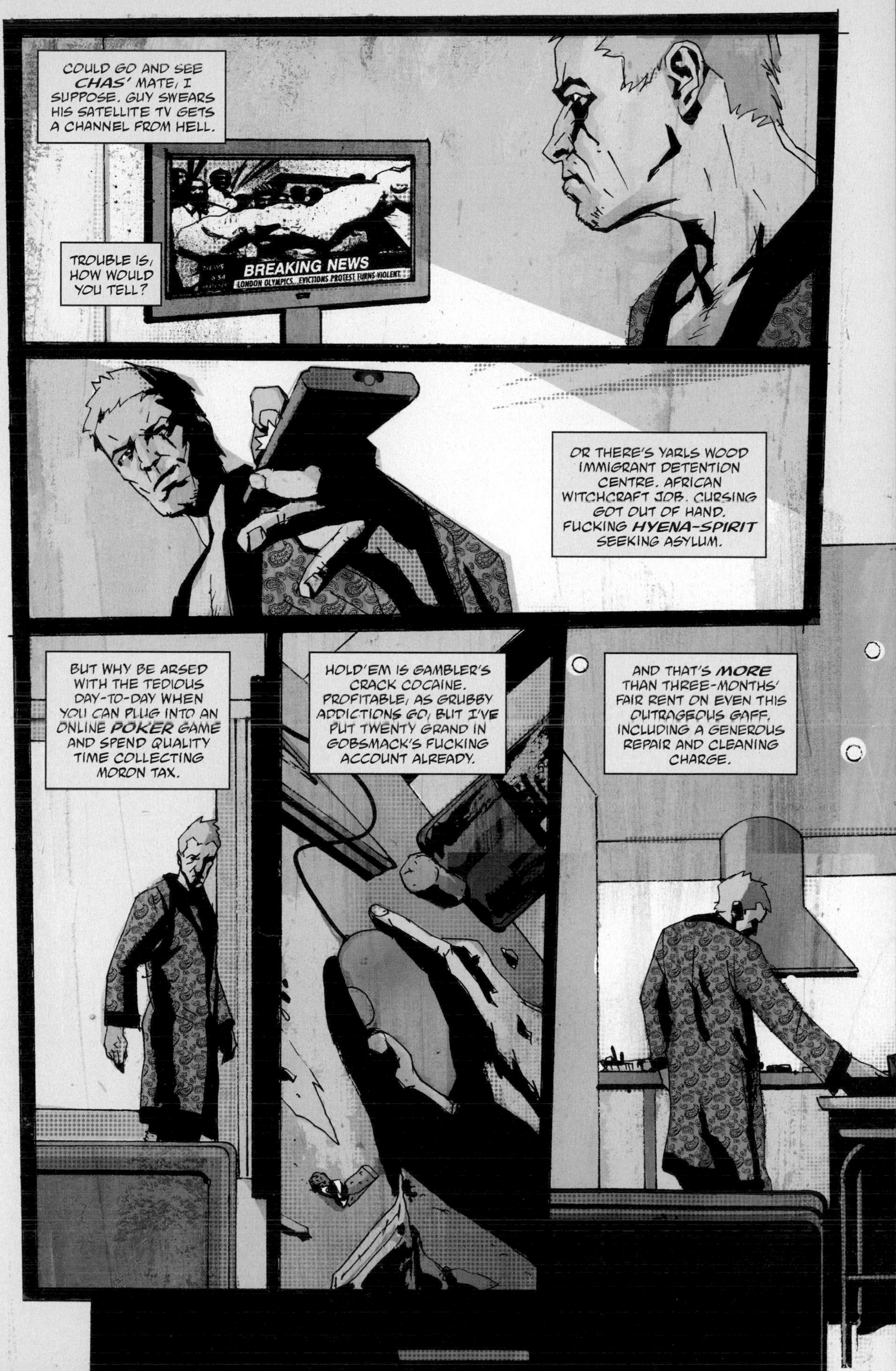
COULD GO AND SEE CHAS' MATE, I SUPPOSE. GUY SWEARS HIS SATELLITE TV GETS A CHANNEL FROM HELL.
BREAKING NEWS
LONDON OLYMPICS...EVICTIONS PROTEST TURNS VIOLENT
TROUBLE IS, HOW WOULD YOU TELL?
OR THERE'S YARLS WOOD IMMIGRANT DETENTION CENTRE. AFRICAN WITCHCRAFT JOB. CURSING GOT OUT OF HAND. FUCKING HYENA-SPIRIT SEEKING ASYLUM.
BUT WHY BE ARSED WITH THE TEDIOUS DAY-TO-DAY WHEN YOU CAN PLUG INTO AN ONLINE POKER GAME AND SPEND QUALITY TIME COLLECTING MORON TAX.
HOLD'EM IS GAMBLER'S CRACK COCAINE. PROFITABLE, AS GRUBBY ADDICTIONS GO, BUT I'VE PUT TWENTY GRAND IN GOBSMACK'S FUCKING ACCOUNT ALREADY.
AND THAT'S MORE THAN THREE-MONTHS' FAIR RENT ON EVEN THIS OUTRAGEOUS GAFF, INCLUDING A GENEROUS REPAIR AND CLEANING CHARGE.

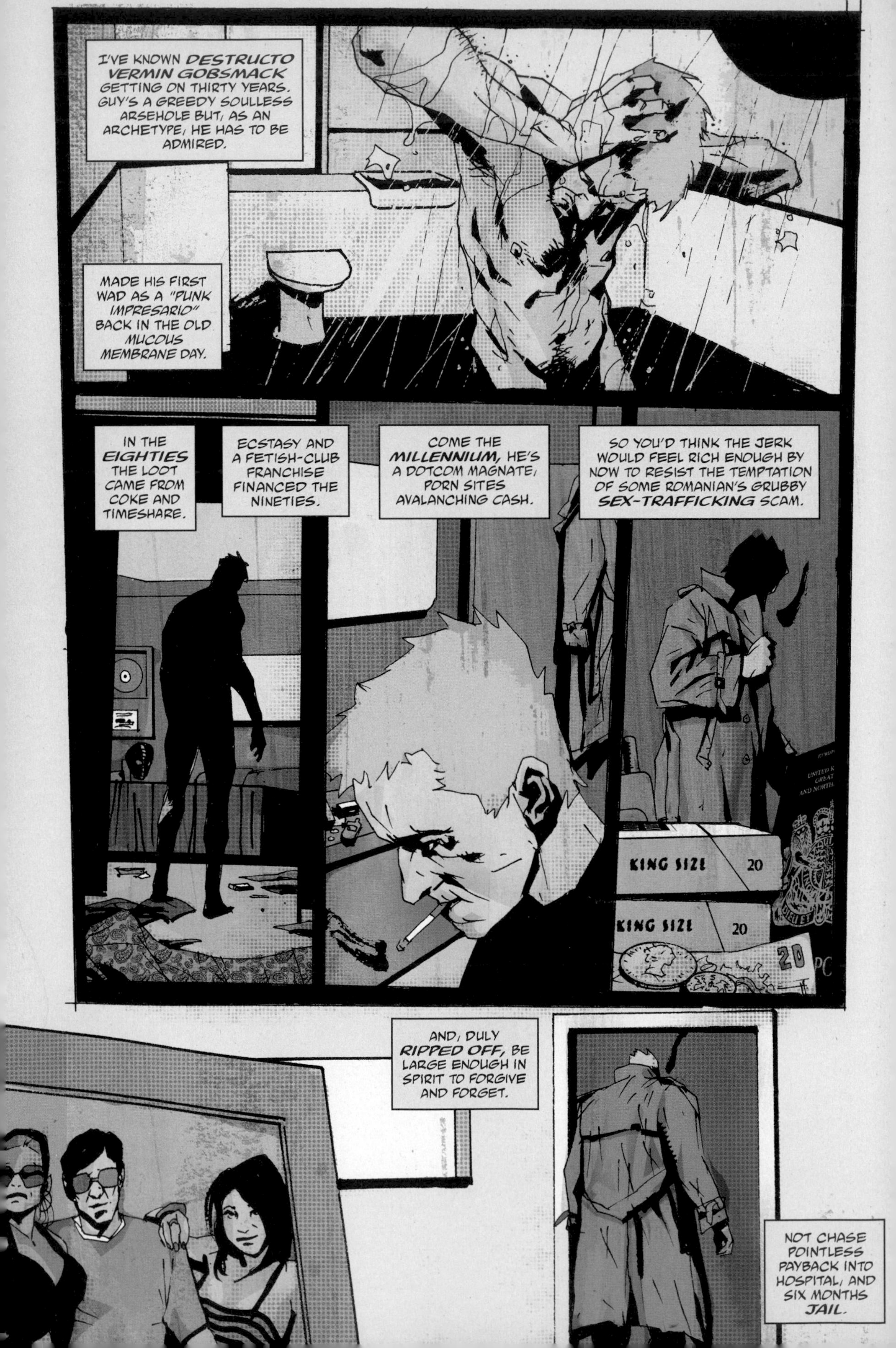
I'VE KNOWN DESTRUCTO VERMIN GOBSMACK GETTING ON THIRTY YEARS. GUY'S A GREEDY SOULLESS ARSEHOLE BUT, AS AN ARCHETYPE, HE HAS TO BE ADMIRED.
MADE HIS FIRST WAD AS A "PUNK IMPRESARIO" BACK IN THE OLD MUCOUS MEMBRANE DAY.
IN THE EIGHTIES THE LOOT CAME FROM COKE AND TIMESHARE.
ECSTASY AND A FETISH-CLUB FRANCHISE FINANCED THE NINETIES.
COME THE MILLENNIUM, HE'S A DOTCOM MAGNATE, PORN SITES AVALANCHING CASH.
SO YOU'D THINK THE JERK WOULD FEEL RICH ENOUGH BY NOW TO RESIST THE TEMPTATION OF SOME ROMANIAN'S GRUBBY SEX-TRAFFICKING SCAM.
KING SIZE 20
KING SIZE 20
AND, DULY RIPPED OFF, BE LARGE ENOUGH IN SPIRIT TO FORGIVE AND FORGET.
NOT CHASE POINTLESS PAYBACK INTO HOSPITAL, AND SIX MONTHS JAIL.

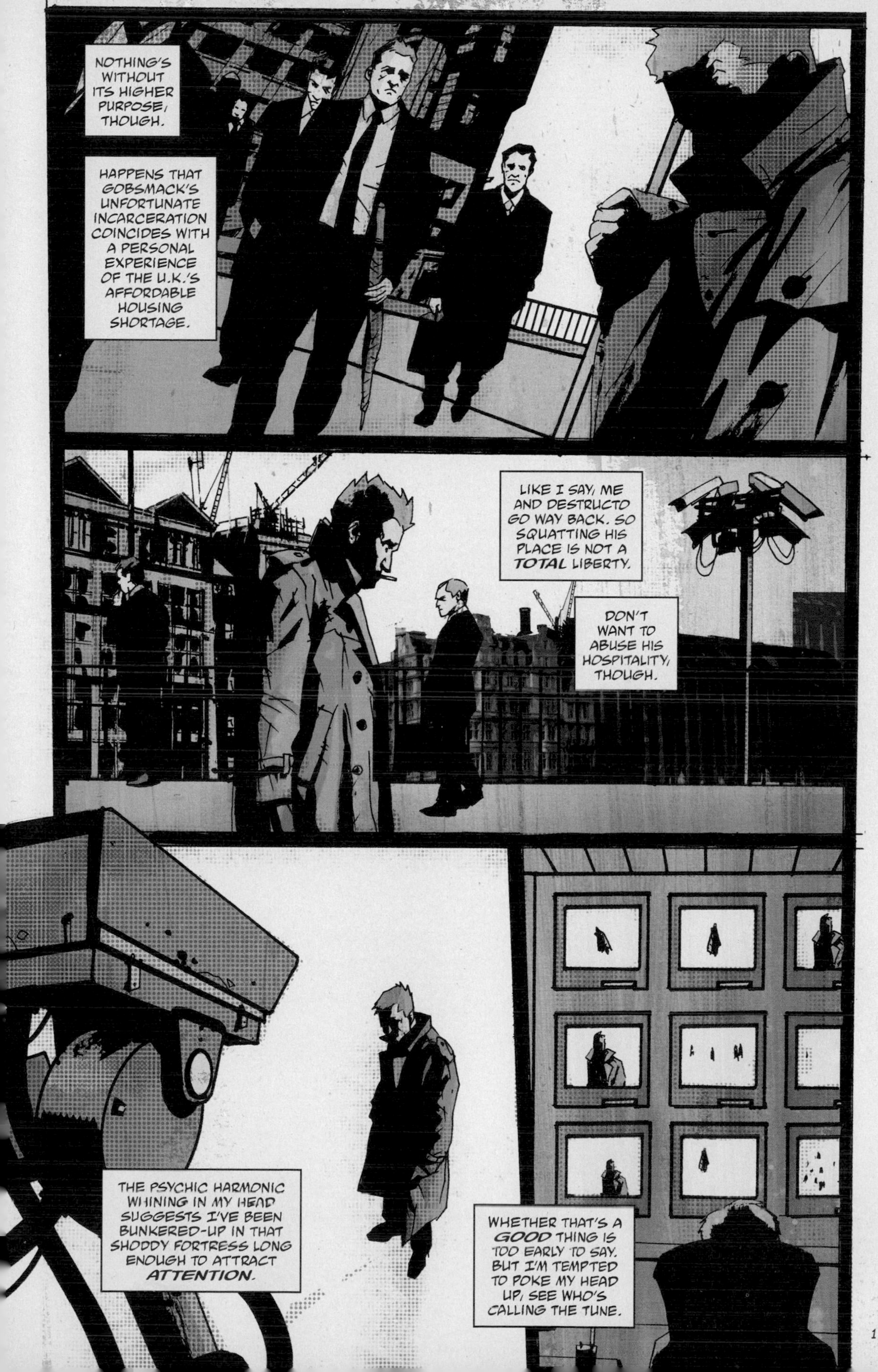
NOTHING'S WITHOUT ITS HIGHER PURPOSE, THOUGH.
HAPPENS THAT GOBSMACK'S UNFORTUNATE INCARCERATION COINCIDES WITH A PERSONAL EXPERIENCE OF THE U.K.'S AFFORDABLE HOUSING SHORTAGE.
LIKE I SAY, ME AND DESTRUCTO GO WAY BACK. SO SQUATTING HIS PLACE IS NOT A TOTAL LIBERTY.
DON'T WANT TO ABUSE HIS HOSPITALITY, THOUGH.
THE PSYCHIC HARMONIC WHINING IN MY HEAD SUGGESTS I'VE BEEN BUNKERED-UP IN THAT SHODDY FORTRESS LONG ENOUGH TO ATTRACT ATTENTION.
WHETHER THAT'S A GOOD THING IS TOO EARLY TO SAY. BUT I'M TEMPTED TO POKE MY HEAD UP, SEE WHO'S CALLING THE TUNE.

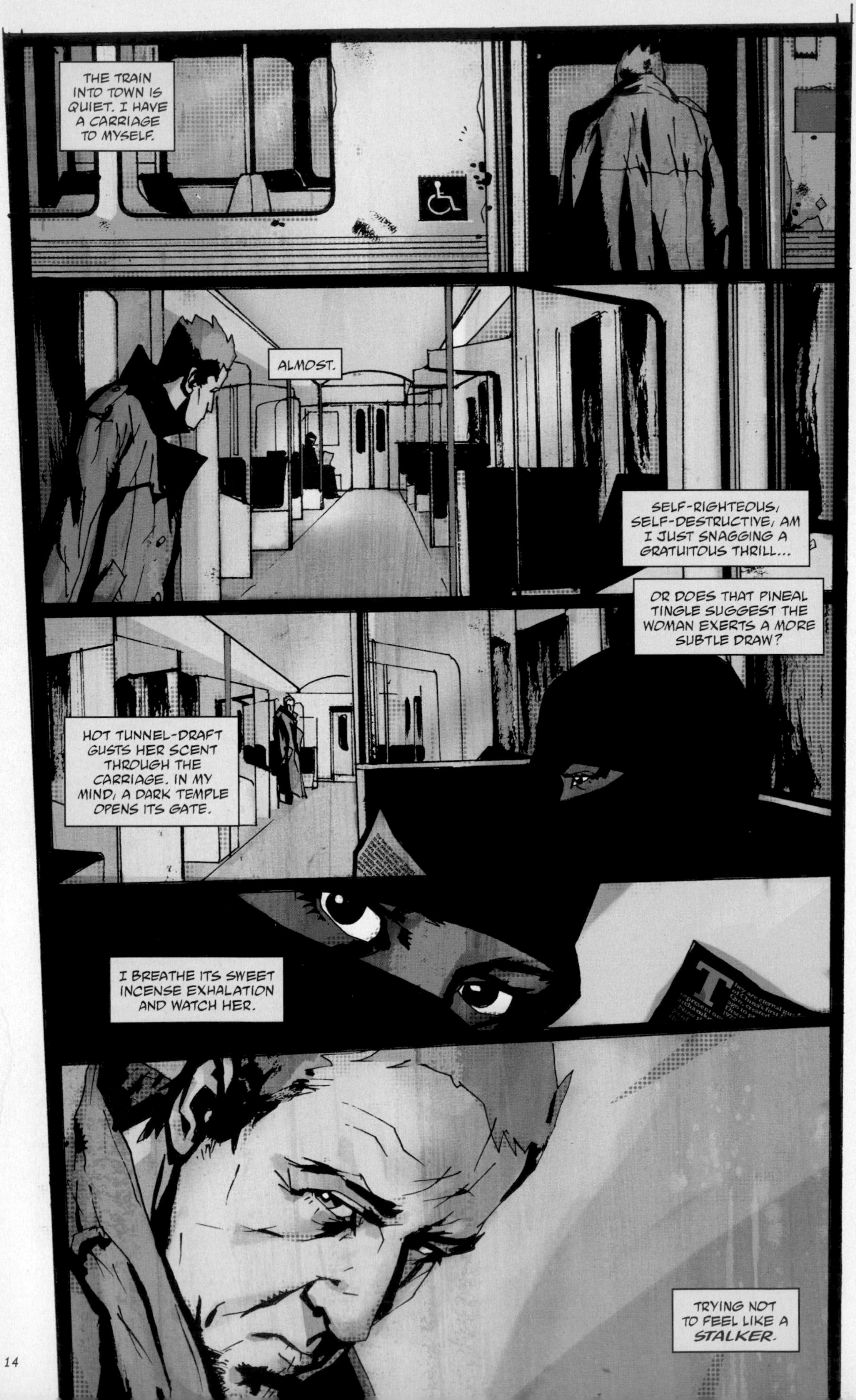
THE TRAIN INTO TOWN IS QUIET. I HAVE A CARRIAGE TO MYSELF.
ALMOST.
SELF-RIGHTEOUS, SELF-DESTRUCTIVE, AM I JUST SNAGGING A GRATUITOUS THRILL...
OR DOES THAT PINEAL TINGLE SUGGEST THE WOMAN EXERTS A MORE SUBTLE DRAW?
HOT TUNNEL-DRAFT GUSTS HER SCENT THROUGH THE CARRIAGE. IN MY MIND, A DARK TEMPLE OPENS ITS GATE.
I BREATHE ITS SWEET INCENSE EXHALATION AND WATCH HER.
TRYING NOT TO FEEL LIKE A *STALKER*.

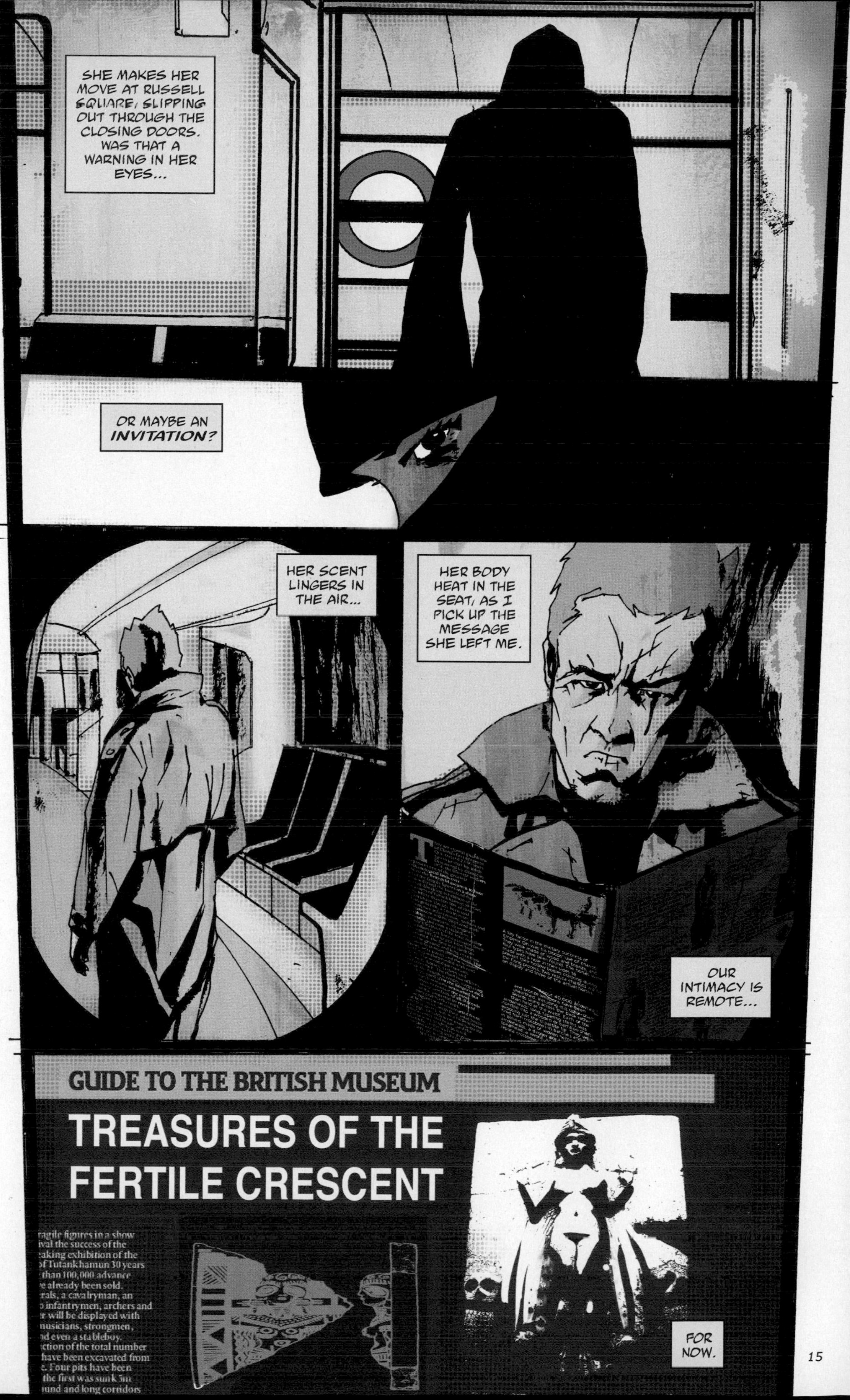
SHE MAKES HER MOVE AT RUSSELL SQUARE, SLIPPING OUT THROUGH THE CLOSING DOORS. WAS THAT A WARNING IN HER EYES...
OR MAYBE AN *INVITATION?*
HER SCENT LINGERS IN THE AIR...
HER BODY HEAT IN THE SEAT, AS I PICK UP THE MESSAGE SHE LEFT ME.
OUR INTIMACY IS REMOTE...
GUIDE TO THE BRITISH MUSEUM
TREASURES OF THE FERTILE CRESCENT
FOR NOW.

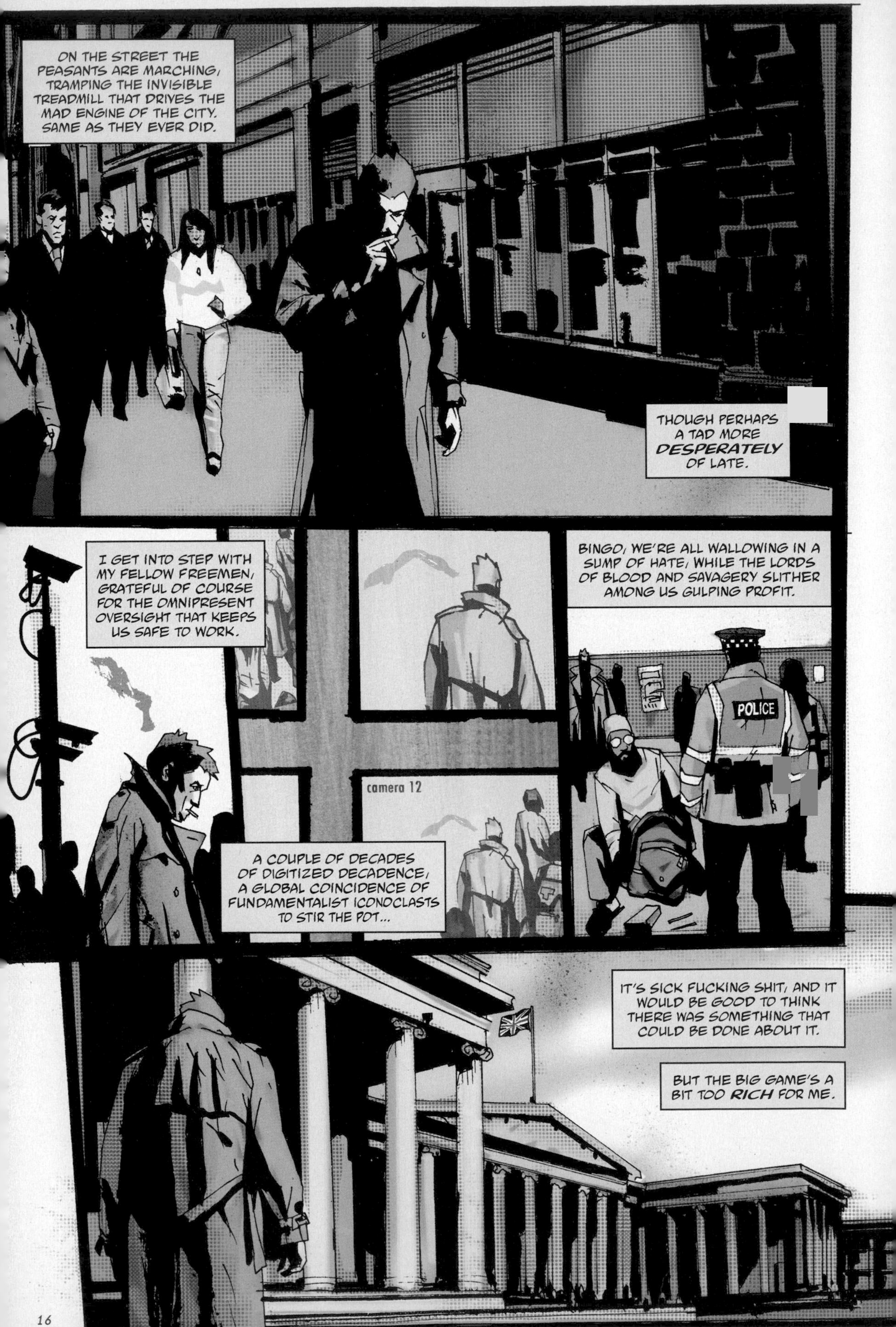
ON THE STREET THE PEASANTS ARE MARCHING, TRAMPING THE INVISIBLE TREADMILL THAT DRIVES THE MAD ENGINE OF THE CITY. SAME AS THEY EVER DID.
THOUGH PERHAPS A TAD MORE DESPERATELY OF LATE.
I GET INTO STEP WITH MY FELLOW FREEMEN, GRATEFUL OF COURSE FOR THE OMNIPRESENT OVERSIGHT THAT KEEPS US SAFE TO WORK.
camera 12
A COUPLE OF DECADES OF DIGITIZED DECADENCE, A GLOBAL COINCIDENCE OF FUNDAMENTALIST ICONOCLASTS TO STIR THE POT...
BINGO, WE'RE ALL WALLOWING IN A SUMP OF HATE, WHILE THE LORDS OF BLOOD AND SAVAGERY SLITHER AMONG US GULPING PROFIT.
POLICE
IT'S SICK FUCKING SHIT, AND IT WOULD BE GOOD TO THINK THERE WAS SOMETHING THAT COULD BE DONE ABOUT IT.
BUT THE BIG GAME'S A BIT TOO RICH FOR ME.

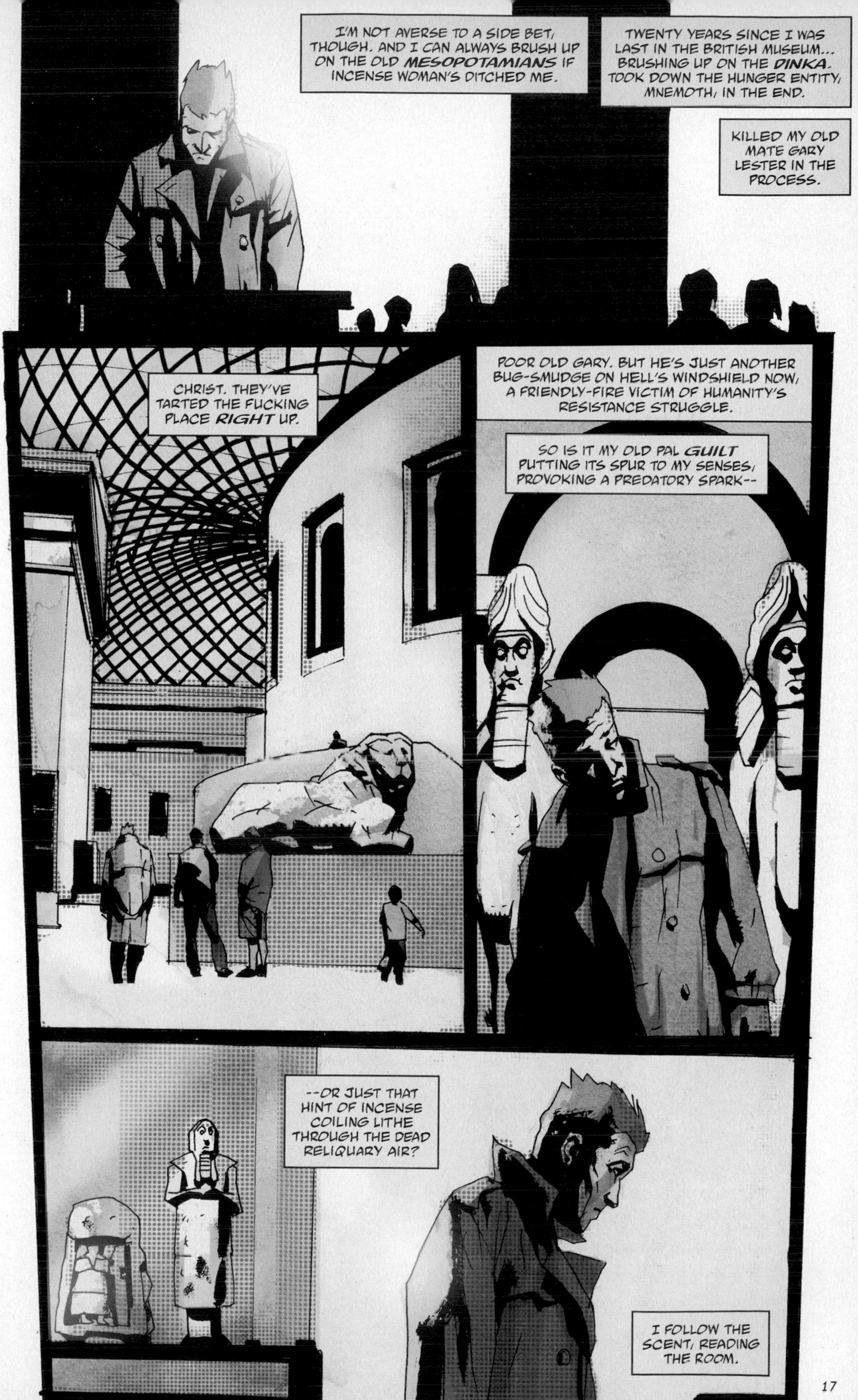
I'M NOT AVERSE TO A SIDE BET, THOUGH. AND I CAN ALWAYS BRUSH UP ON THE OLD MESOPOTAMIANS IF INCENSE WOMAN'S DITCHED ME.
TWENTY YEARS SINCE I WAS LAST IN THE BRITISH MUSEUM... BRUSHING UP ON THE DINKA. TOOK DOWN THE HUNGER ENTITY, MNEMOTH, IN THE END.
KILLED MY OLD MATE GARY LESTER IN THE PROCESS.
CHRIST. THEY'VE TARTED THE FUCKING PLACE RIGHT UP.
POOR OLD GARY. BUT HE'S JUST ANOTHER BUG-SMUDGE ON HELL'S WINDSHIELD NOW, A FRIENDLY-FIRE VICTIM OF HUMANITY'S RESISTANCE STRUGGLE.
SO IS IT MY OLD PAL GUILT PUTTING ITS SPUR TO MY SENSES, PROVOKING A PREDATORY SPARK--
--OR JUST THAT HINT OF INCENSE COILING LITHE THROUGH THE DEAD RELIQUARY AIR?
I FOLLOW THE SCENT, READING THE ROOM.

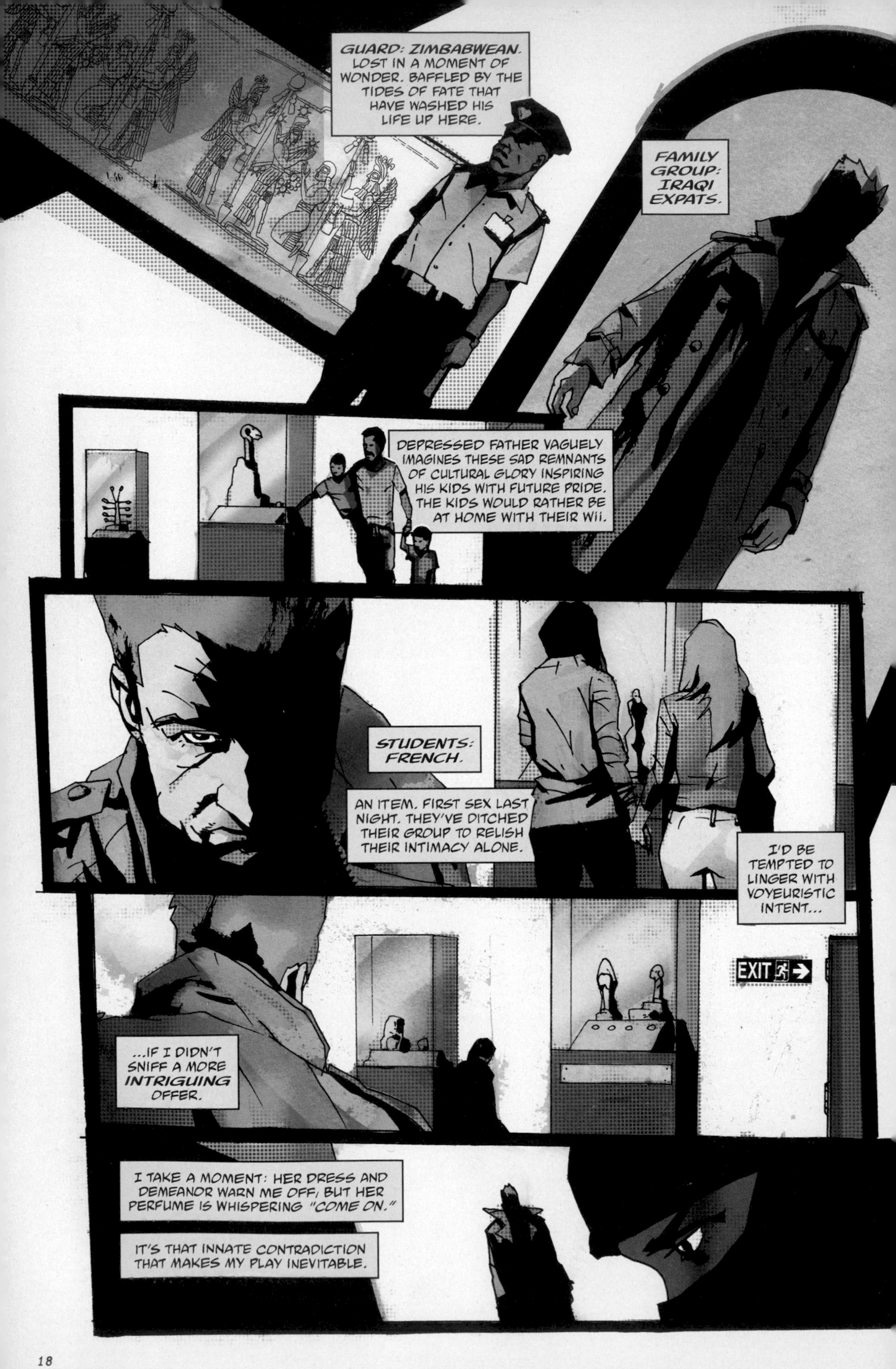
GUARD: ZIMBABWEAN. LOST IN A MOMENT OF WONDER. BAFFLED BY THE TIDES OF FATE THAT HAVE WASHED HIS LIFE UP HERE.
FAMILY GROUP: IRAQI EXPATS.
DEPRESSED FATHER VAGUELY IMAGINES THESE SAD REMNANTS OF CULTURAL GLORY INSPIRING HIS KIDS WITH FUTURE PRIDE. THE KIDS WOULD RATHER BE AT HOME WITH THEIR Wii.
STUDENTS: FRENCH.
AN ITEM. FIRST SEX LAST NIGHT. THEY'VE DITCHED THEIR GROUP TO RELISH THEIR INTIMACY ALONE.
I'D BE TEMPTED TO LINGER WITH VOYEURISTIC INTENT...
EXIT
...IF I DIDN'T SNIFF A MORE INTRIGUING OFFER.
I TAKE A MOMENT: HER DRESS AND DEMEANOR WARN ME OFF; BUT HER PERFUME IS WHISPERING "COME ON."
IT'S THAT INNATE CONTRADICTION THAT MAKES MY PLAY INEVITABLE.

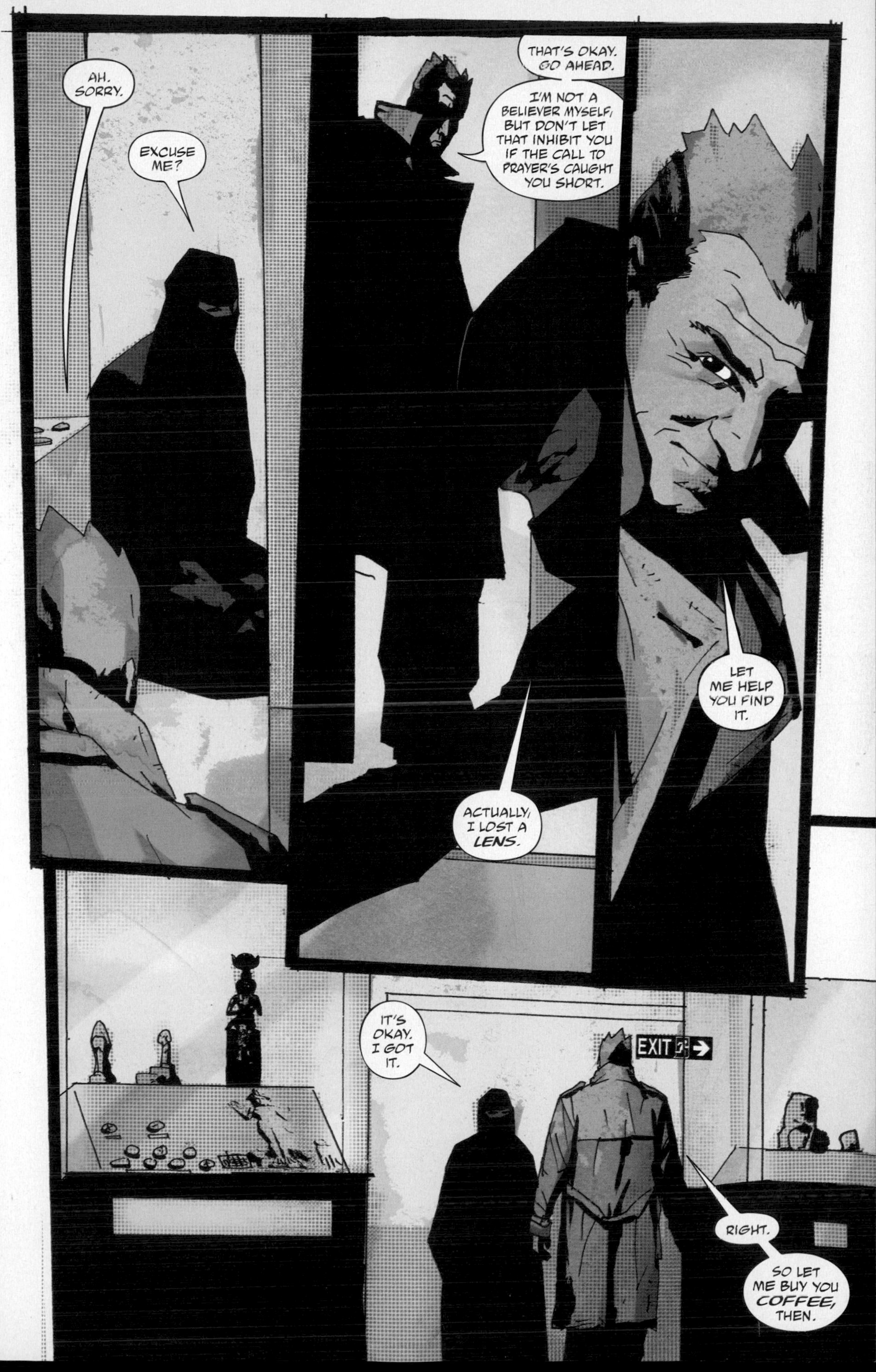
AH. SORRY.
EXCUSE ME?
THAT'S OKAY. GO AHEAD.
I'M NOT A BELIEVER MYSELF, BUT DON'T LET THAT INHIBIT YOU IF THE CALL TO PRAYER'S CAUGHT YOU SHORT.
ACTUALLY, I LOST A LENS.
LET ME HELP YOU FIND IT.
IT'S OKAY. I GOT IT.
EXIT
RIGHT.
SO LET ME BUY YOU COFFEE, THEN.

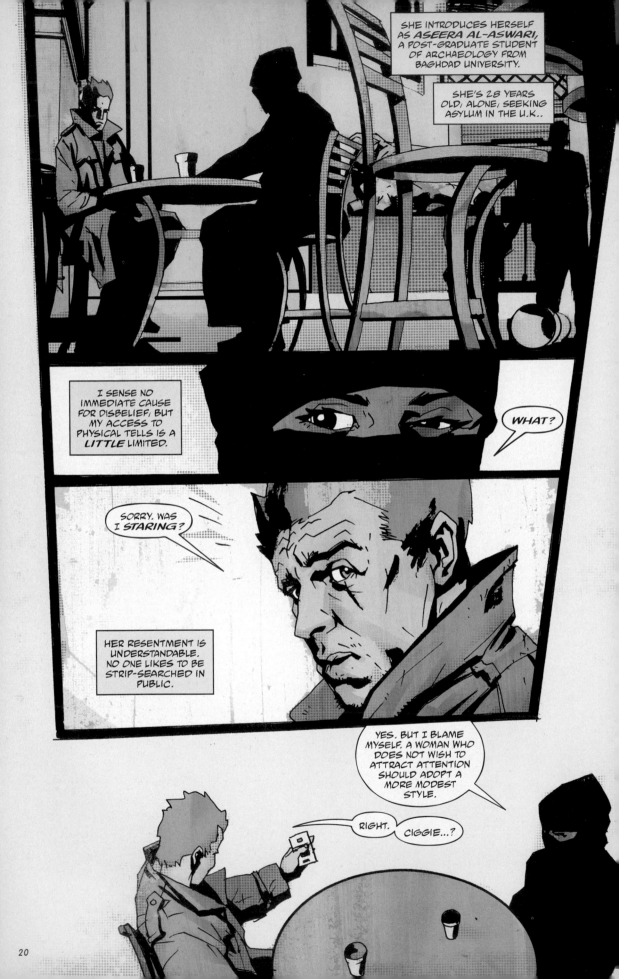

SHE INTRODUCES HERSELF AS *ASEERA AL-ASWARI*, A POST-GRADUATE STUDENT OF ARCHAEOLOGY FROM BAGHDAD UNIVERSITY.

SHE'S 28 YEARS OLD, ALONE, SEEKING ASYLUM IN THE U.K..

I SENSE NO IMMEDIATE CAUSE FOR DISBELIEF, BUT MY ACCESS TO PHYSICAL TELLS IS A *LITTLE* LIMITED.

WHAT?

SORRY. WAS I *STARING?*

HER RESENTMENT IS UNDERSTANDABLE. NO ONE LIKES TO BE STRIP-SEARCHED IN PUBLIC.

YES. BUT I BLAME MYSELF. A WOMAN WHO DOES NOT WISH TO ATTRACT ATTENTION SHOULD ADOPT A MORE MODEST STYLE.

RIGHT. CIGGIE...?

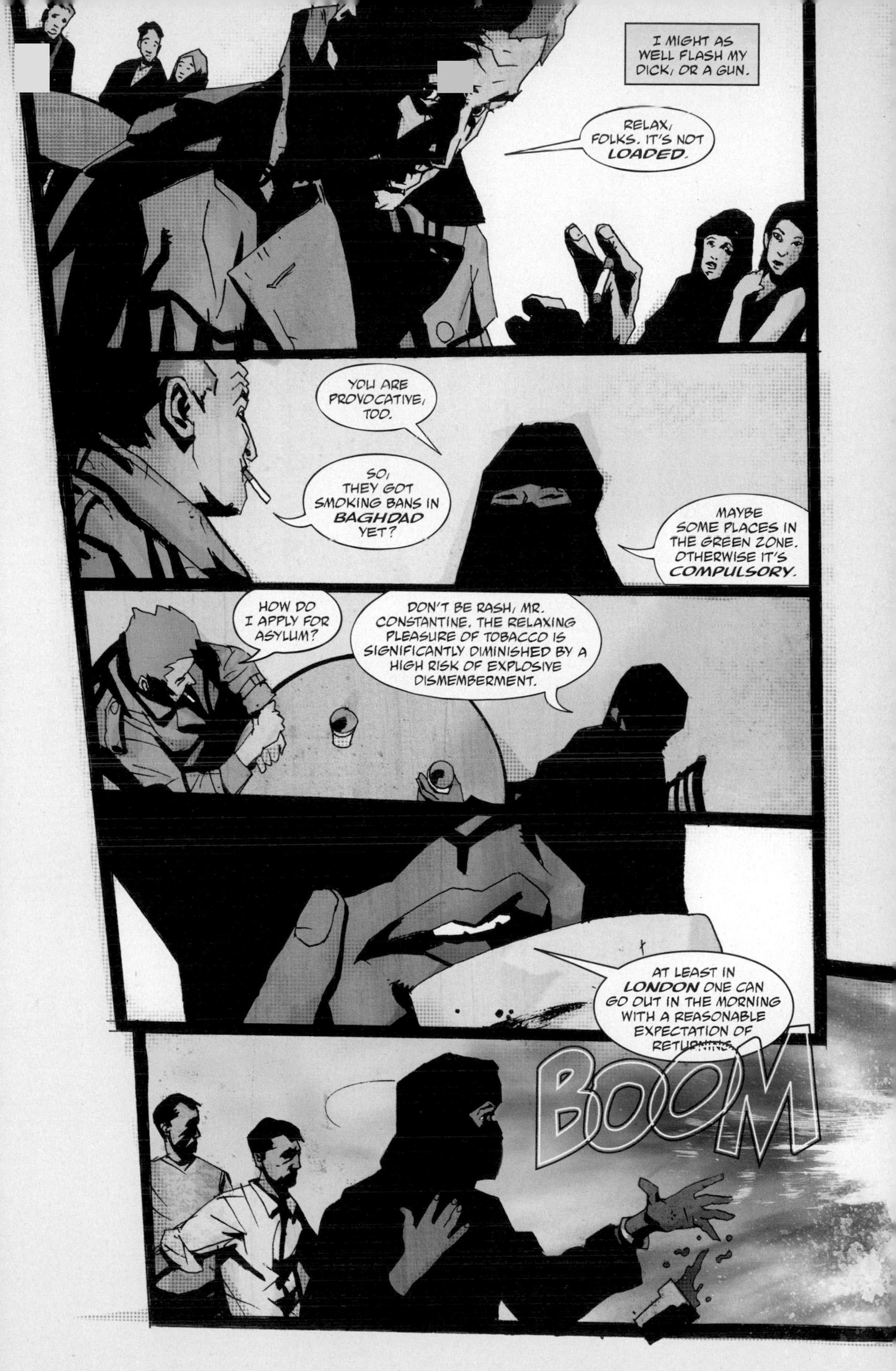
I MIGHT AS WELL FLASH MY DICK, OR A GUN.
RELAX, FOLKS. IT'S NOT *LOADED*.
YOU ARE PROVOCATIVE, TOO.
SO, THEY GOT SMOKING BANS IN *BAGHDAD* YET?
MAYBE SOME PLACES IN THE GREEN ZONE. OTHERWISE IT'S *COMPULSORY*.
HOW DO I APPLY FOR ASYLUM?
DON'T BE RASH, MR. CONSTANTINE. THE RELAXING PLEASURE OF TOBACCO IS SIGNIFICANTLY DIMINISHED BY A HIGH RISK OF EXPLOSIVE DISMEMBERMENT.
AT LEAST IN *LONDON* ONE CAN GO OUT IN THE MORNING WITH A REASONABLE EXPECTATION OF RETURNING.
BOOM

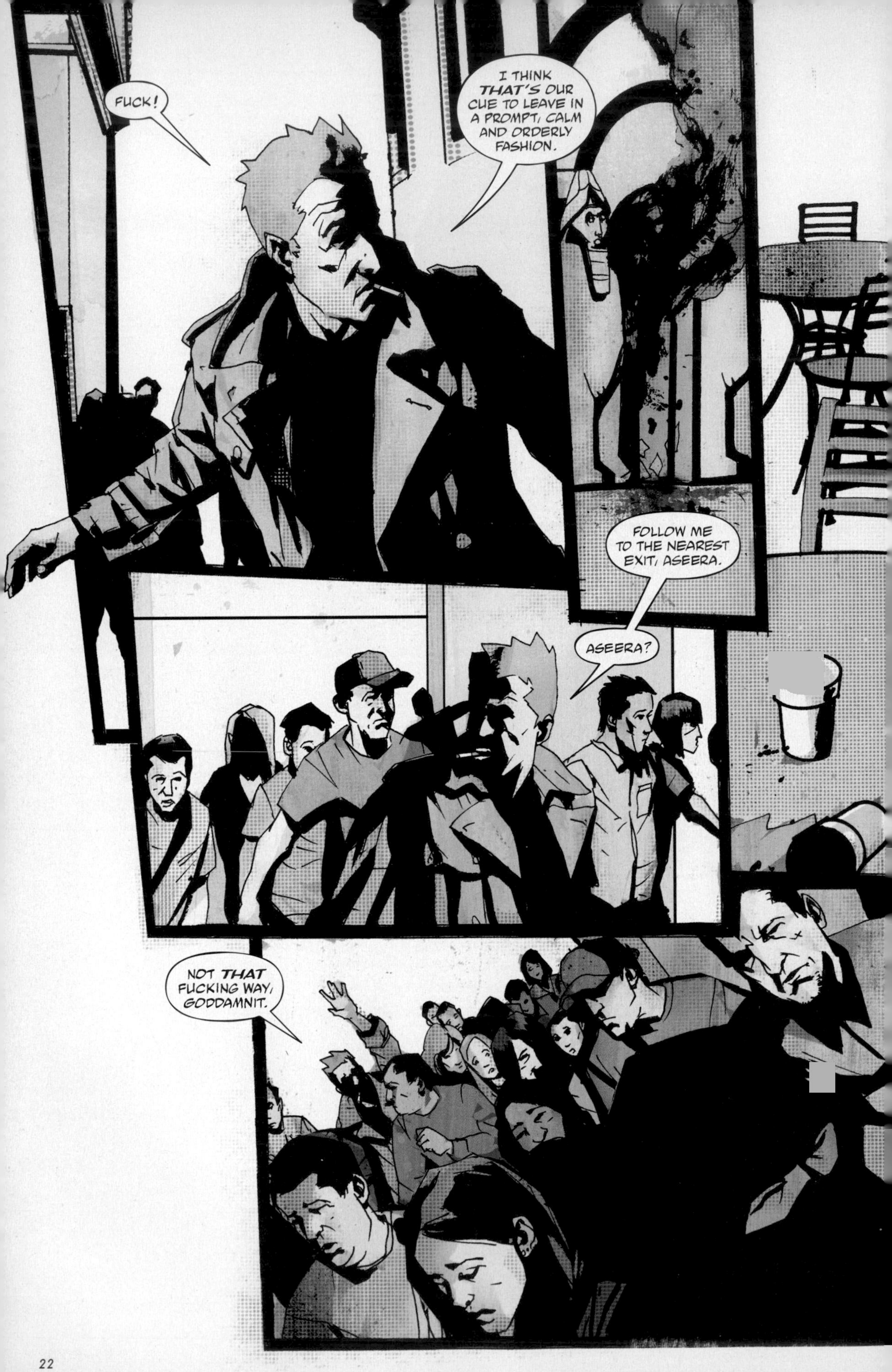
FUCK!
I THINK *THAT'S* OUR CUE TO LEAVE IN A PROMPT, CALM AND ORDERLY FASHION.
FOLLOW ME TO THE NEAREST EXIT, ASEERA.
ASEERA?
NOT *THAT* FUCKING WAY, GODDAMNIT.

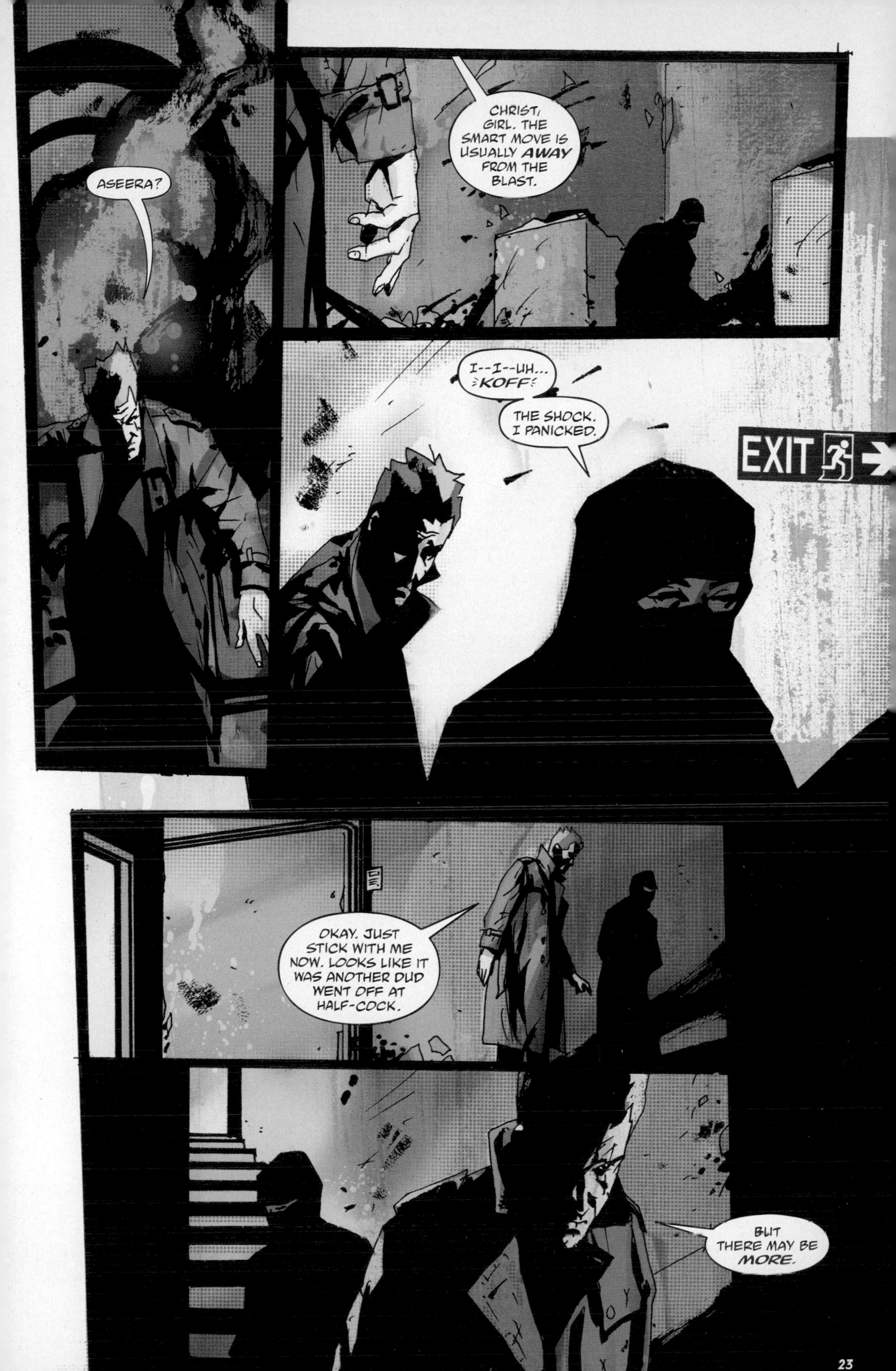
ASEERA?
CHRIST, GIRL. THE SMART MOVE IS USUALLY AWAY FROM THE BLAST.
I--I--UH... KOFF
THE SHOCK. I PANICKED.
EXIT
OKAY. JUST STICK WITH ME NOW. LOOKS LIKE IT WAS ANOTHER DUD WENT OFF AT HALF-COCK.
BUT THERE MAY BE MORE.

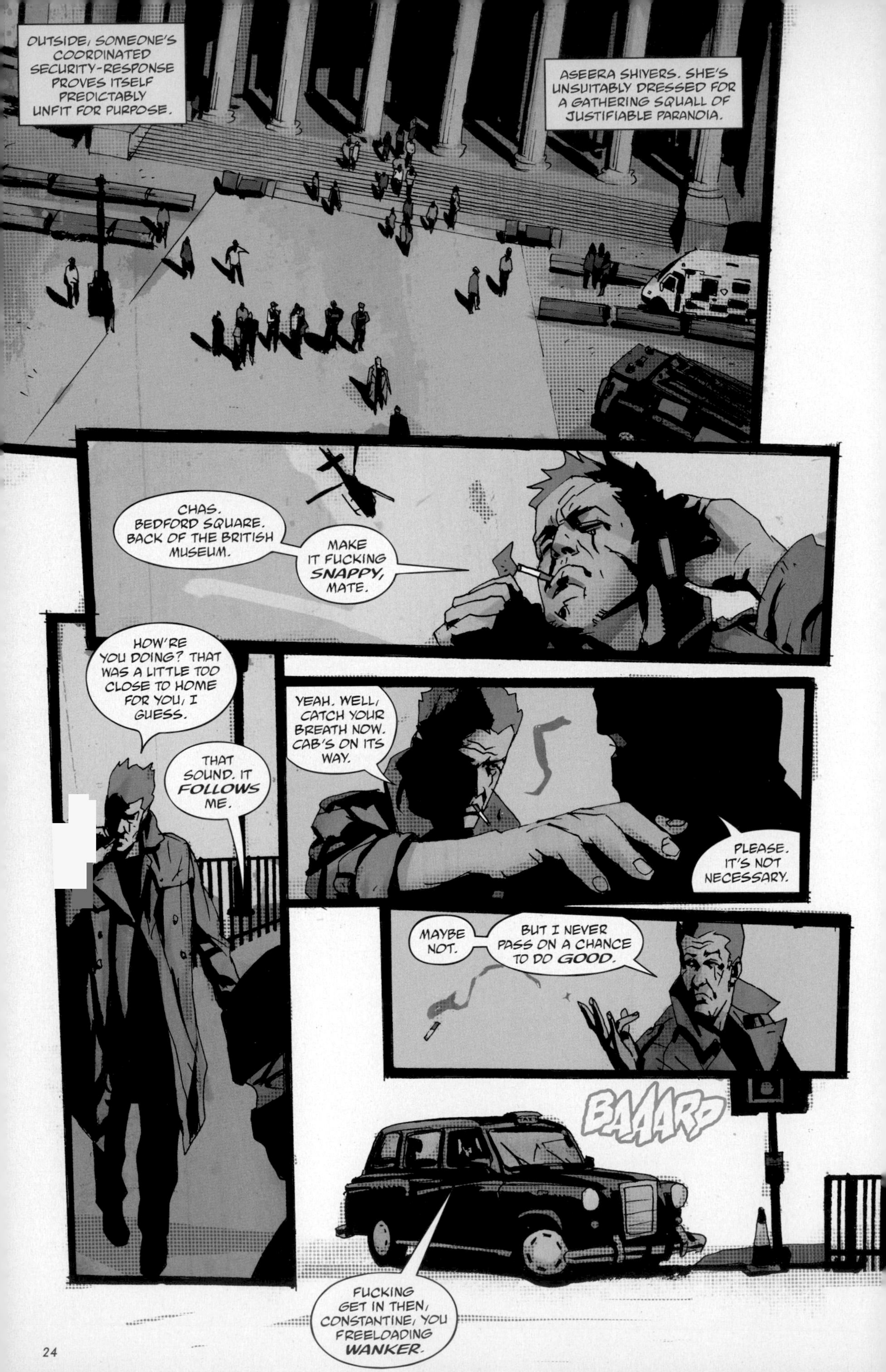
OUTSIDE, SOMEONE'S COORDINATED SECURITY-RESPONSE PROVES ITSELF PREDICTABLY UNFIT FOR PURPOSE.
ASEERA SHIVERS. SHE'S UNSUITABLY DRESSED FOR A GATHERING SQUALL OF JUSTIFIABLE PARANOIA.
CHAS. BEDFORD SQUARE. BACK OF THE BRITISH MUSEUM.
MAKE IT FUCKING SNAPPY, MATE.
HOW'RE YOU DOING? THAT WAS A LITTLE TOO CLOSE TO HOME FOR YOU, I GUESS.
THAT SOUND. IT FOLLOWS ME.
YEAH. WELL, CATCH YOUR BREATH NOW. CAB'S ON ITS WAY.
PLEASE. IT'S NOT NECESSARY.
MAYBE NOT.
BUT I NEVER PASS ON A CHANCE TO DO GOOD.
BAAARP
FUCKING GET IN THEN, CONSTANTINE, YOU FREELOADING WANKER.

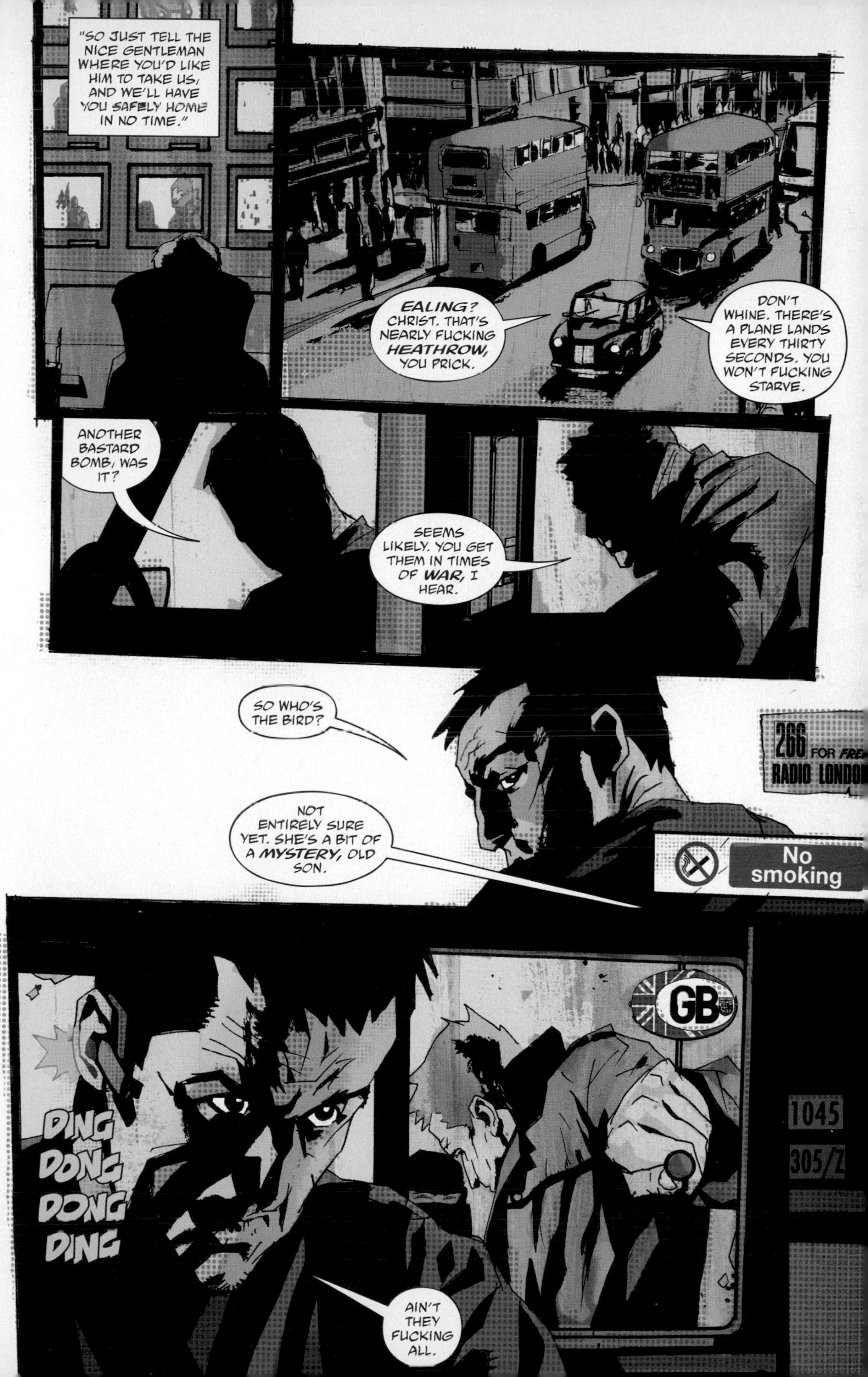
"SO JUST TELL THE NICE GENTLEMAN WHERE YOU'D LIKE HIM TO TAKE US, AND WE'LL HAVE YOU SAFELY HOME IN NO TIME."
EALING? CHRIST. THAT'S NEARLY FUCKING HEATHROW, YOU PRICK.
DON'T WHINE. THERE'S A PLANE LANDS EVERY THIRTY SECONDS. YOU WON'T FUCKING STARVE.
ANOTHER BASTARD BOMB, WAS IT?
SEEMS LIKELY. YOU GET THEM IN TIMES OF WAR, I HEAR.
SO WHO'S THE BIRD?
266 FOR FRE
RADIO LONDON
NOT ENTIRELY SURE YET. SHE'S A BIT OF A MYSTERY, OLD SON.
No smoking
GB
1045
305/Z
DING DONG DONG DING
AIN'T THEY FUCKING ALL.

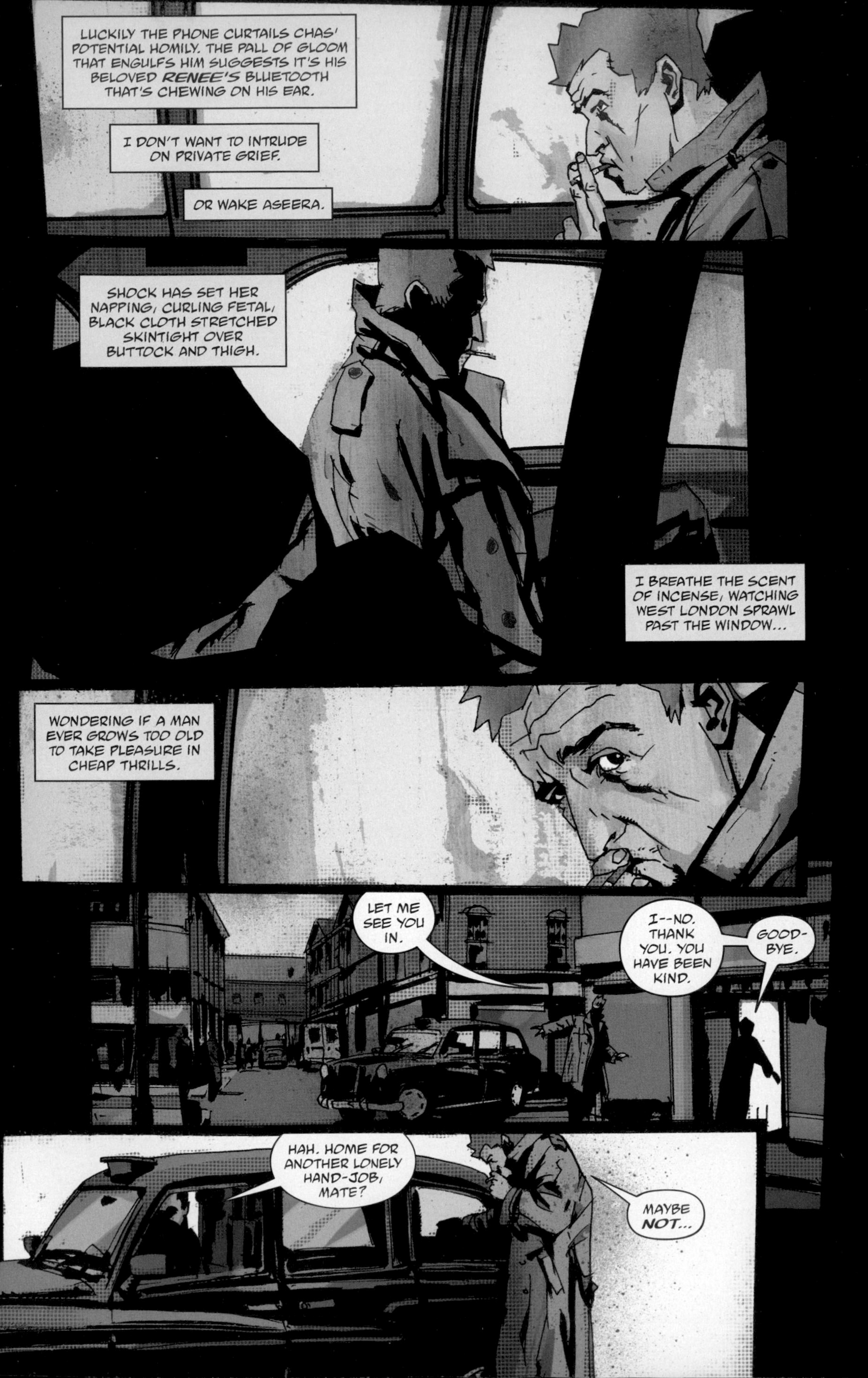
LUCKILY THE PHONE CURTAILS CHAS' POTENTIAL HOMILY. THE PALL OF GLOOM THAT ENGULFS HIM SUGGESTS IT'S HIS BELOVED RENEE'S BLUETOOTH THAT'S CHEWING ON HIS EAR.
I DON'T WANT TO INTRUDE ON PRIVATE GRIEF.
OR WAKE ASEERA.
SHOCK HAS SET HER NAPPING, CURLING FETAL, BLACK CLOTH STRETCHED SKINTIGHT OVER BUTTOCK AND THIGH.
I BREATHE THE SCENT OF INCENSE, WATCHING WEST LONDON SPRAWL PAST THE WINDOW...
WONDERING IF A MAN EVER GROWS TOO OLD TO TAKE PLEASURE IN CHEAP THRILLS.
LET ME SEE YOU IN.
I--NO. THANK YOU. YOU HAVE BEEN KIND.
GOOD-BYE.
HAH. HOME FOR ANOTHER LONELY HAND-JOB, MATE?
MAYBE NOT...

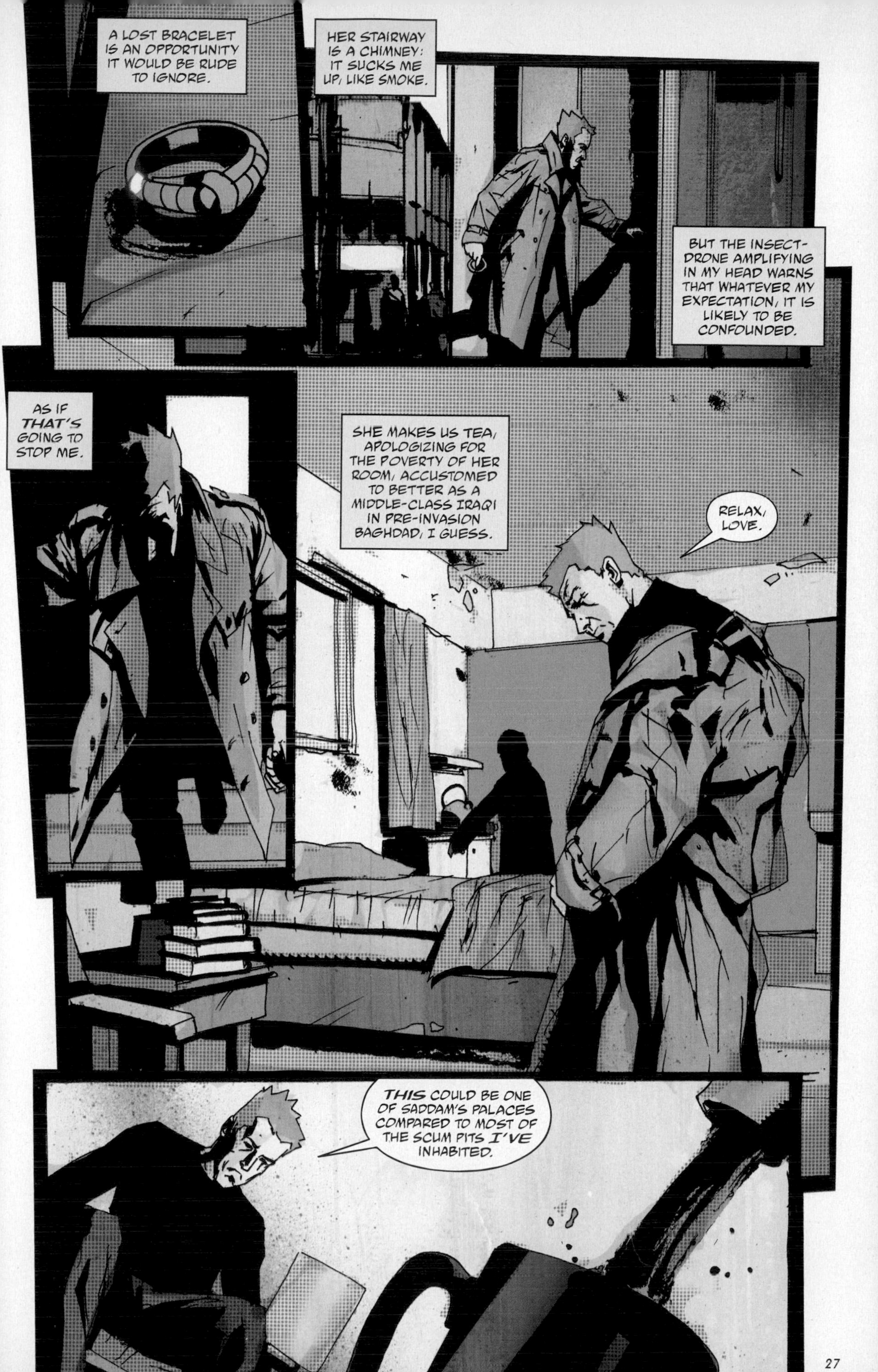
A LOST BRACELET IS AN OPPORTUNITY IT WOULD BE RUDE TO IGNORE.
HER STAIRWAY IS A CHIMNEY: IT SUCKS ME UP, LIKE SMOKE.
BUT THE INSECT-DRONE AMPLIFYING IN MY HEAD WARNS THAT WHATEVER MY EXPECTATION, IT IS LIKELY TO BE CONFOUNDED.
AS IF THAT'S GOING TO STOP ME.
SHE MAKES US TEA, APOLOGIZING FOR THE POVERTY OF HER ROOM, ACCUSTOMED TO BETTER AS A MIDDLE-CLASS IRAQI IN PRE-INVASION BAGHDAD, I GUESS.
RELAX, LOVE.
THIS COULD BE ONE OF SADDAM'S PALACES COMPARED TO MOST OF THE SCUM PITS I'VE INHABITED.

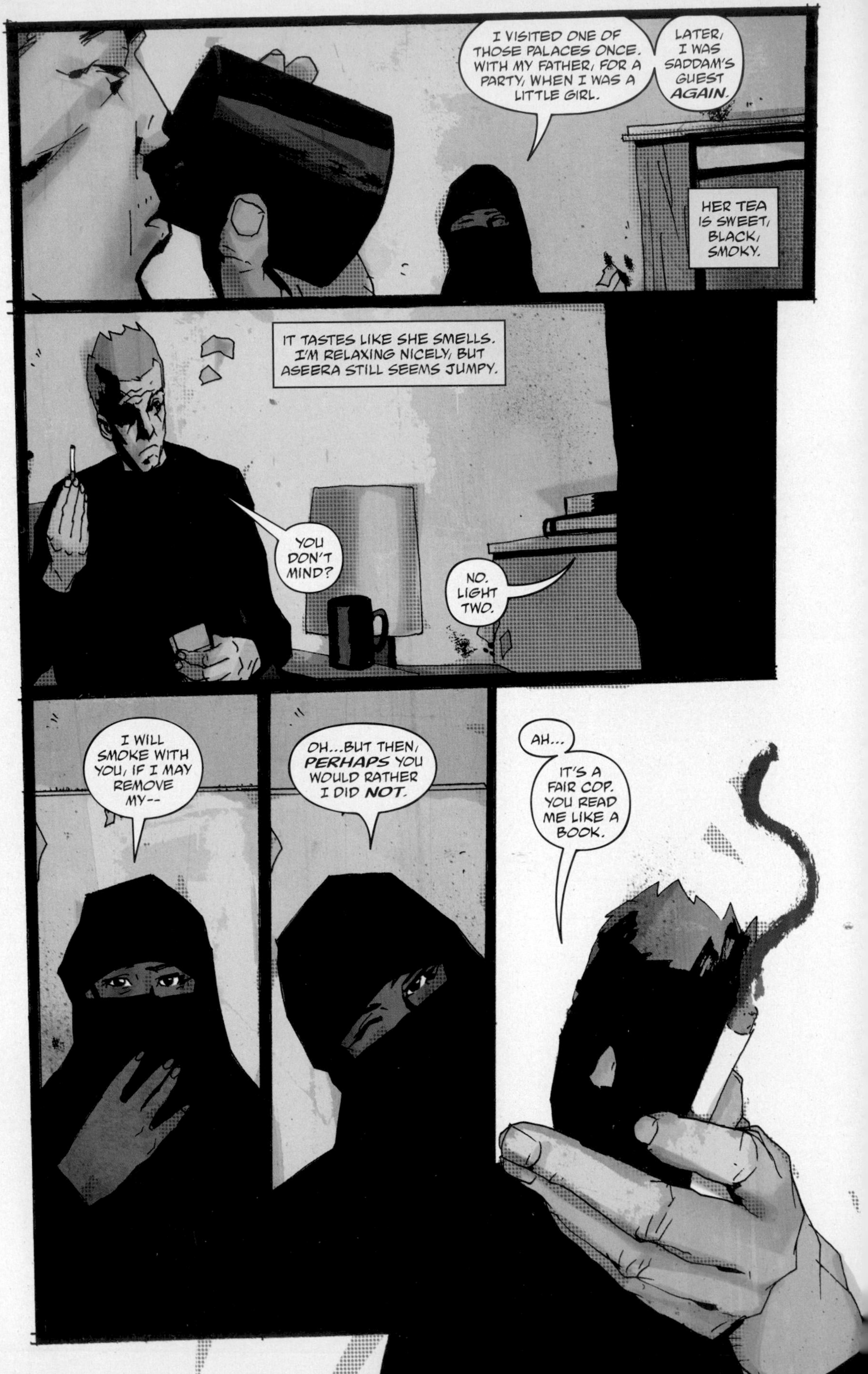

I VISITED ONE OF THOSE PALACES ONCE. WITH MY FATHER, FOR A PARTY, WHEN I WAS A LITTLE GIRL.
LATER, I WAS SADDAM'S GUEST *AGAIN*.
HER TEA IS SWEET, BLACK, SMOKY.
IT TASTES LIKE SHE SMELLS. I'M RELAXING NICELY, BUT ASEERA STILL SEEMS JUMPY.
YOU DON'T MIND?
NO. LIGHT TWO.
I WILL SMOKE WITH YOU, IF I MAY REMOVE MY--
OH...BUT THEN, *PERHAPS* YOU WOULD RATHER I DID **NOT**.
AH...
IT'S A FAIR COP. YOU READ ME LIKE A BOOK.

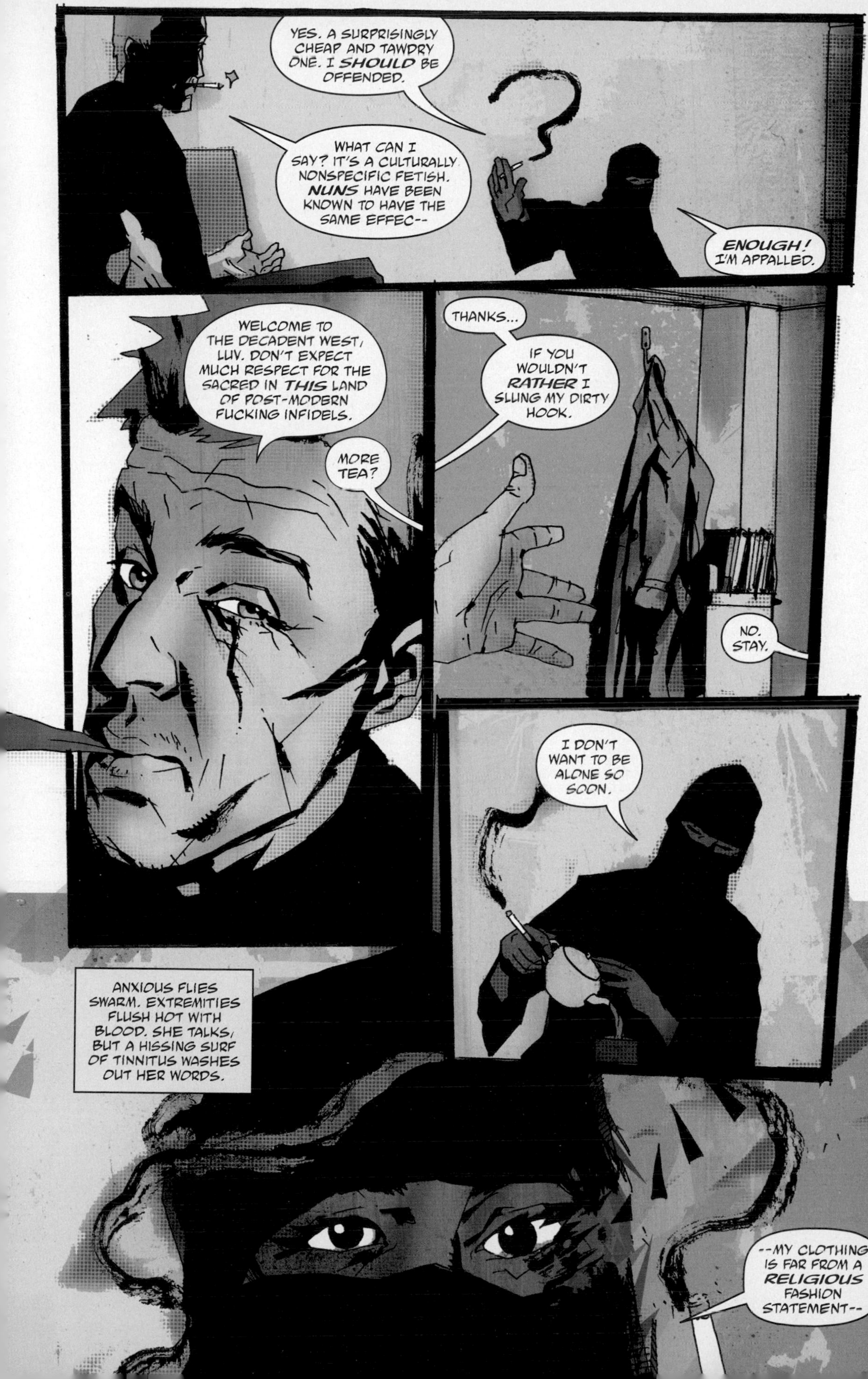
YES. A SURPRISINGLY CHEAP AND TAWDRY ONE. I SHOULD BE OFFENDED.
WHAT CAN I SAY? IT'S A CULTURALLY NONSPECIFIC FETISH. NUNS HAVE BEEN KNOWN TO HAVE THE SAME EFFEC--
ENOUGH! I'M APPALLED.
WELCOME TO THE DECADENT WEST, LUV. DON'T EXPECT MUCH RESPECT FOR THE SACRED IN THIS LAND OF POST-MODERN FUCKING INFIDELS.
MORE TEA?
THANKS...
IF YOU WOULDN'T RATHER I SLUNG MY DIRTY HOOK.
NO. STAY.
I DON'T WANT TO BE ALONE SO SOON.
ANXIOUS FLIES SWARM. EXTREMITIES FLUSH HOT WITH BLOOD. SHE TALKS, BUT A HISSING SURF OF TINNITUS WASHES OUT HER WORDS.
--MY CLOTHING IS FAR FROM A RELIGIOUS FASHION STATEMENT--

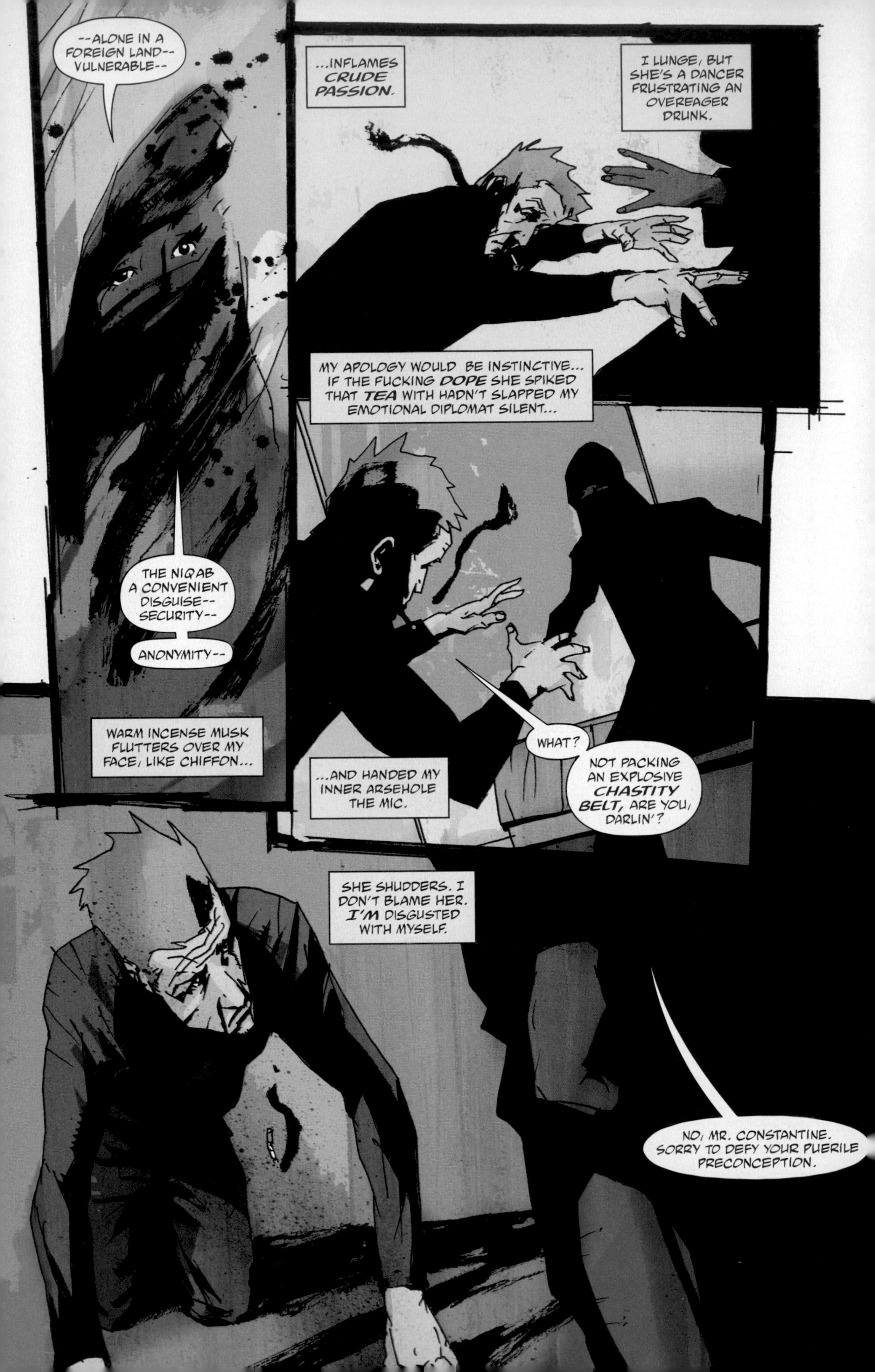
--ALONE IN A FOREIGN LAND--VULNERABLE--
THE NIQAB A CONVENIENT DISGUISE--SECURITY--
ANONYMITY--
WARM INCENSE MUSK FLUTTERS OVER MY FACE, LIKE CHIFFON...
...INFLAMES CRUDE PASSION.
I LUNGE, BUT SHE'S A DANCER FRUSTRATING AN OVEREAGER DRUNK.
MY APOLOGY WOULD BE INSTINCTIVE... IF THE FUCKING DOPE SHE SPIKED THAT TEA WITH HADN'T SLAPPED MY EMOTIONAL DIPLOMAT SILENT...
...AND HANDED MY INNER ARSEHOLE THE MIC.
WHAT?
NOT PACKING AN EXPLOSIVE CHASTITY BELT, ARE YOU, DARLIN'?
SHE SHUDDERS. I DON'T BLAME HER. I'M DISGUSTED WITH MYSELF.
NO, MR. CONSTANTINE. SORRY TO DEFY YOUR PUERILE PRECONCEPTION.

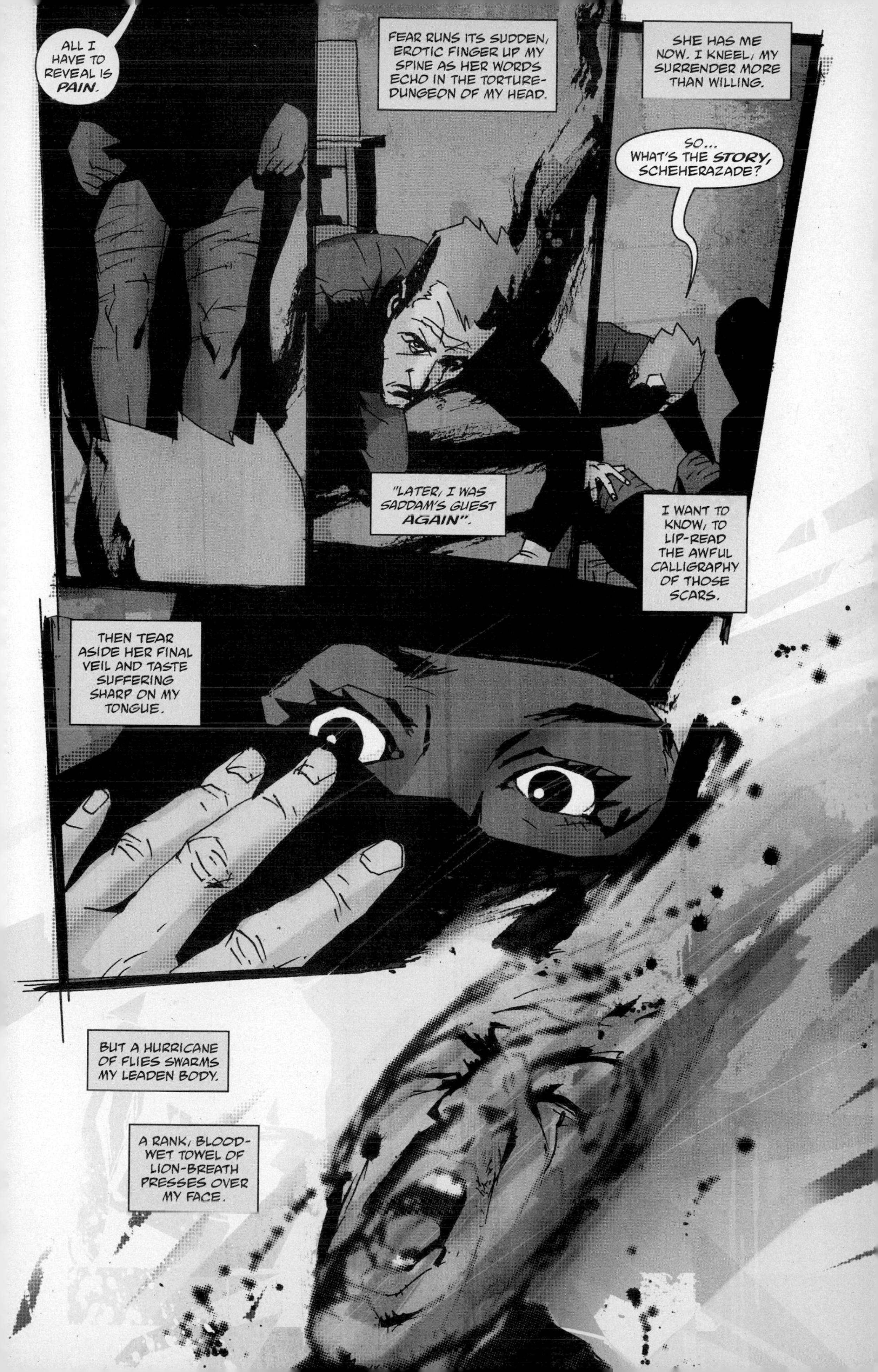
ALL I HAVE TO REVEAL IS *PAIN*.
FEAR RUNS ITS SUDDEN, EROTIC FINGER UP MY SPINE AS HER WORDS ECHO IN THE TORTURE-DUNGEON OF MY HEAD.
"LATER, I WAS SADDAM'S GUEST *AGAIN*".
SHE HAS ME NOW. I KNEEL, MY SURRENDER MORE THAN WILLING.
SO... WHAT'S THE *STORY,* SCHEHERAZADE?
I WANT TO KNOW, TO LIP-READ THE AWFUL CALLIGRAPHY OF THOSE SCARS.
THEN TEAR ASIDE HER FINAL VEIL AND TASTE SUFFERING SHARP ON MY TONGUE.
BUT A HURRICANE OF FLIES SWARMS MY LEADEN BODY.
A RANK, BLOOD-WET TOWEL OF LION-BREATH PRESSES OVER MY FACE.

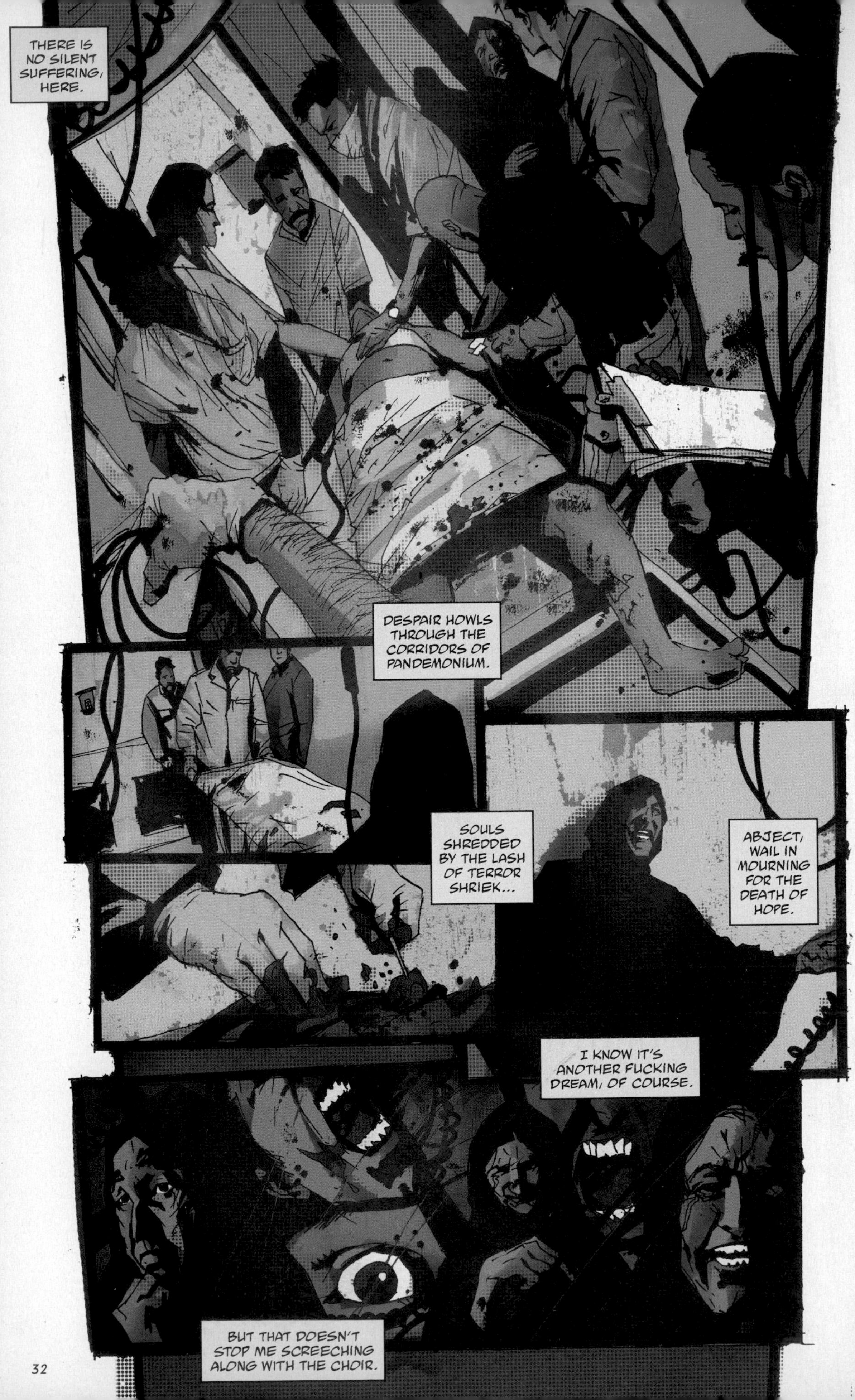
THERE IS NO SILENT SUFFERING, HERE.
DESPAIR HOWLS THROUGH THE CORRIDORS OF PANDEMONIUM.
SOULS SHREDDED BY THE LASH OF TERROR SHRIEK...
ABJECT, WAIL IN MOURNING FOR THE DEATH OF HOPE.
I KNOW IT'S ANOTHER FUCKING DREAM, OF COURSE.
BUT THAT DOESN'T STOP ME SCREECHING ALONG WITH THE CHOIR.

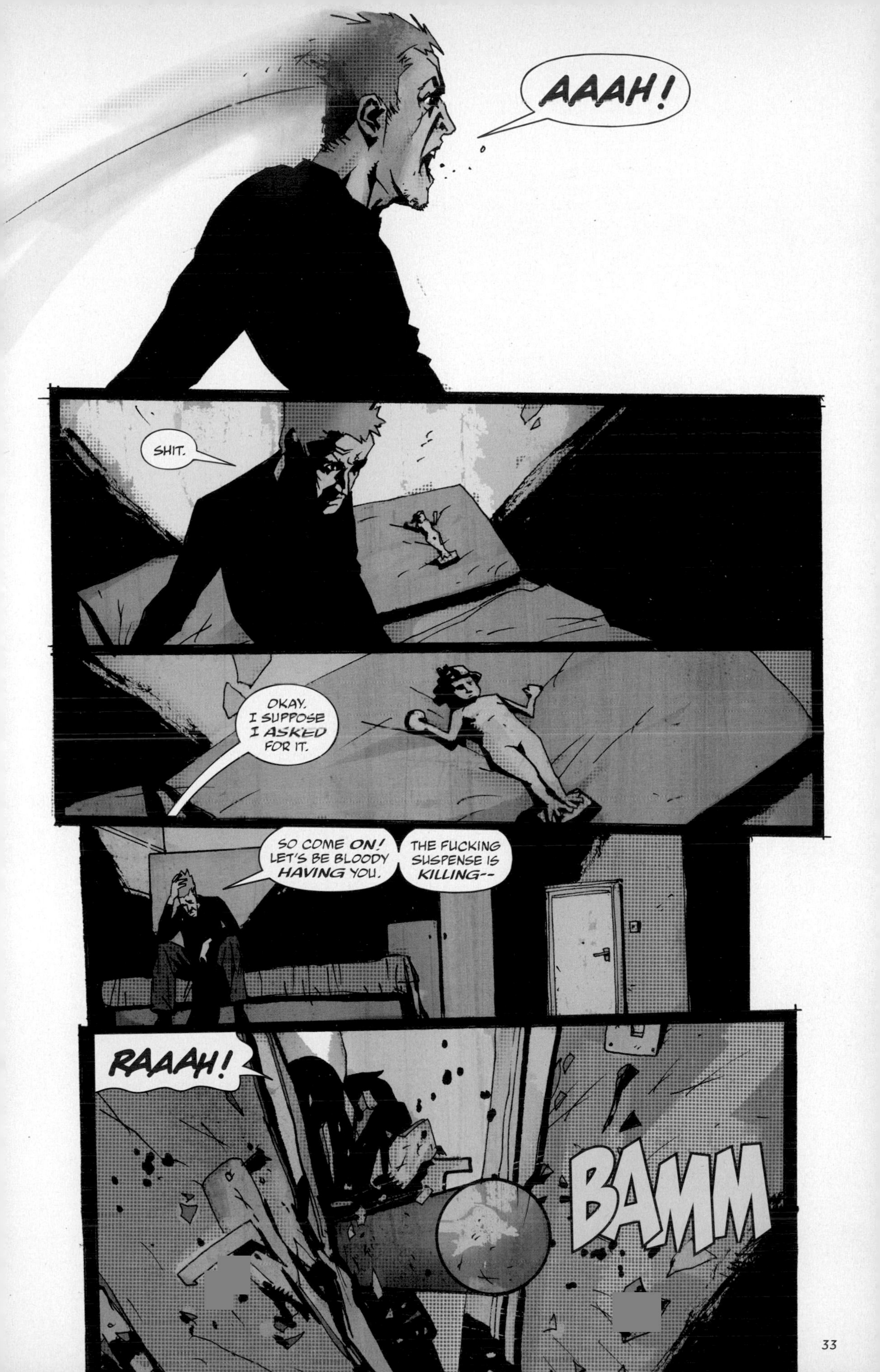
AAAH!
SHIT.
OKAY. I SUPPOSE I ASKED FOR IT.
SO COME ON! LET'S BE BLOODY HAVING YOU.
THE FUCKING SUSPENSE IS KILLING--
RAAAH!
BAMM

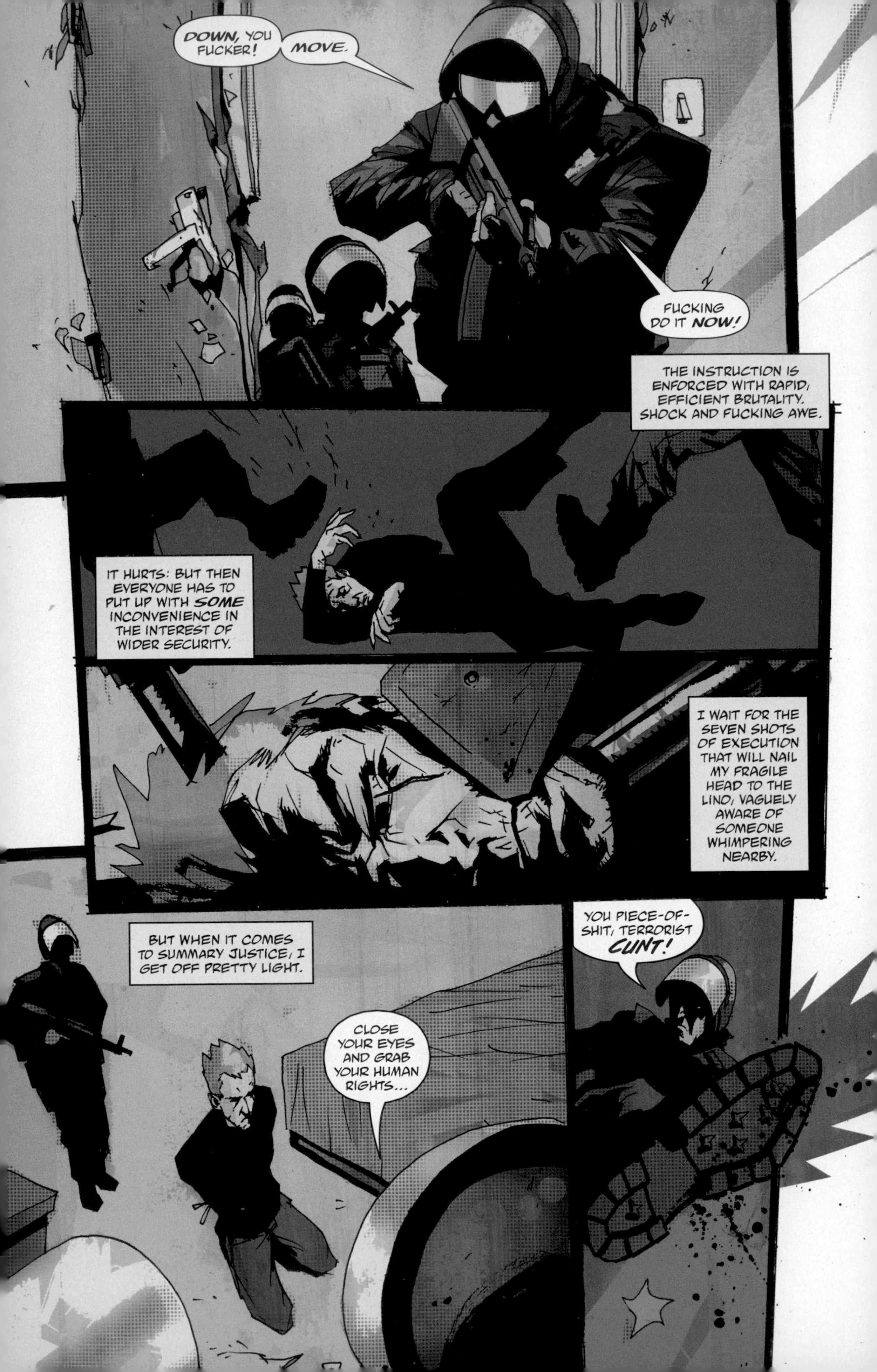
DOWN, YOU FUCKER!
MOVE.
FUCKING DO IT NOW!
THE INSTRUCTION IS ENFORCED WITH RAPID, EFFICIENT BRUTALITY. SHOCK AND FUCKING AWE.
IT HURTS: BUT THEN EVERYONE HAS TO PUT UP WITH SOME INCONVENIENCE IN THE INTEREST OF WIDER SECURITY.
I WAIT FOR THE SEVEN SHOTS OF EXECUTION THAT WILL NAIL MY FRAGILE HEAD TO THE LINO, VAGUELY AWARE OF SOMEONE WHIMPERING NEARBY.
BUT WHEN IT COMES TO SUMMARY JUSTICE, I GET OFF PRETTY LIGHT.
CLOSE YOUR EYES AND GRAB YOUR HUMAN RIGHTS...
YOU PIECE-OF-SHIT, TERRORIST CUNT!

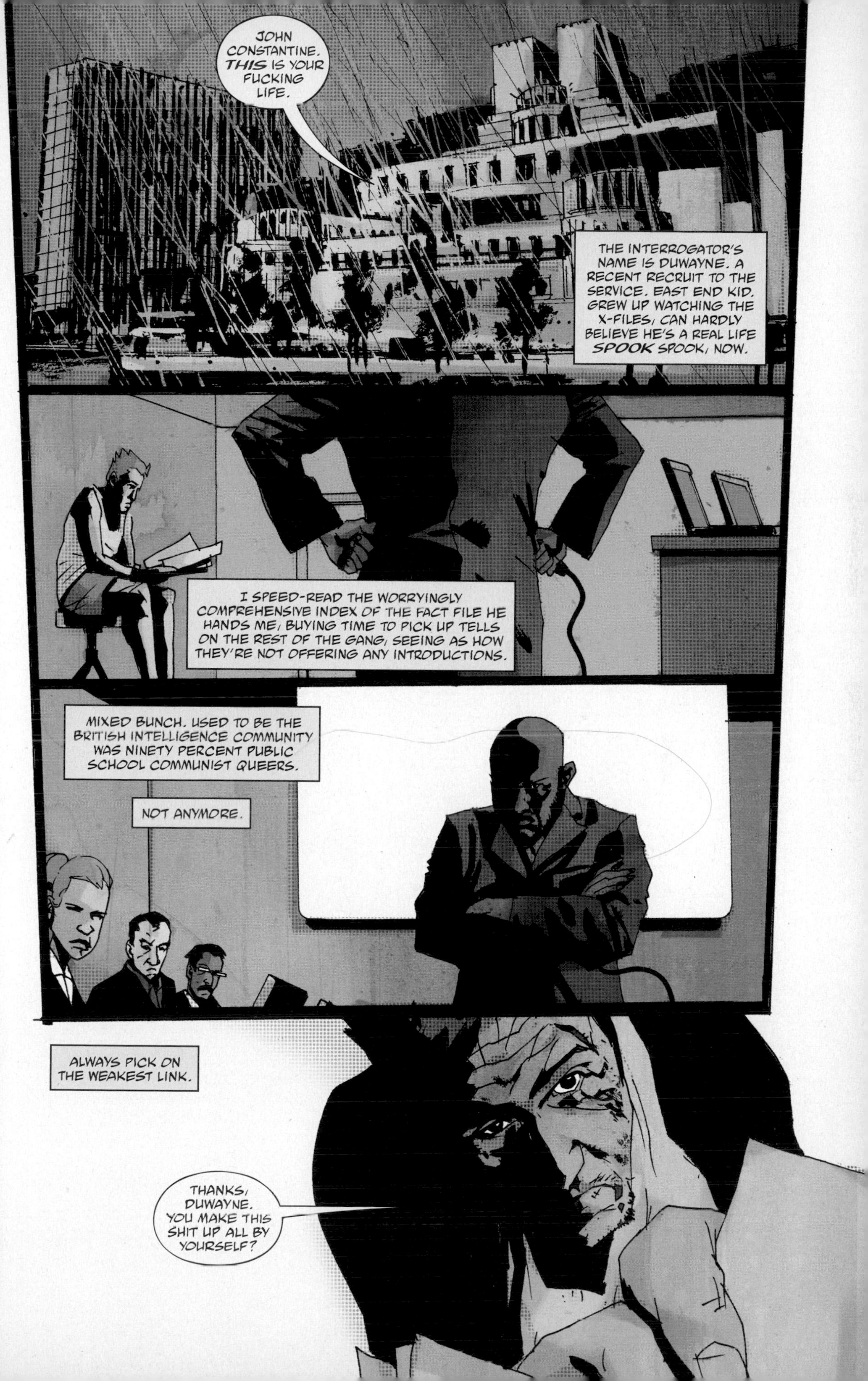
JOHN CONSTANTINE. THIS IS YOUR FUCKING LIFE.
THE INTERROGATOR'S NAME IS DUWAYNE. A RECENT RECRUIT TO THE SERVICE. EAST END KID. GREW UP WATCHING THE X-FILES, CAN HARDLY BELIEVE HE'S A REAL LIFE SPOOK SPOOK, NOW.
I SPEED-READ THE WORRYINGLY COMPREHENSIVE INDEX OF THE FACT FILE HE HANDS ME, BUYING TIME TO PICK UP TELLS ON THE REST OF THE GANG, SEEING AS HOW THEY'RE NOT OFFERING ANY INTRODUCTIONS.
MIXED BUNCH. USED TO BE THE BRITISH INTELLIGENCE COMMUNITY WAS NINETY PERCENT PUBLIC SCHOOL COMMUNIST QUEERS.
NOT ANYMORE.
ALWAYS PICK ON THE WEAKEST LINK.
THANKS, DUWAYNE. YOU MAKE THIS SHIT UP ALL BY YOURSELF?

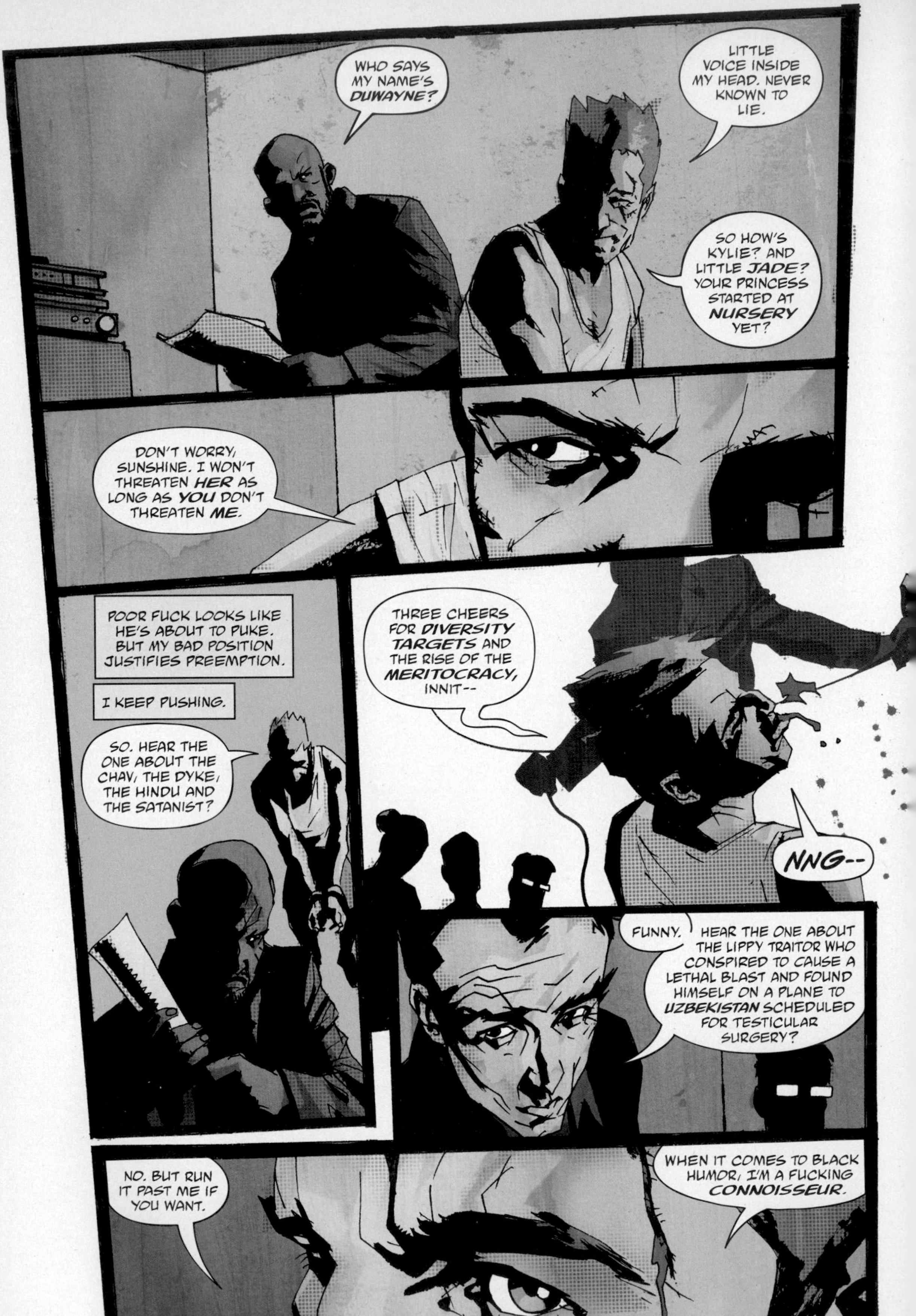
WHO SAYS MY NAME'S DUWAYNE?
LITTLE VOICE INSIDE MY HEAD. NEVER KNOWN TO LIE.
SO HOW'S KYLIE? AND LITTLE JADE? YOUR PRINCESS STARTED AT NURSERY YET?
DON'T WORRY, SUNSHINE. I WON'T THREATEN HER AS LONG AS YOU DON'T THREATEN ME.
POOR FUCK LOOKS LIKE HE'S ABOUT TO PUKE. BUT MY BAD POSITION JUSTIFIES PREEMPTION.
I KEEP PUSHING.
SO. HEAR THE ONE ABOUT THE CHAV, THE DYKE, THE HINDU AND THE SATANIST?
THREE CHEERS FOR DIVERSITY TARGETS AND THE RISE OF THE MERITOCRACY, INNIT--
NNG--
FUNNY.
HEAR THE ONE ABOUT THE LIPPY TRAITOR WHO CONSPIRED TO CAUSE A LETHAL BLAST AND FOUND HIMSELF ON A PLANE TO UZBEKISTAN SCHEDULED FOR TESTICULAR SURGERY?
NO. BUT RUN IT PAST ME IF YOU WANT.
WHEN IT COMES TO BLACK HUMOR, I'M A FUCKING CONNOISSEUR.

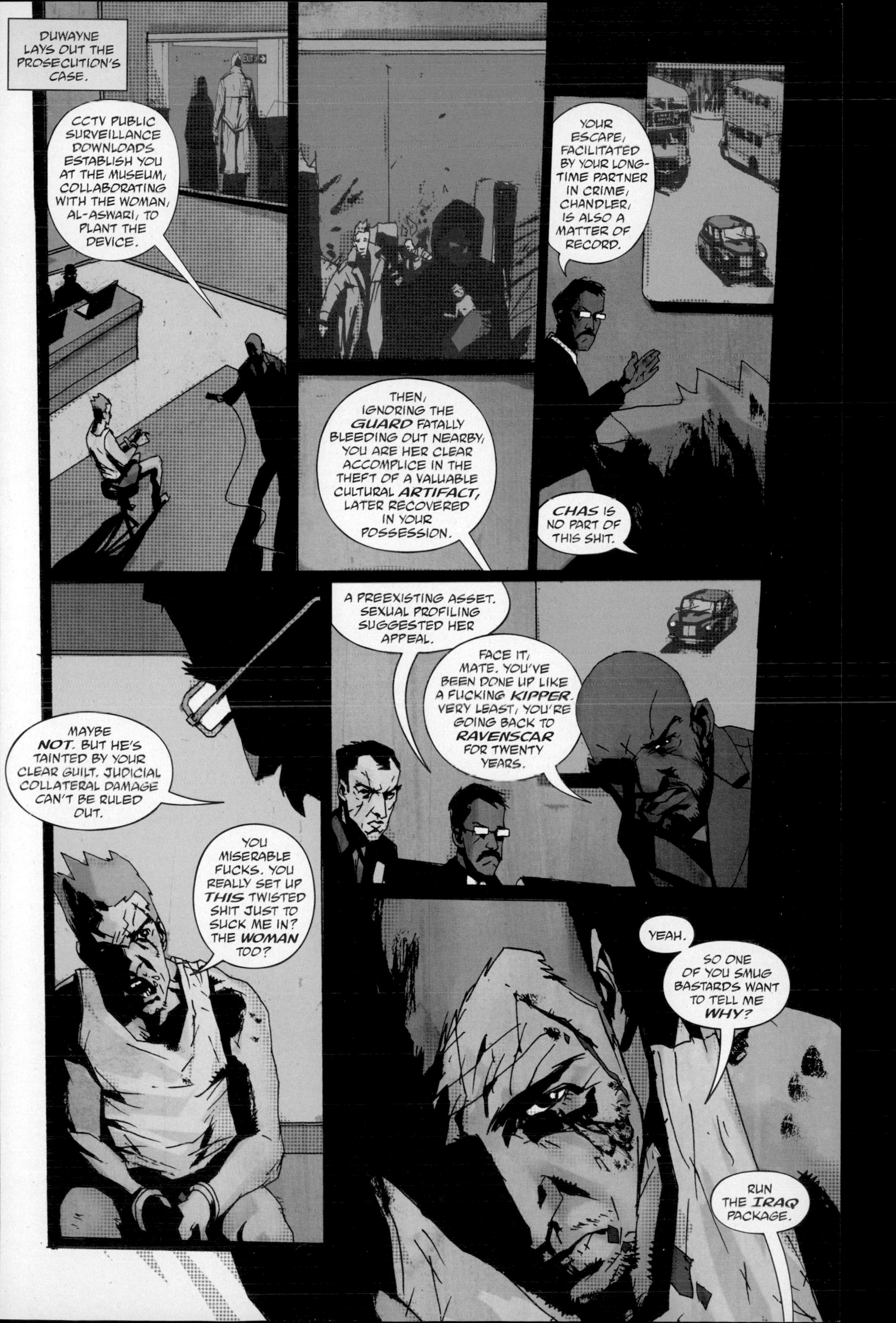
DUWAYNE LAYS OUT THE PROSECUTION'S CASE.
CCTV PUBLIC SURVEILLANCE DOWNLOADS ESTABLISH YOU AT THE MUSEUM, COLLABORATING WITH THE WOMAN, AL-ASWARI, TO PLANT THE DEVICE.
YOUR ESCAPE, FACILITATED BY YOUR LONG-TIME PARTNER IN CRIME, CHANDLER, IS ALSO A MATTER OF RECORD.
THEN, IGNORING THE GUARD FATALLY BLEEDING OUT NEARBY, YOU ARE HER CLEAR ACCOMPLICE IN THE THEFT OF A VALUABLE CULTURAL ARTIFACT, LATER RECOVERED IN YOUR POSSESSION.
CHAS IS NO PART OF THIS SHIT.
MAYBE NOT. BUT HE'S TAINTED BY YOUR CLEAR GUILT. JUDICIAL COLLATERAL DAMAGE CAN'T BE RULED OUT.
YOU MISERABLE FUCKS. YOU REALLY SET UP THIS TWISTED SHIT JUST TO SUCK ME IN? THE WOMAN TOO?
A PREEXISTING ASSET. SEXUAL PROFILING SUGGESTED HER APPEAL.
FACE IT, MATE. YOU'VE BEEN DONE UP LIKE A FUCKING KIPPER. VERY LEAST, YOU'RE GOING BACK TO RAVENSCAR FOR TWENTY YEARS.
YEAH.
SO ONE OF YOU SMUG BASTARDS WANT TO TELL ME WHY?
RUN THE IRAQ PACKAGE.

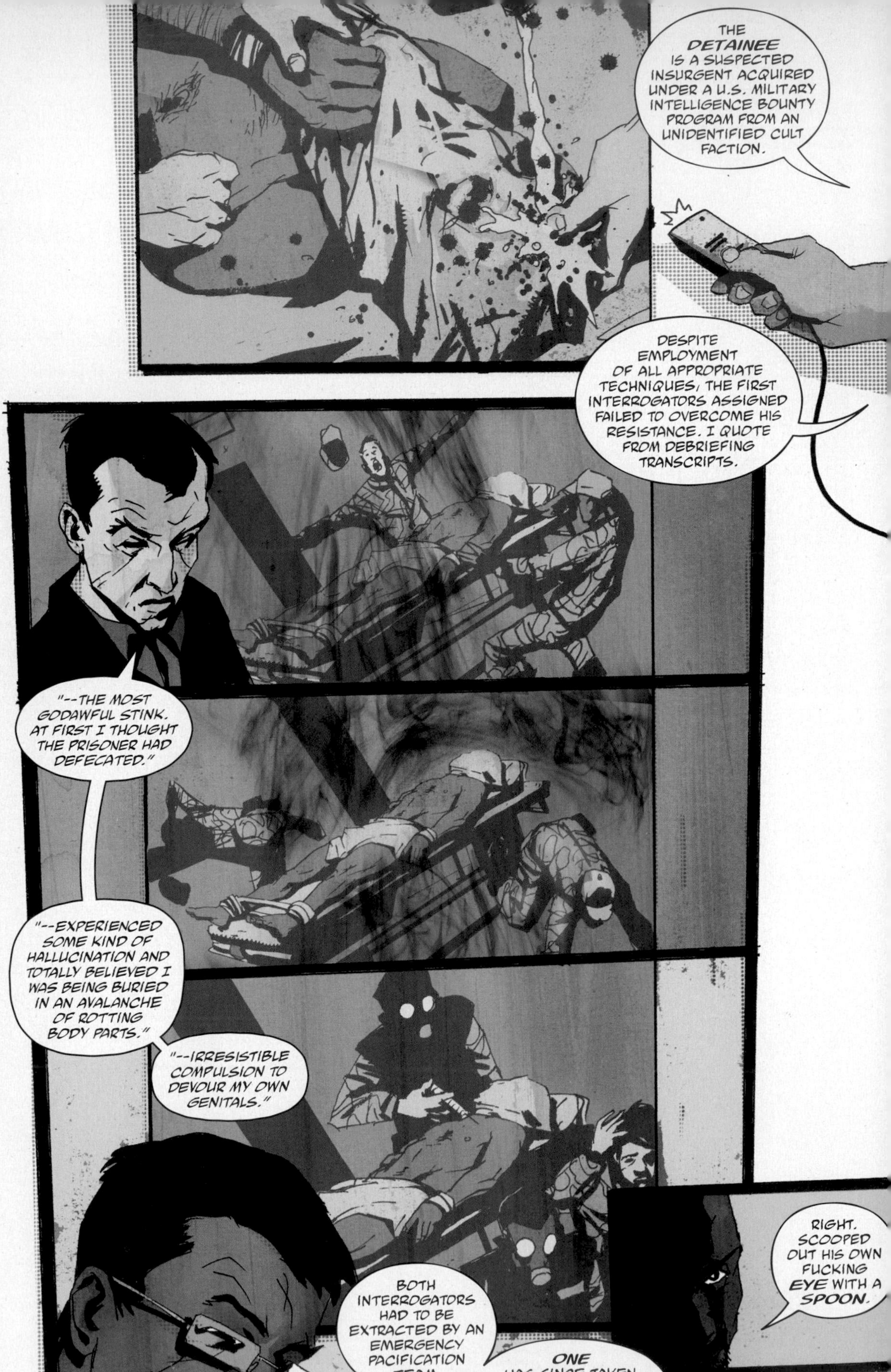
THE DETAINEE IS A SUSPECTED INSURGENT ACQUIRED UNDER A U.S. MILITARY INTELLIGENCE BOUNTY PROGRAM FROM AN UNIDENTIFIED CULT FACTION.
DESPITE EMPLOYMENT OF ALL APPROPRIATE TECHNIQUES, THE FIRST INTERROGATORS ASSIGNED FAILED TO OVERCOME HIS RESISTANCE. I QUOTE FROM DEBRIEFING TRANSCRIPTS.
"--THE MOST GODAWFUL STINK. AT FIRST I THOUGHT THE PRISONER HAD DEFECATED."
"--EXPERIENCED SOME KIND OF HALLUCINATION AND TOTALLY BELIEVED I WAS BEING BURIED IN AN AVALANCHE OF ROTTING BODY PARTS."
"--IRRESISTIBLE COMPULSION TO DEVOUR MY OWN GENITALS."
BOTH INTERROGATORS HAD TO BE EXTRACTED BY AN EMERGENCY PACIFICATION TEAM.
ONE HAS SINCE TAKEN HIS OWN LIFE. THE OTHER IS ON SUICIDE WATCH IN A MILITARY HOSPITAL.
RIGHT. SCOOPED OUT HIS OWN FUCKING EYE WITH A SPOON.

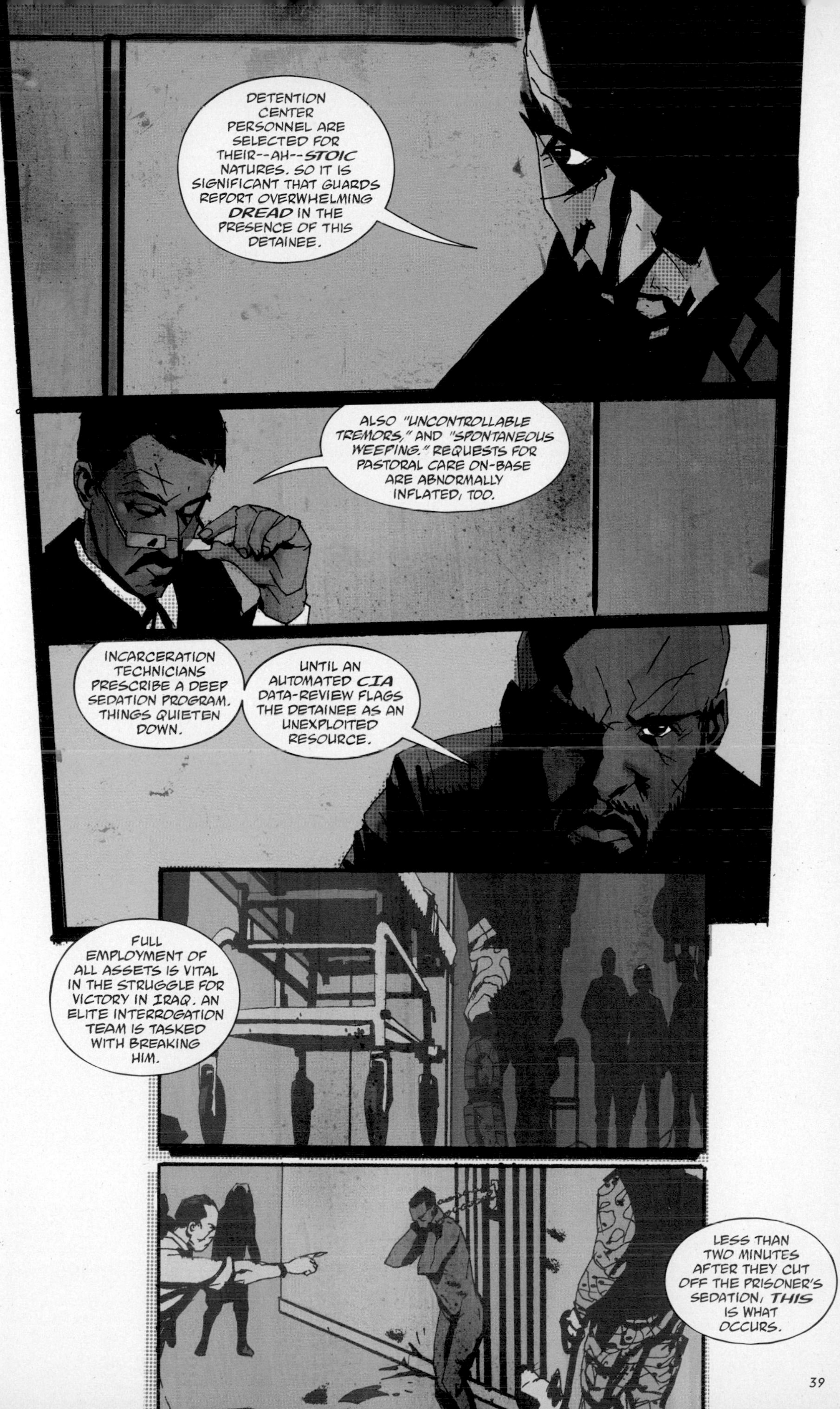

DETENTION CENTER PERSONNEL ARE SELECTED FOR THEIR--AH--STOIC NATURES. SO IT IS SIGNIFICANT THAT GUARDS REPORT OVERWHELMING DREAD IN THE PRESENCE OF THIS DETAINEE.
ALSO "UNCONTROLLABLE TREMORS," AND "SPONTANEOUS WEEPING." REQUESTS FOR PASTORAL CARE ON-BASE ARE ABNORMALLY INFLATED, TOO.
INCARCERATION TECHNICIANS PRESCRIBE A DEEP SEDATION PROGRAM. THINGS QUIETEN DOWN.
UNTIL AN AUTOMATED CIA DATA-REVIEW FLAGS THE DETAINEE AS AN UNEXPLOITED RESOURCE.
FULL EMPLOYMENT OF ALL ASSETS IS VITAL IN THE STRUGGLE FOR VICTORY IN IRAQ. AN ELITE INTERROGATION TEAM IS TASKED WITH BREAKING HIM.
LESS THAN TWO MINUTES AFTER THEY CUT OFF THE PRISONER'S SEDATION, THIS IS WHAT OCCURS.

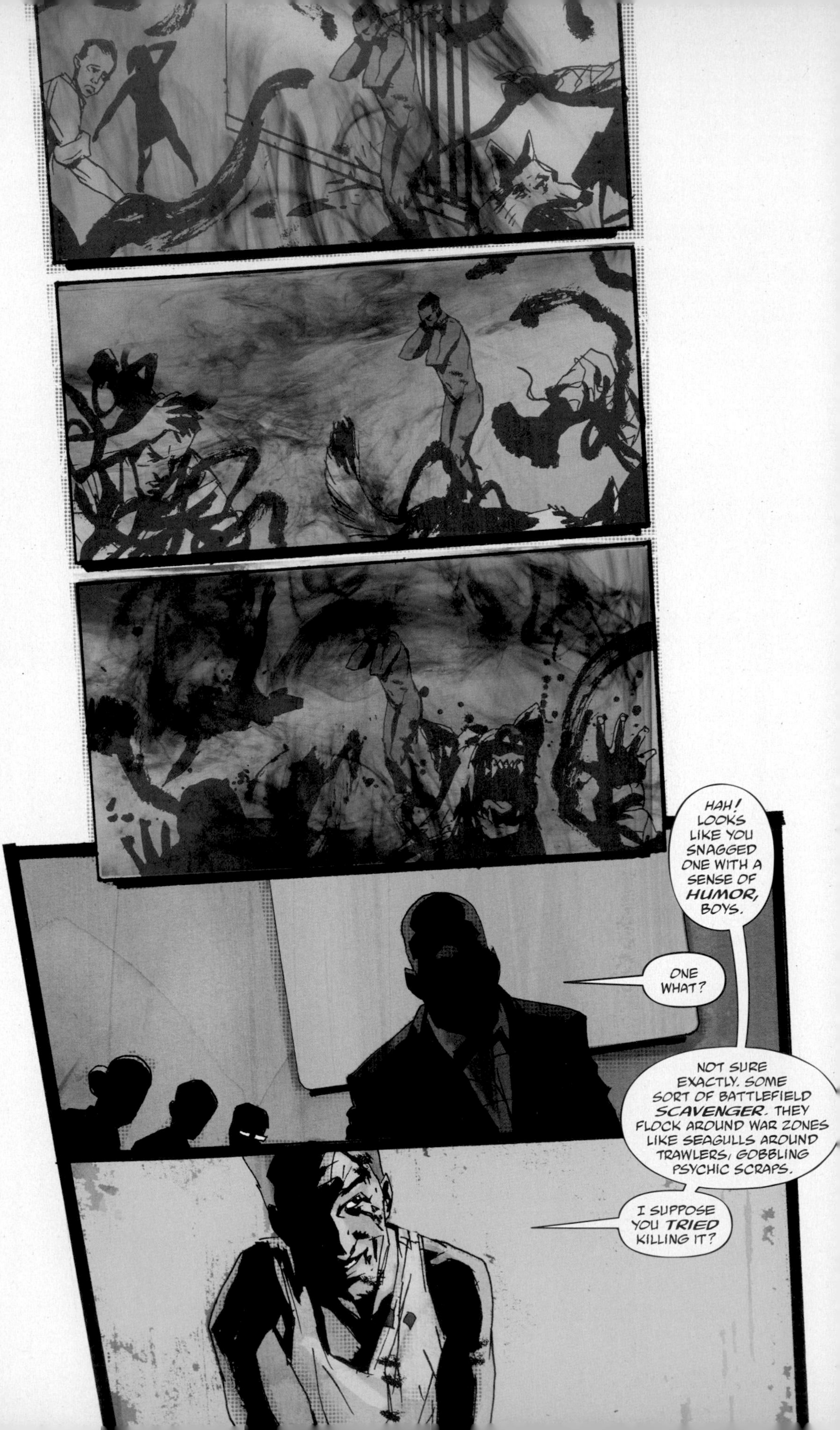
HAH! LOOKS LIKE YOU SNAGGED ONE WITH A SENSE OF HUMOR, BOYS.
ONE WHAT?
NOT SURE EXACTLY. SOME SORT OF BATTLEFIELD SCAVENGER. THEY FLOCK AROUND WAR ZONES LIKE SEAGULLS AROUND TRAWLERS, GOBBLING PSYCHIC SCRAPS.
I SUPPOSE YOU TRIED KILLING IT?

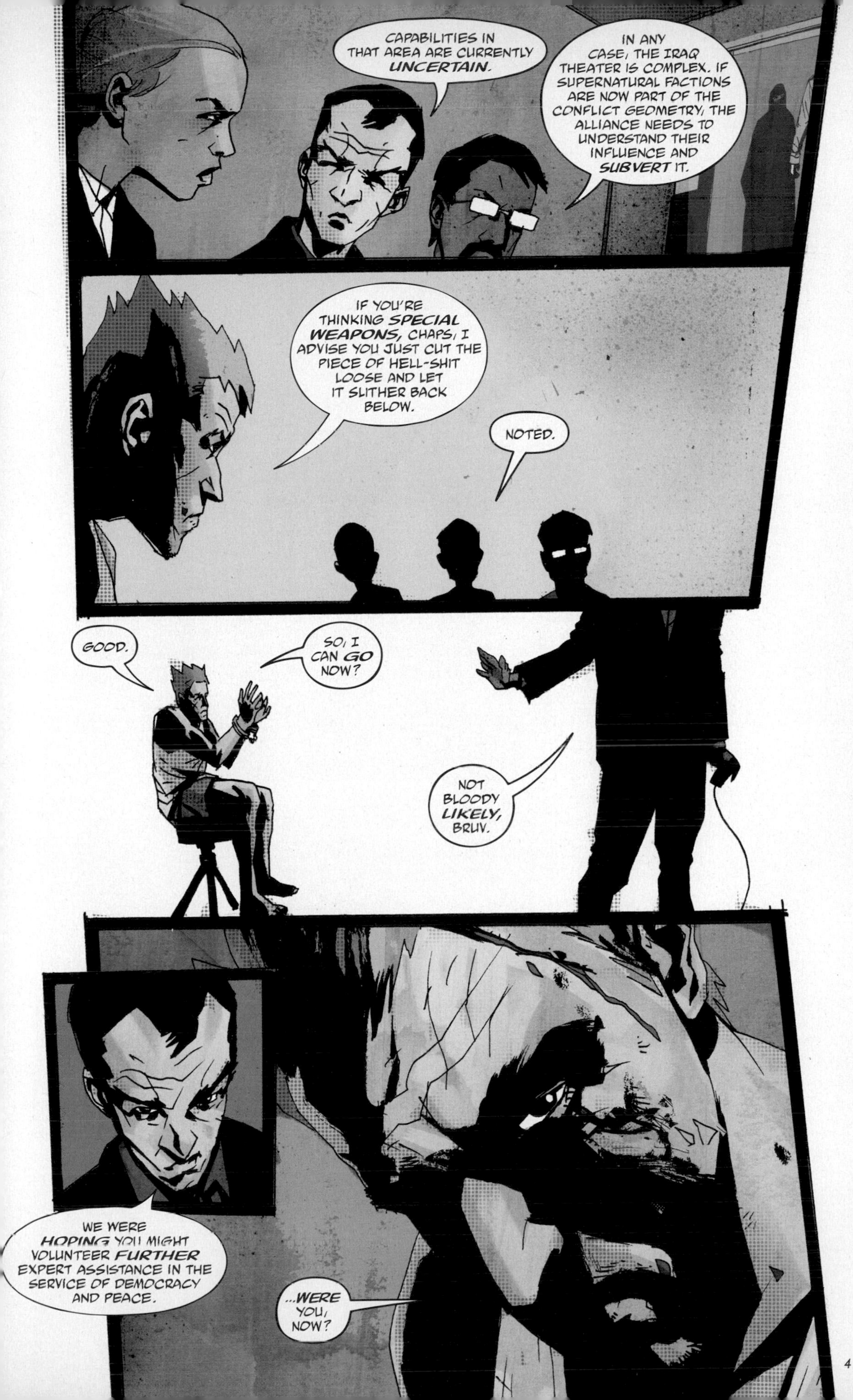
CAPABILITIES IN THAT AREA ARE CURRENTLY UNCERTAIN.
IN ANY CASE, THE IRAQ THEATER IS COMPLEX. IF SUPERNATURAL FACTIONS ARE NOW PART OF THE CONFLICT GEOMETRY, THE ALLIANCE NEEDS TO UNDERSTAND THEIR INFLUENCE AND SUBVERT IT.
IF YOU'RE THINKING SPECIAL WEAPONS, CHAPS, I ADVISE YOU JUST CUT THE PIECE OF HELL-SHIT LOOSE AND LET IT SLITHER BACK BELOW.
NOTED.
GOOD.
SO, I CAN GO NOW?
NOT BLOODY LIKELY, BRUV.
WE WERE HOPING YOU MIGHT VOLUNTEER FURTHER EXPERT ASSISTANCE IN THE SERVICE OF DEMOCRACY AND PEACE.
...WERE YOU, NOW?

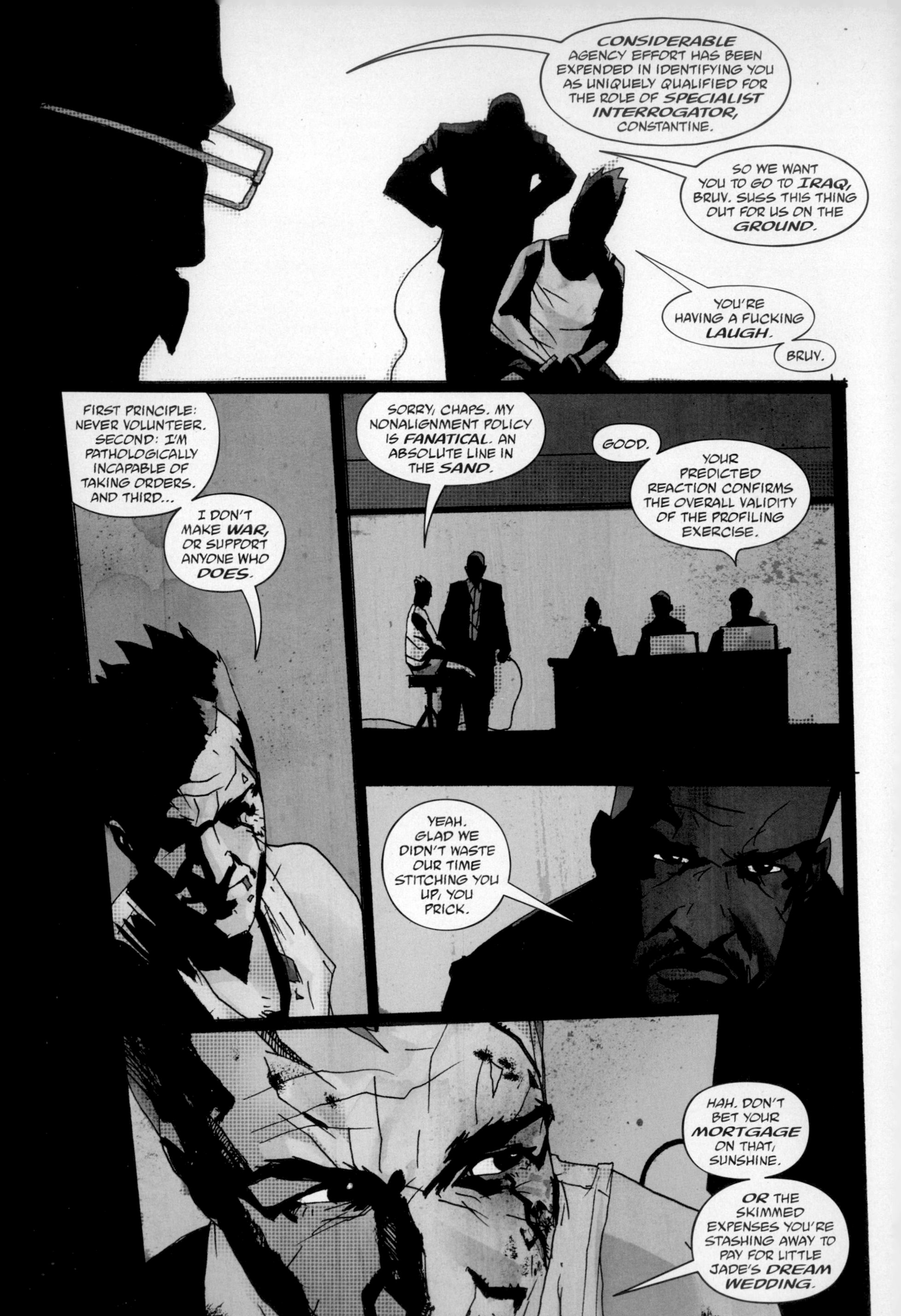
CONSIDERABLE AGENCY EFFORT HAS BEEN EXPENDED IN IDENTIFYING YOU AS UNIQUELY QUALIFIED FOR THE ROLE OF SPECIALIST INTERROGATOR, CONSTANTINE.
SO WE WANT YOU TO GO TO IRAQ, BRUV. SUSS THIS THING OUT FOR US ON THE GROUND.
YOU'RE HAVING A FUCKING LAUGH.
BRUV.
FIRST PRINCIPLE: NEVER VOLUNTEER. SECOND: I'M PATHOLOGICALLY INCAPABLE OF TAKING ORDERS. AND THIRD...
I DON'T MAKE WAR, OR SUPPORT ANYONE WHO DOES.
SORRY, CHAPS. MY NONALIGNMENT POLICY IS FANATICAL. AN ABSOLUTE LINE IN THE SAND.
GOOD.
YOUR PREDICTED REACTION CONFIRMS THE OVERALL VALIDITY OF THE PROFILING EXERCISE.
YEAH. GLAD WE DIDN'T WASTE OUR TIME STITCHING YOU UP, YOU PRICK.
HAH. DON'T BET YOUR MORTGAGE ON THAT, SUNSHINE.
OR THE SKIMMED EXPENSES YOU'RE STASHING AWAY TO PAY FOR LITTLE JADE'S DREAM WEDDING.

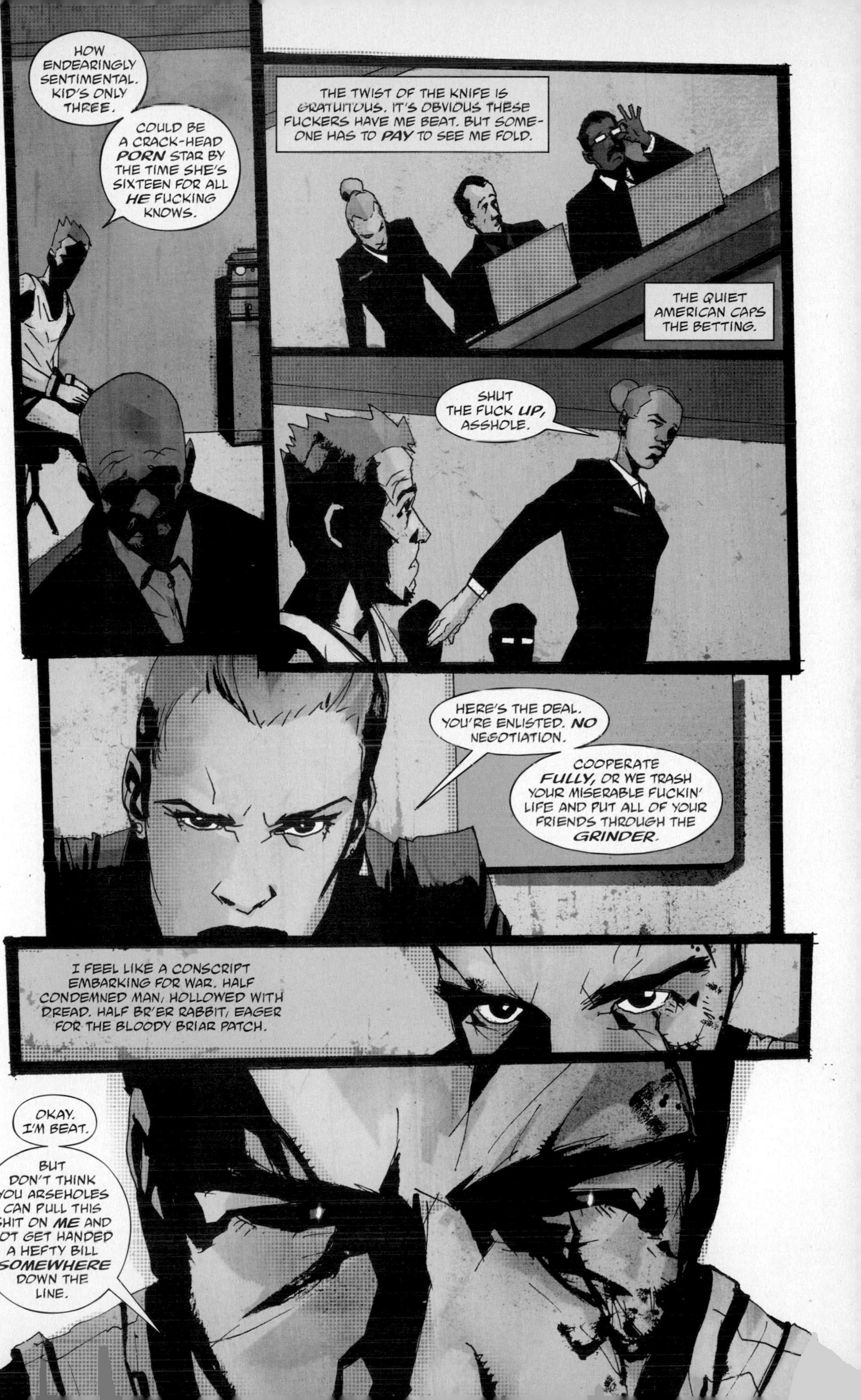
HOW ENDEARINGLY SENTIMENTAL. KID'S ONLY THREE.
COULD BE A CRACK-HEAD PORN STAR BY THE TIME SHE'S SIXTEEN FOR ALL HE FUCKING KNOWS.
THE TWIST OF THE KNIFE IS GRATUITOUS. IT'S OBVIOUS THESE FUCKERS HAVE ME BEAT. BUT SOME-ONE HAS TO PAY TO SEE ME FOLD.
THE QUIET AMERICAN CAPS THE BETTING.
SHUT THE FUCK UP, ASSHOLE.
HERE'S THE DEAL. YOU'RE ENLISTED. NO NEGOTIATION.
COOPERATE FULLY, OR WE TRASH YOUR MISERABLE FUCKIN' LIFE AND PUT ALL OF YOUR FRIENDS THROUGH THE GRINDER.
I FEEL LIKE A CONSCRIPT EMBARKING FOR WAR. HALF CONDEMNED MAN, HOLLOWED WITH DREAD. HALF BR'ER RABBIT, EAGER FOR THE BLOODY BRIAR PATCH.
OKAY. I'M BEAT.
BUT DON'T THINK YOU ARSEHOLES CAN PULL THIS SHIT ON ME AND NOT GET HANDED A HEFTY BILL SOMEWHERE DOWN THE LINE.

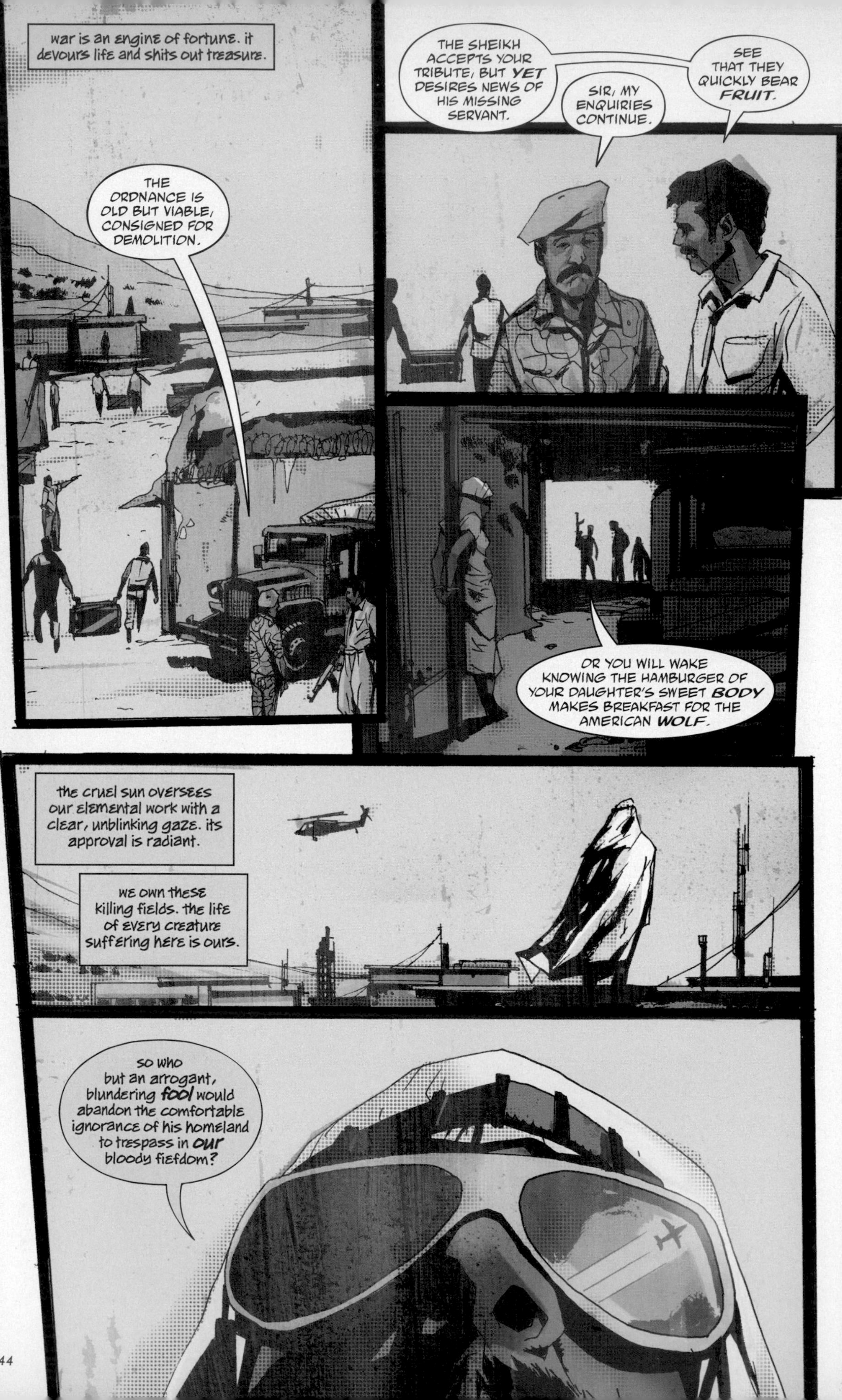
war is an engine of fortune. it devours life and shits out treasure.
THE ORDNANCE IS OLD BUT VIABLE, CONSIGNED FOR DEMOLITION.
THE SHEIKH ACCEPTS YOUR TRIBUTE, BUT YET DESIRES NEWS OF HIS MISSING SERVANT.
SIR, MY ENQUIRIES CONTINUE.
SEE THAT THEY QUICKLY BEAR FRUIT.
OR YOU WILL WAKE KNOWING THE HAMBURGER OF YOUR DAUGHTER'S SWEET BODY MAKES BREAKFAST FOR THE AMERICAN WOLF.
the cruel sun oversees our elemental work with a clear, unblinking gaze. its approval is radiant.
we own these killing fields. the life of every creature suffering here is ours.
so who but an arrogant, blundering fool would abandon the comfortable ignorance of his homeland to trespass in our bloody fiefdom?

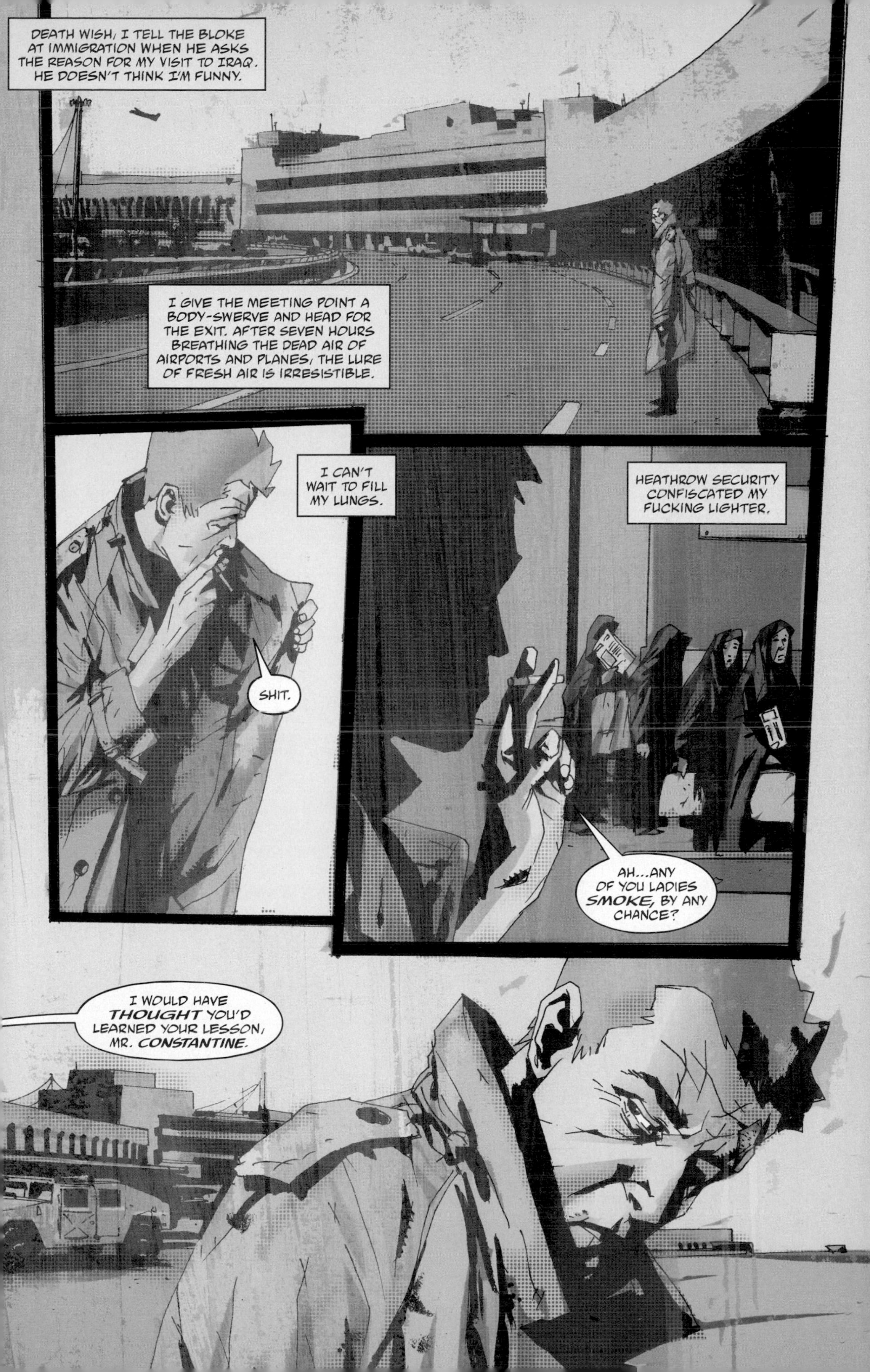
DEATH WISH, I TELL THE BLOKE AT IMMIGRATION WHEN HE ASKS THE REASON FOR MY VISIT TO IRAQ. HE DOESN'T THINK I'M FUNNY.
I GIVE THE MEETING POINT A BODY-SWERVE AND HEAD FOR THE EXIT. AFTER SEVEN HOURS BREATHING THE DEAD AIR OF AIRPORTS AND PLANES, THE LURE OF FRESH AIR IS IRRESISTIBLE.
I CAN'T WAIT TO FILL MY LUNGS.
SHIT.
HEATHROW SECURITY CONFISCATED MY FUCKING LIGHTER.
AH...ANY OF YOU LADIES SMOKE, BY ANY CHANCE?
I WOULD HAVE THOUGHT YOU'D LEARNED YOUR LESSON, MR. CONSTANTINE.

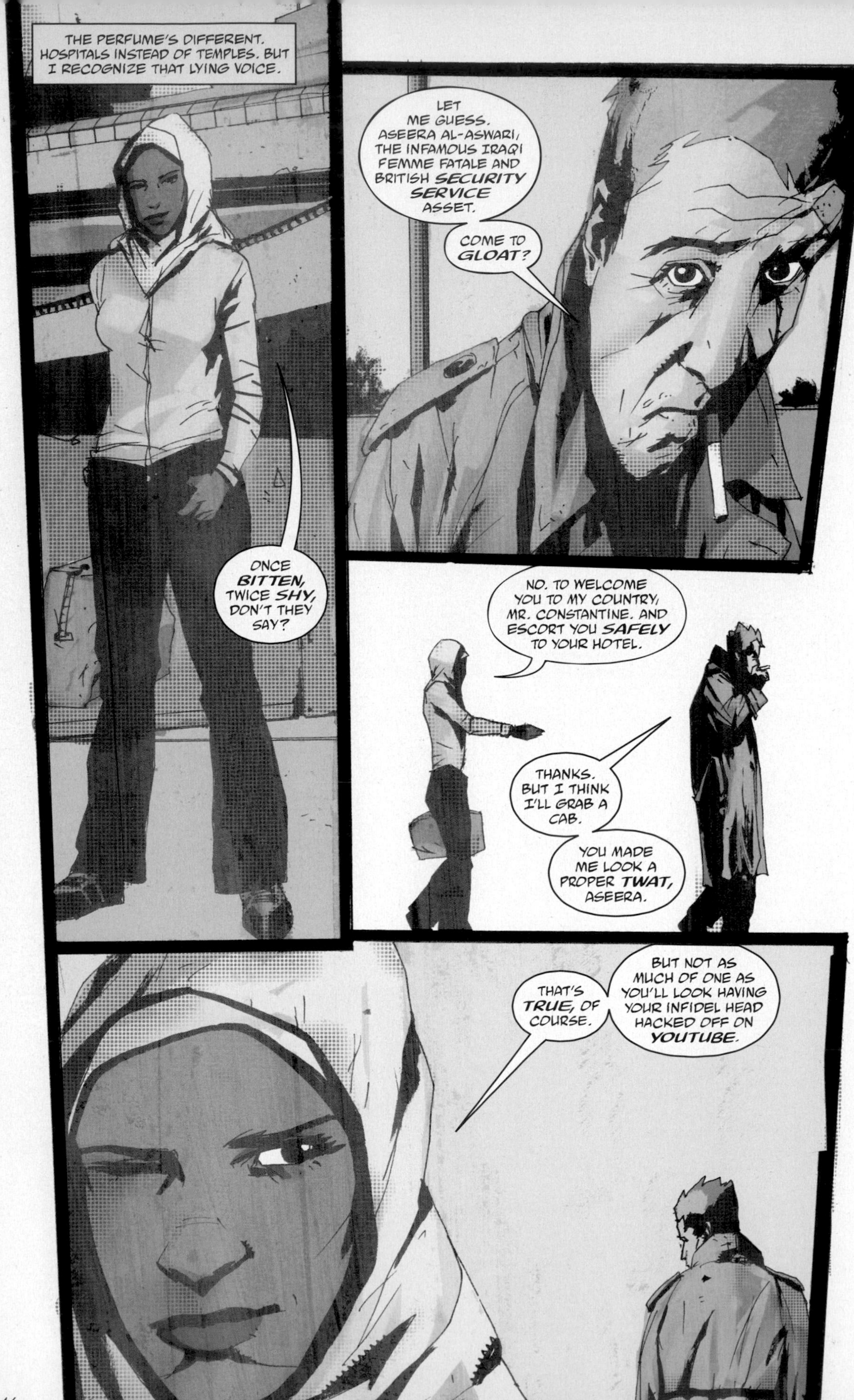
THE PERFUME'S DIFFERENT. HOSPITALS INSTEAD OF TEMPLES. BUT I RECOGNIZE THAT LYING VOICE.
LET ME GUESS. ASEERA AL-ASWARI, THE INFAMOUS IRAQI FEMME FATALE AND BRITISH SECURITY SERVICE ASSET.
COME TO GLOAT?
ONCE BITTEN, TWICE SHY, DON'T THEY SAY?
NO. TO WELCOME YOU TO MY COUNTRY, MR. CONSTANTINE. AND ESCORT YOU SAFELY TO YOUR HOTEL.
THANKS. BUT I THINK I'LL GRAB A CAB.
YOU MADE ME LOOK A PROPER TWAT, ASEERA.
THAT'S TRUE, OF COURSE.
BUT NOT AS MUCH OF ONE AS YOU'LL LOOK HAVING YOUR INFIDEL HEAD HACKED OFF ON YOUTUBE.

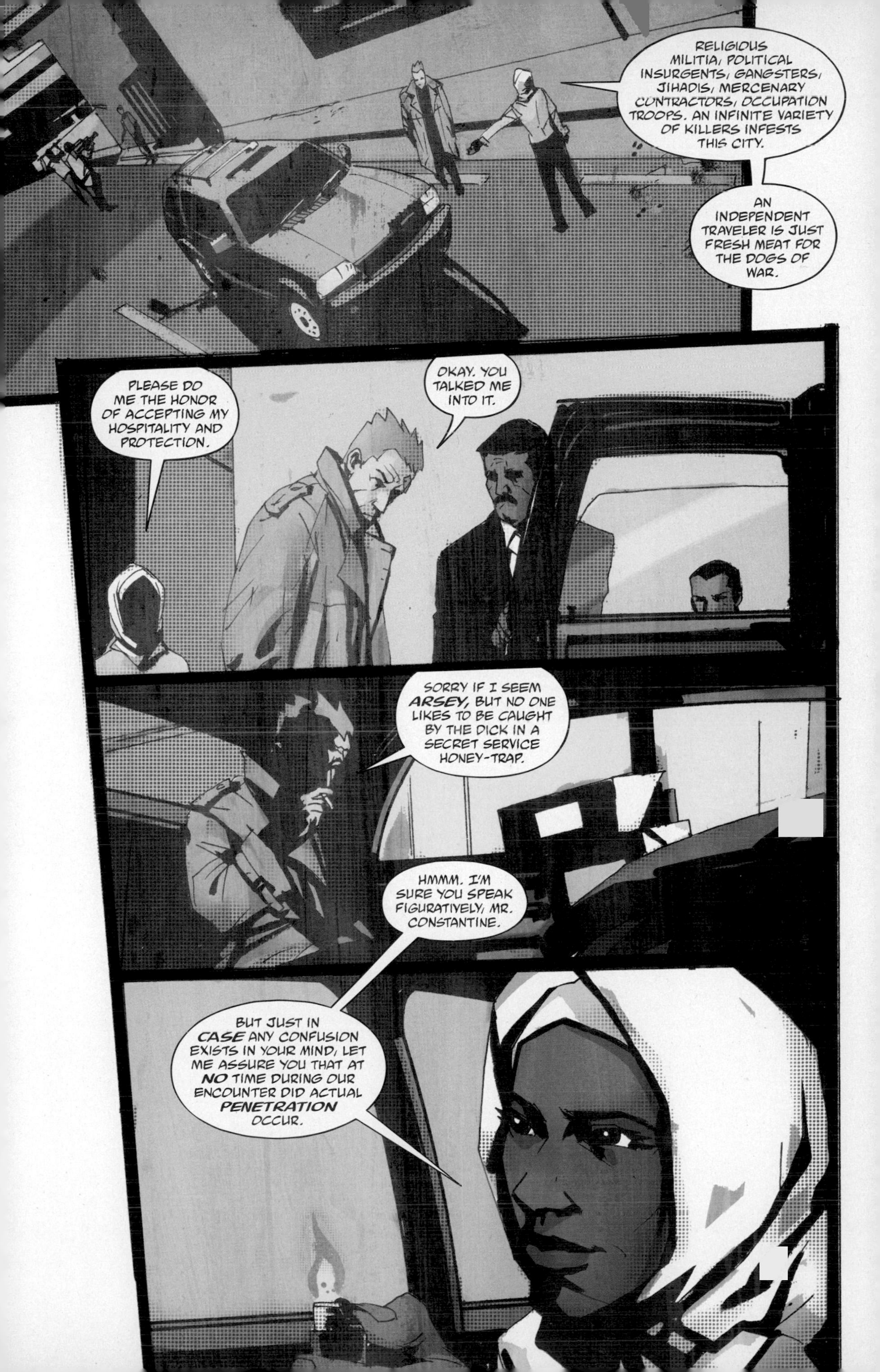
RELIGIOUS MILITIA, POLITICAL INSURGENTS, GANGSTERS, JIHADIS, MERCENARY CONTRACTORS, OCCUPATION TROOPS. AN INFINITE VARIETY OF KILLERS INFESTS THIS CITY.
AN INDEPENDENT TRAVELER IS JUST FRESH MEAT FOR THE DOGS OF WAR.
PLEASE DO ME THE HONOR OF ACCEPTING MY HOSPITALITY AND PROTECTION.
OKAY. YOU TALKED ME INTO IT.
SORRY IF I SEEM ARSEY, BUT NO ONE LIKES TO BE CAUGHT BY THE DICK IN A SECRET SERVICE HONEY-TRAP.
HMMM. I'M SURE YOU SPEAK FIGURATIVELY, MR. CONSTANTINE.
BUT JUST IN CASE ANY CONFUSION EXISTS IN YOUR MIND, LET ME ASSURE YOU THAT AT NO TIME DURING OUR ENCOUNTER DID ACTUAL PENETRATION OCCUR.

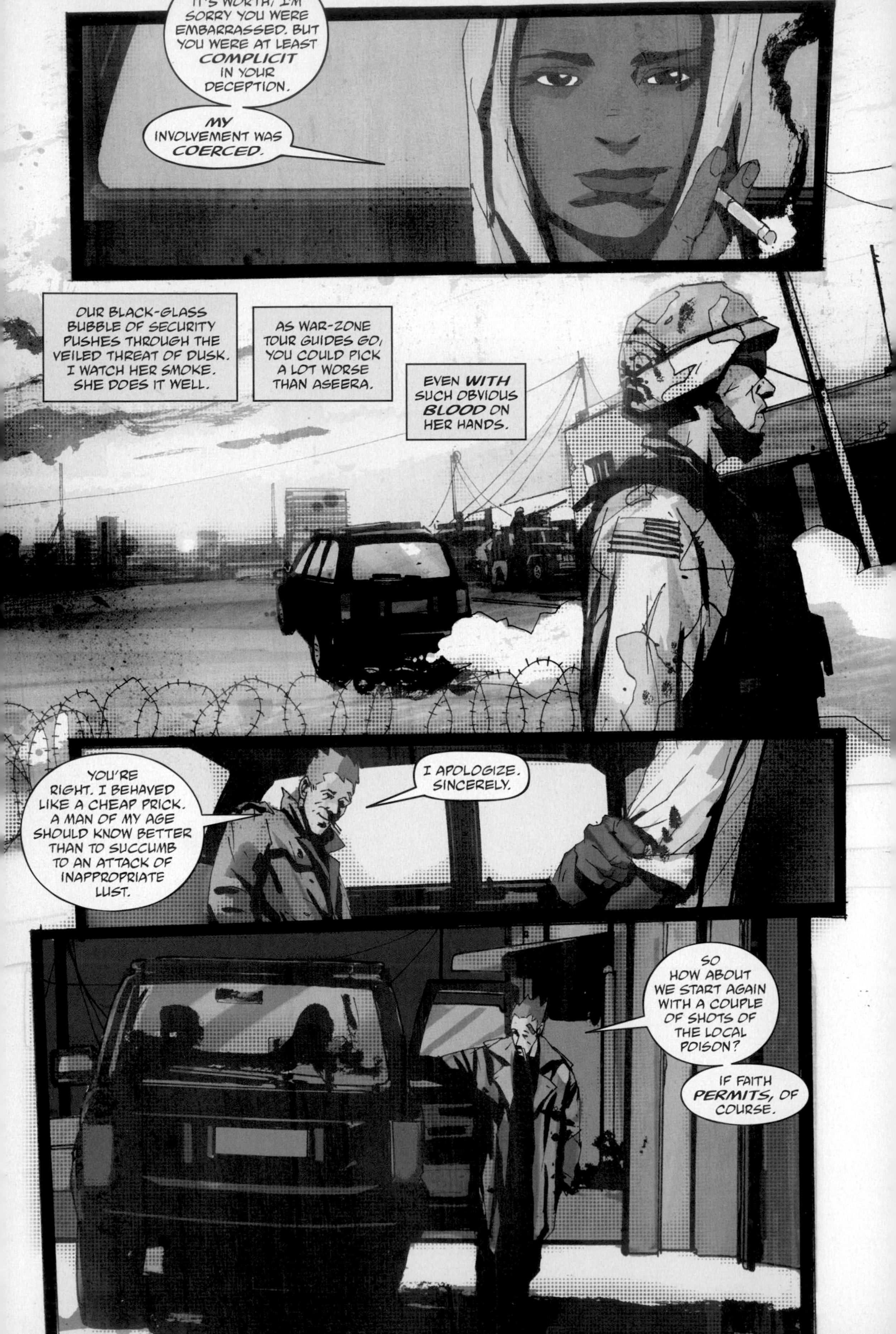
FOR WHAT IT'S WORTH, I'M SORRY YOU WERE EMBARRASSED. BUT YOU WERE AT LEAST COMPLICIT IN YOUR DECEPTION.
MY INVOLVEMENT WAS COERCED.
OUR BLACK-GLASS BUBBLE OF SECURITY PUSHES THROUGH THE VEILED THREAT OF DUSK. I WATCH HER SMOKE. SHE DOES IT WELL.
AS WAR-ZONE TOUR GUIDES GO, YOU COULD PICK A LOT WORSE THAN ASEERA.
EVEN WITH SUCH OBVIOUS BLOOD ON HER HANDS.
YOU'RE RIGHT. I BEHAVED LIKE A CHEAP PRICK. A MAN OF MY AGE SHOULD KNOW BETTER THAN TO SUCCUMB TO AN ATTACK OF INAPPROPRIATE LUST.
I APOLOGIZE. SINCERELY.
SO HOW ABOUT WE START AGAIN WITH A COUPLE OF SHOTS OF THE LOCAL POISON?
IF FAITH PERMITS, OF COURSE.

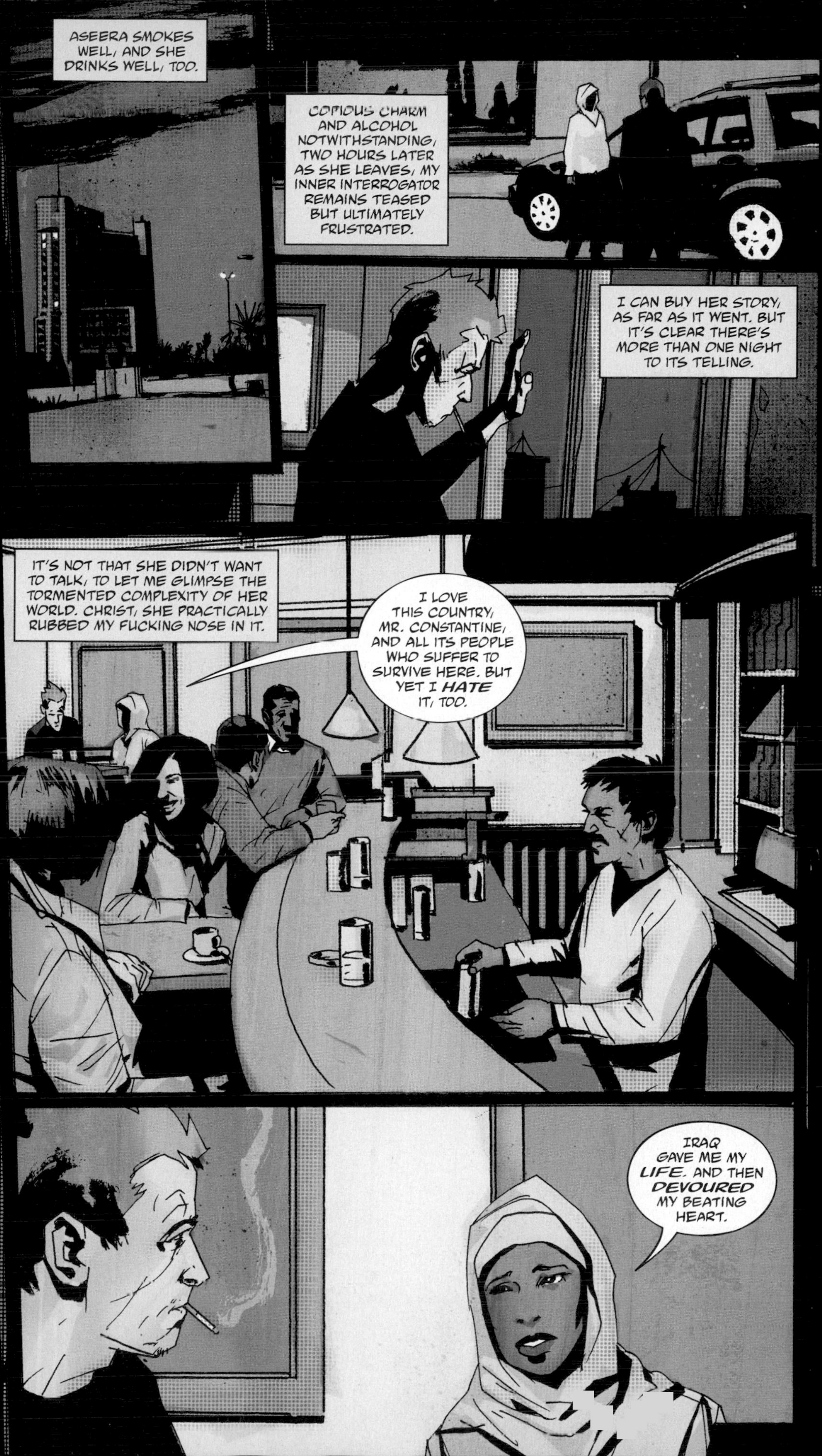
ASEERA SMOKES WELL, AND SHE DRINKS WELL, TOO.
COPIOUS CHARM AND ALCOHOL NOTWITHSTANDING, TWO HOURS LATER AS SHE LEAVES, MY INNER INTERROGATOR REMAINS TEASED BUT ULTIMATELY FRUSTRATED.
I CAN BUY HER STORY, AS FAR AS IT WENT. BUT IT'S CLEAR THERE'S MORE THAN ONE NIGHT TO ITS TELLING.
IT'S NOT THAT SHE DIDN'T WANT TO TALK, TO LET ME GLIMPSE THE TORMENTED COMPLEXITY OF HER WORLD. CHRIST, SHE PRACTICALLY RUBBED MY FUCKING NOSE IN IT.
I LOVE THIS COUNTRY, MR. CONSTANTINE, AND ALL ITS PEOPLE WHO SUFFER TO SURVIVE HERE. BUT YET I HATE IT, TOO.
IRAQ GAVE ME MY LIFE. AND THEN DEVOURED MY BEATING HEART.

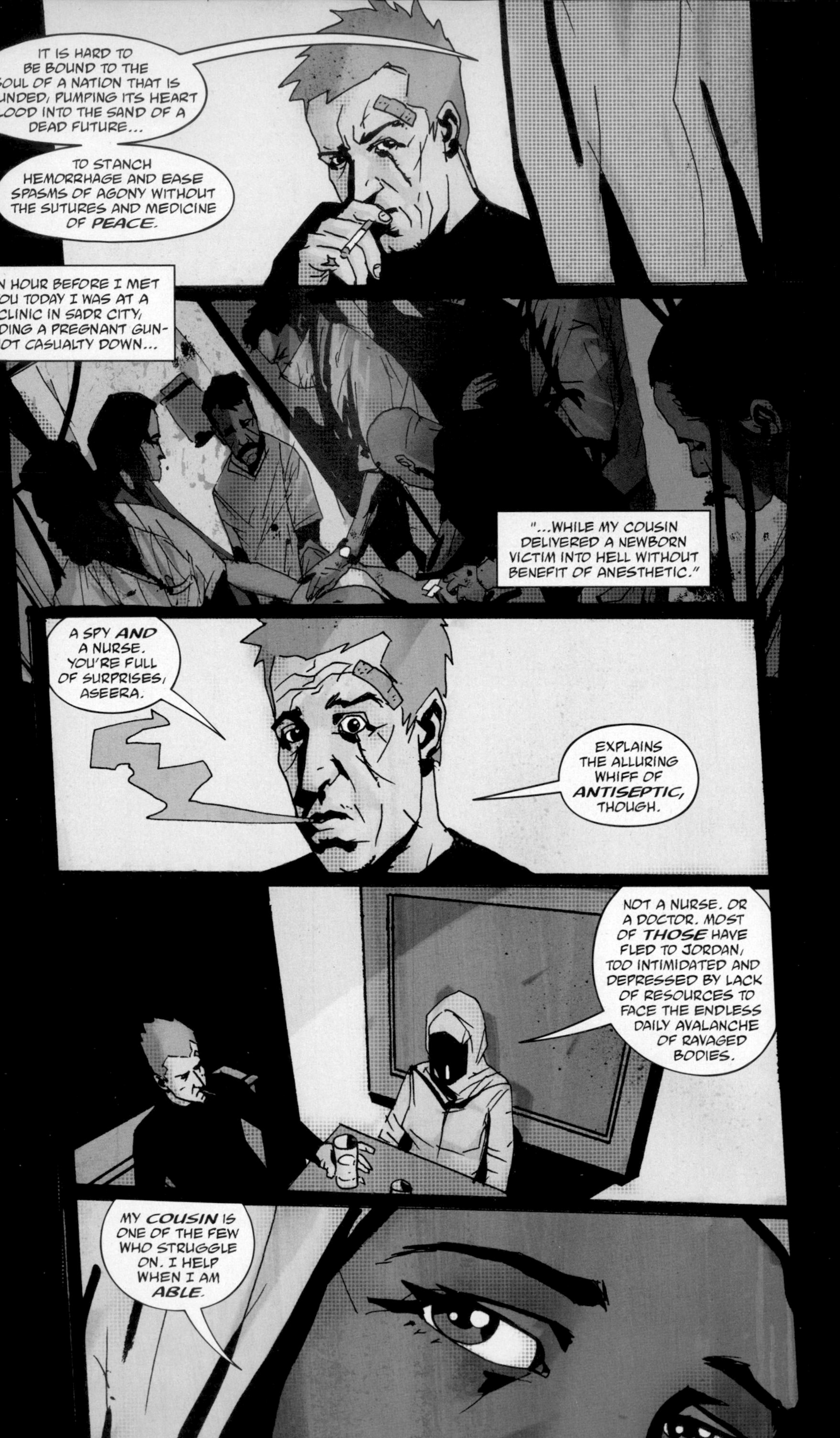
IT IS HARD TO BE BOUND TO THE SOUL OF A NATION THAT IS WOUNDED, PUMPING ITS HEART BLOOD INTO THE SAND OF A DEAD FUTURE...
TO STANCH HEMORRHAGE AND EASE SPASMS OF AGONY WITHOUT THE SUTURES AND MEDICINE OF *PEACE*.
"AN HOUR BEFORE I MET YOU TODAY I WAS AT A CLINIC IN SADR CITY, HOLDING A PREGNANT GUN-SHOT CASUALTY DOWN...
"...WHILE MY COUSIN DELIVERED A NEWBORN VICTIM INTO HELL WITHOUT BENEFIT OF ANESTHETIC."
A SPY *AND* A NURSE. YOU'RE FULL OF SURPRISES, ASEERA.
EXPLAINS THE ALLURING WHIFF OF *ANTISEPTIC*, THOUGH.
NOT A NURSE. OR A DOCTOR. MOST OF *THOSE* HAVE FLED TO JORDAN, TOO INTIMIDATED AND DEPRESSED BY LACK OF RESOURCES TO FACE THE ENDLESS DAILY AVALANCHE OF RAVAGED BODIES.
MY *COUSIN* IS ONE OF THE FEW WHO STRUGGLE ON. I HELP WHEN I AM *ABLE*.

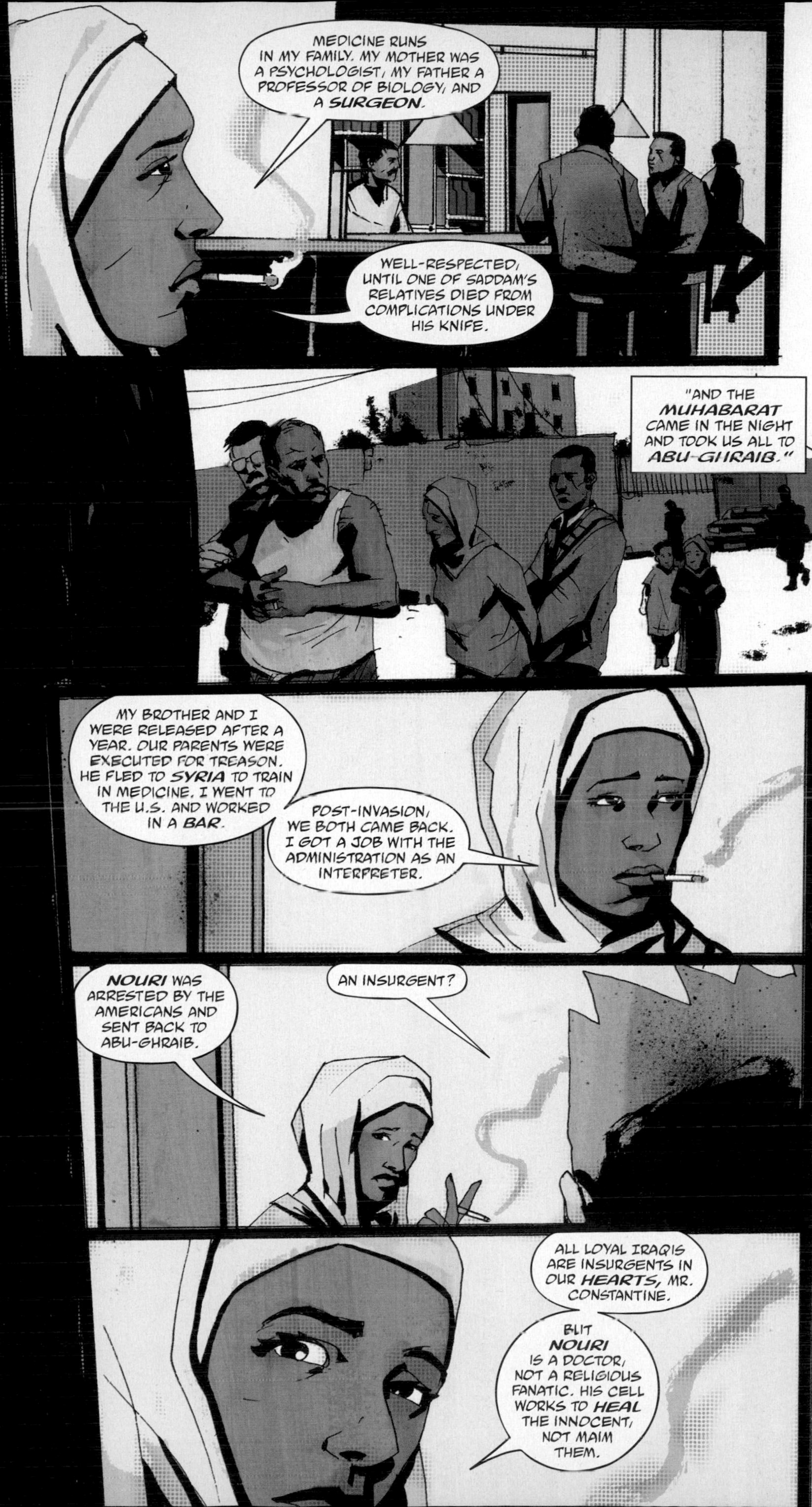

MEDICINE RUNS IN MY FAMILY. MY MOTHER WAS A PSYCHOLOGIST, MY FATHER A PROFESSOR OF BIOLOGY, AND A SURGEON.
WELL-RESPECTED, UNTIL ONE OF SADDAM'S RELATIVES DIED FROM COMPLICATIONS UNDER HIS KNIFE.
"AND THE MUHABARAT CAME IN THE NIGHT AND TOOK US ALL TO ABU-GHRAIB."
MY BROTHER AND I WERE RELEASED AFTER A YEAR. OUR PARENTS WERE EXECUTED FOR TREASON. HE FLED TO SYRIA TO TRAIN IN MEDICINE. I WENT TO THE U.S. AND WORKED IN A BAR.
POST-INVASION, WE BOTH CAME BACK. I GOT A JOB WITH THE ADMINISTRATION AS AN INTERPRETER.
NOURI WAS ARRESTED BY THE AMERICANS AND SENT BACK TO ABU-GHRAIB.
AN INSURGENT?
ALL LOYAL IRAQIS ARE INSURGENTS IN OUR HEARTS, MR. CONSTANTINE.
BUT NOURI IS A DOCTOR, NOT A RELIGIOUS FANATIC. HIS CELL WORKS TO HEAL THE INNOCENT, NOT MAIM THEM.

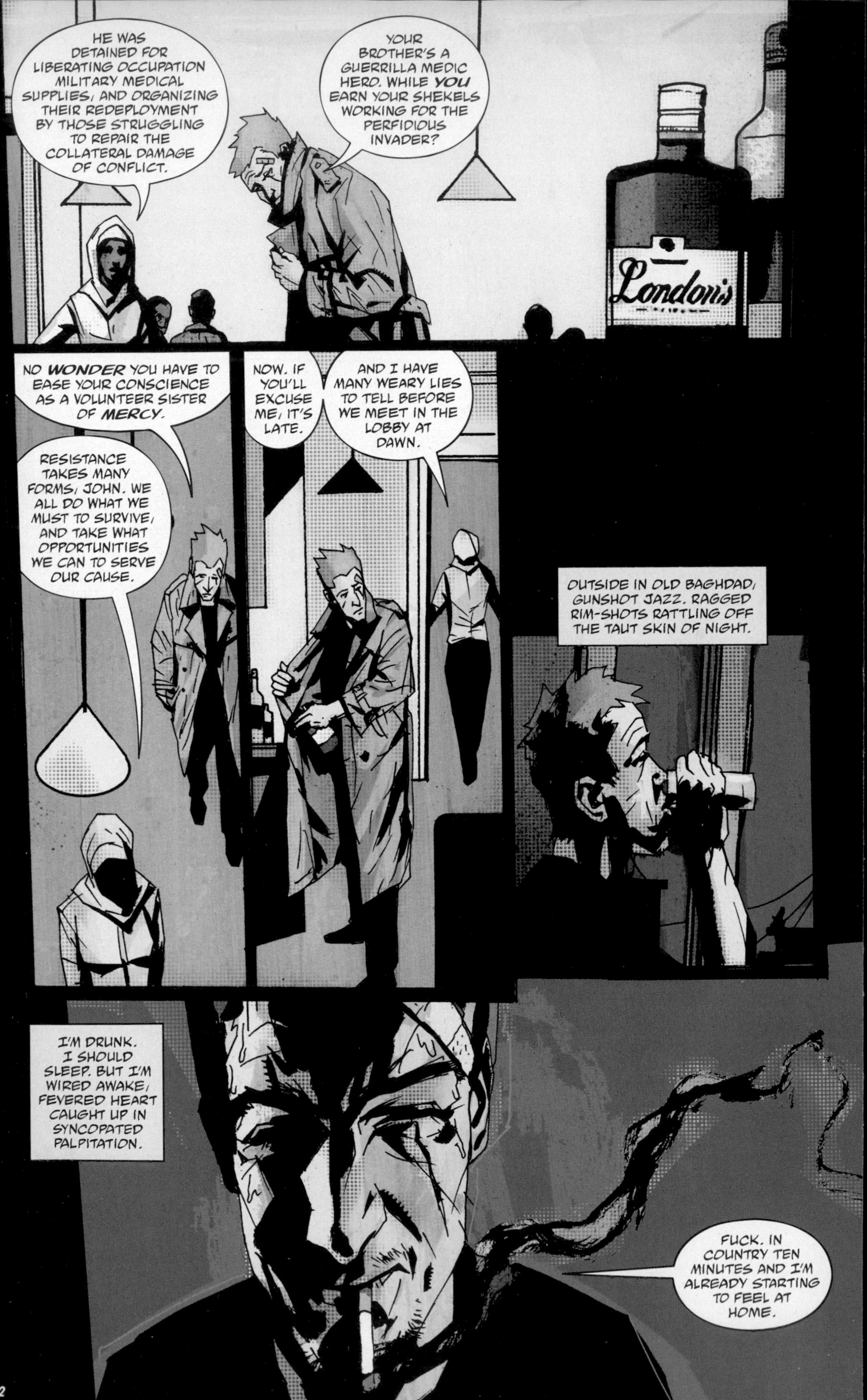
HE WAS DETAINED FOR LIBERATING OCCUPATION MILITARY MEDICAL SUPPLIES, AND ORGANIZING THEIR REDEPLOYMENT BY THOSE STRUGGLING TO REPAIR THE COLLATERAL DAMAGE OF CONFLICT.
YOUR BROTHER'S A GUERRILLA MEDIC HERO. WHILE YOU EARN YOUR SHEKELS WORKING FOR THE PERFIDIOUS INVADER?
Londons
NO WONDER YOU HAVE TO EASE YOUR CONSCIENCE AS A VOLUNTEER SISTER OF MERCY.
RESISTANCE TAKES MANY FORMS, JOHN. WE ALL DO WHAT WE MUST TO SURVIVE, AND TAKE WHAT OPPORTUNITIES WE CAN TO SERVE OUR CAUSE.
NOW. IF YOU'LL EXCUSE ME, IT'S LATE.
AND I HAVE MANY WEARY LIES TO TELL BEFORE WE MEET IN THE LOBBY AT DAWN.
OUTSIDE IN OLD BAGHDAD, GUNSHOT JAZZ. RAGGED RIM-SHOTS RATTLING OFF THE TAUT SKIN OF NIGHT.
I'M DRUNK. I SHOULD SLEEP. BUT I'M WIRED AWAKE, FEVERED HEART CAUGHT UP IN SYNCOPATED PALPITATION.
FUCK. IN COUNTRY TEN MINUTES AND I'M ALREADY STARTING TO FEEL AT HOME.

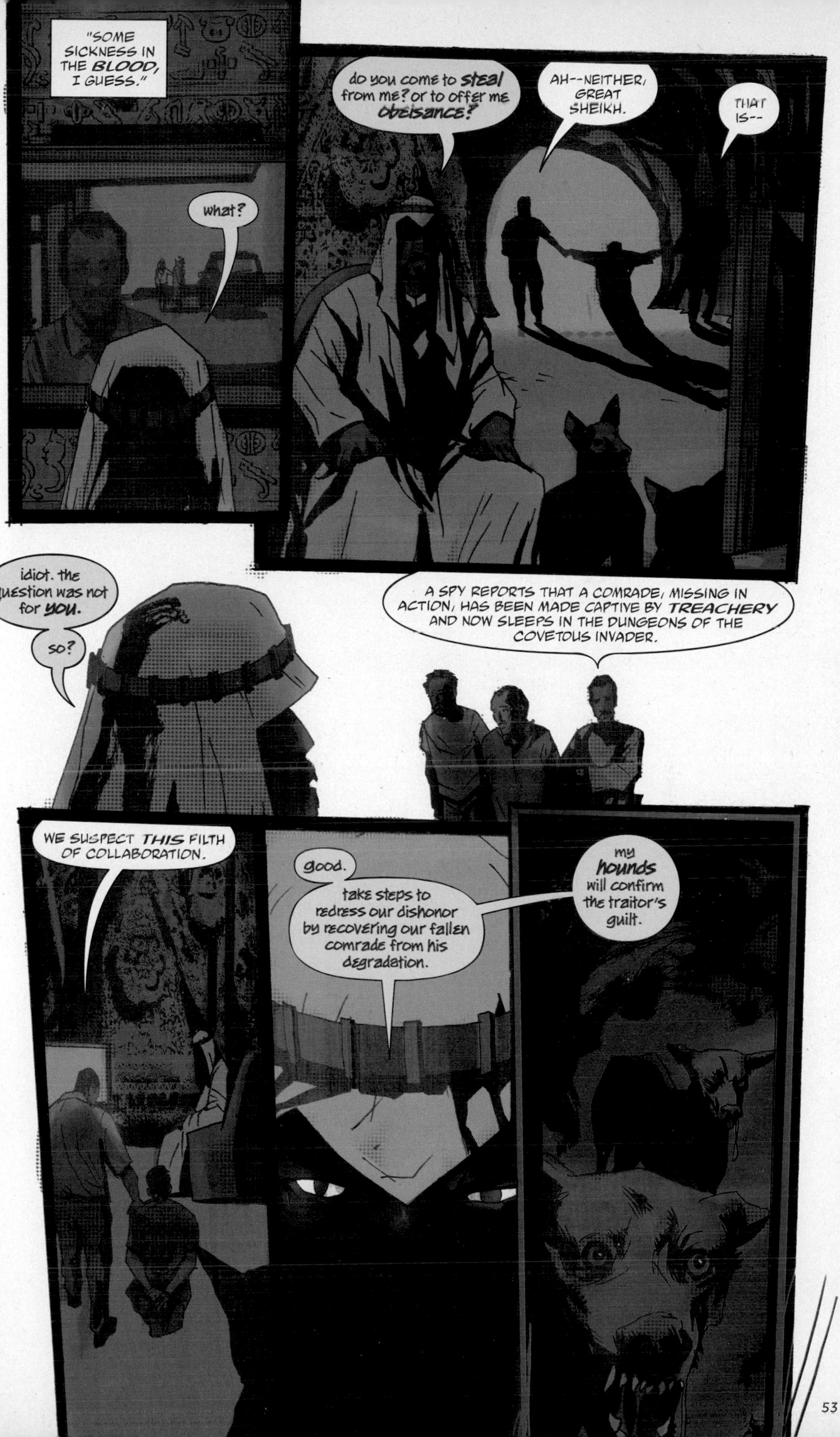
"SOME SICKNESS IN THE BLOOD, I GUESS."
what?
do you come to steal from me? or to offer me obeisance?
AH--NEITHER, GREAT SHEIKH.
THAT IS--
idiot. the question was not for YOU.
so?
A SPY REPORTS THAT A COMRADE, MISSING IN ACTION, HAS BEEN MADE CAPTIVE BY TREACHERY AND NOW SLEEPS IN THE DUNGEONS OF THE COVETOUS INVADER.
WE SUSPECT THIS FILTH OF COLLABORATION.
good.
take steps to redress our dishonor by recovering our fallen comrade from his degradation.
my hounds will confirm the traitor's guilt.

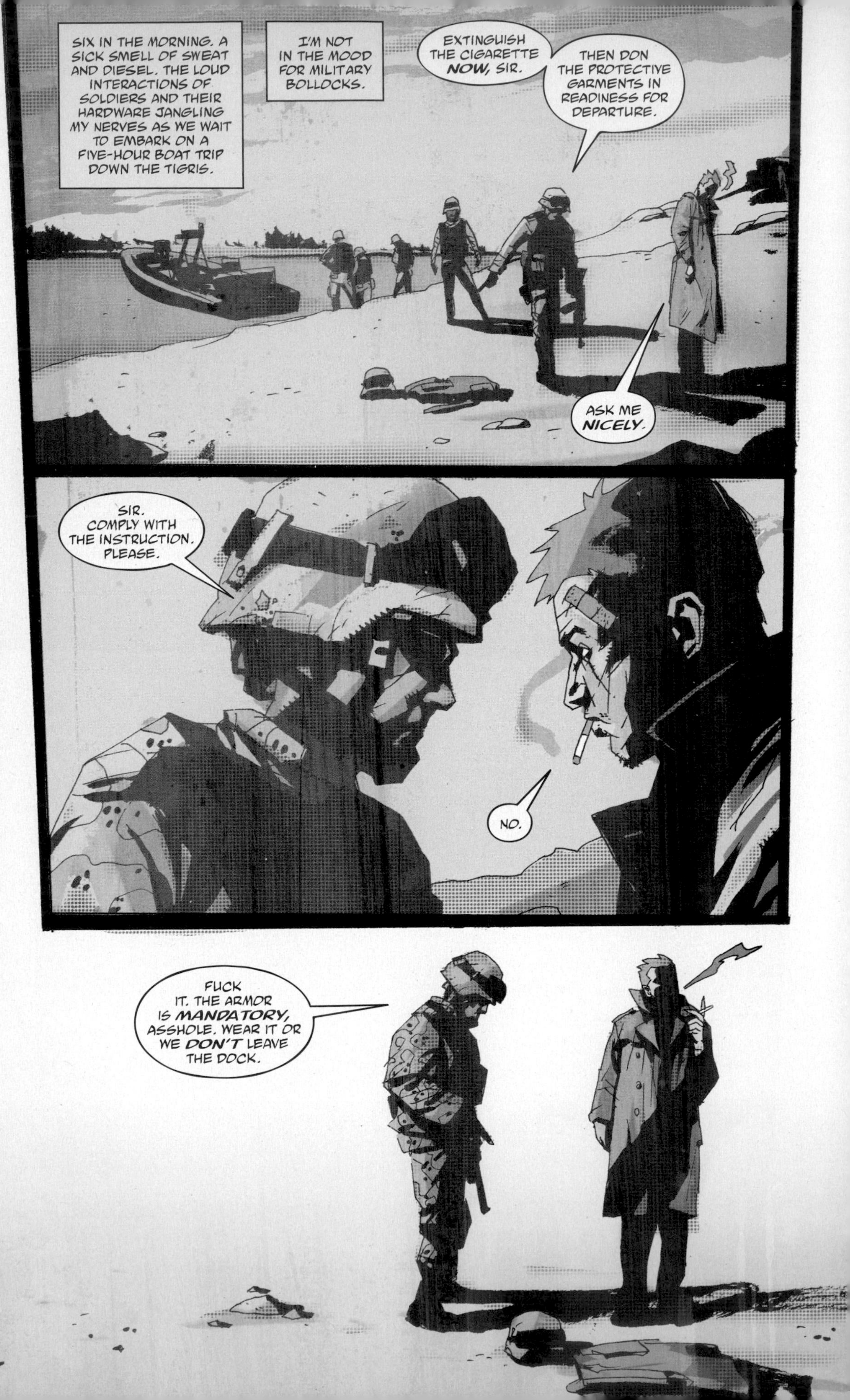
SIX IN THE MORNING. A SICK SMELL OF SWEAT AND DIESEL. THE LOUD INTERACTIONS OF SOLDIERS AND THEIR HARDWARE JANGLING MY NERVES AS WE WAIT TO EMBARK ON A FIVE-HOUR BOAT TRIP DOWN THE TIGRIS.
I'M NOT IN THE MOOD FOR MILITARY BOLLOCKS.
EXTINGUISH THE CIGARETTE NOW, SIR.
THEN DON THE PROTECTIVE GARMENTS IN READINESS FOR DEPARTURE.
ASK ME NICELY.
SIR. COMPLY WITH THE INSTRUCTION. PLEASE.
NO.
FUCK IT. THE ARMOR IS MANDATORY, ASSHOLE. WEAR IT OR WE DON'T LEAVE THE DOCK.

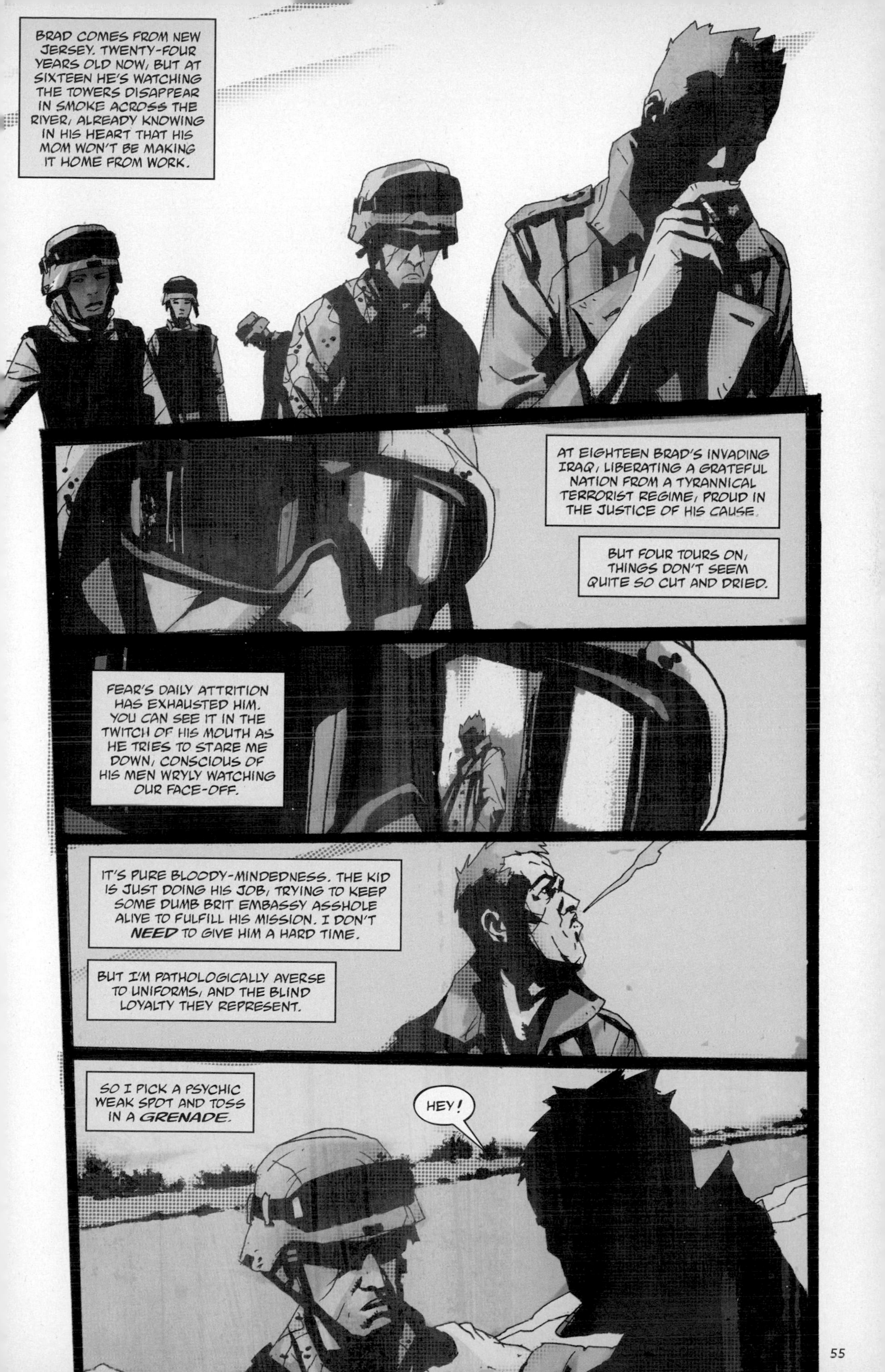
BRAD COMES FROM NEW JERSEY. TWENTY-FOUR YEARS OLD NOW, BUT AT SIXTEEN HE'S WATCHING THE TOWERS DISAPPEAR IN SMOKE ACROSS THE RIVER, ALREADY KNOWING IN HIS HEART THAT HIS MOM WON'T BE MAKING IT HOME FROM WORK.
AT EIGHTEEN BRAD'S INVADING IRAQ, LIBERATING A GRATEFUL NATION FROM A TYRANNICAL TERRORIST REGIME, PROUD IN THE JUSTICE OF HIS CAUSE.
BUT FOUR TOURS ON, THINGS DON'T SEEM QUITE SO CUT AND DRIED.
FEAR'S DAILY ATTRITION HAS EXHAUSTED HIM. YOU CAN SEE IT IN THE TWITCH OF HIS MOUTH AS HE TRIES TO STARE ME DOWN, CONSCIOUS OF HIS MEN WRYLY WATCHING OUR FACE-OFF.
IT'S PURE BLOODY-MINDEDNESS. THE KID IS JUST DOING HIS JOB, TRYING TO KEEP SOME DUMB BRIT EMBASSY ASSHOLE ALIVE TO FULFILL HIS MISSION. I DON'T NEED TO GIVE HIM A HARD TIME.
BUT I'M PATHOLOGICALLY AVERSE TO UNIFORMS, AND THE BLIND LOYALTY THEY REPRESENT.
SO I PICK A PSYCHIC WEAK SPOT AND TOSS IN A GRENADE.
HEY!

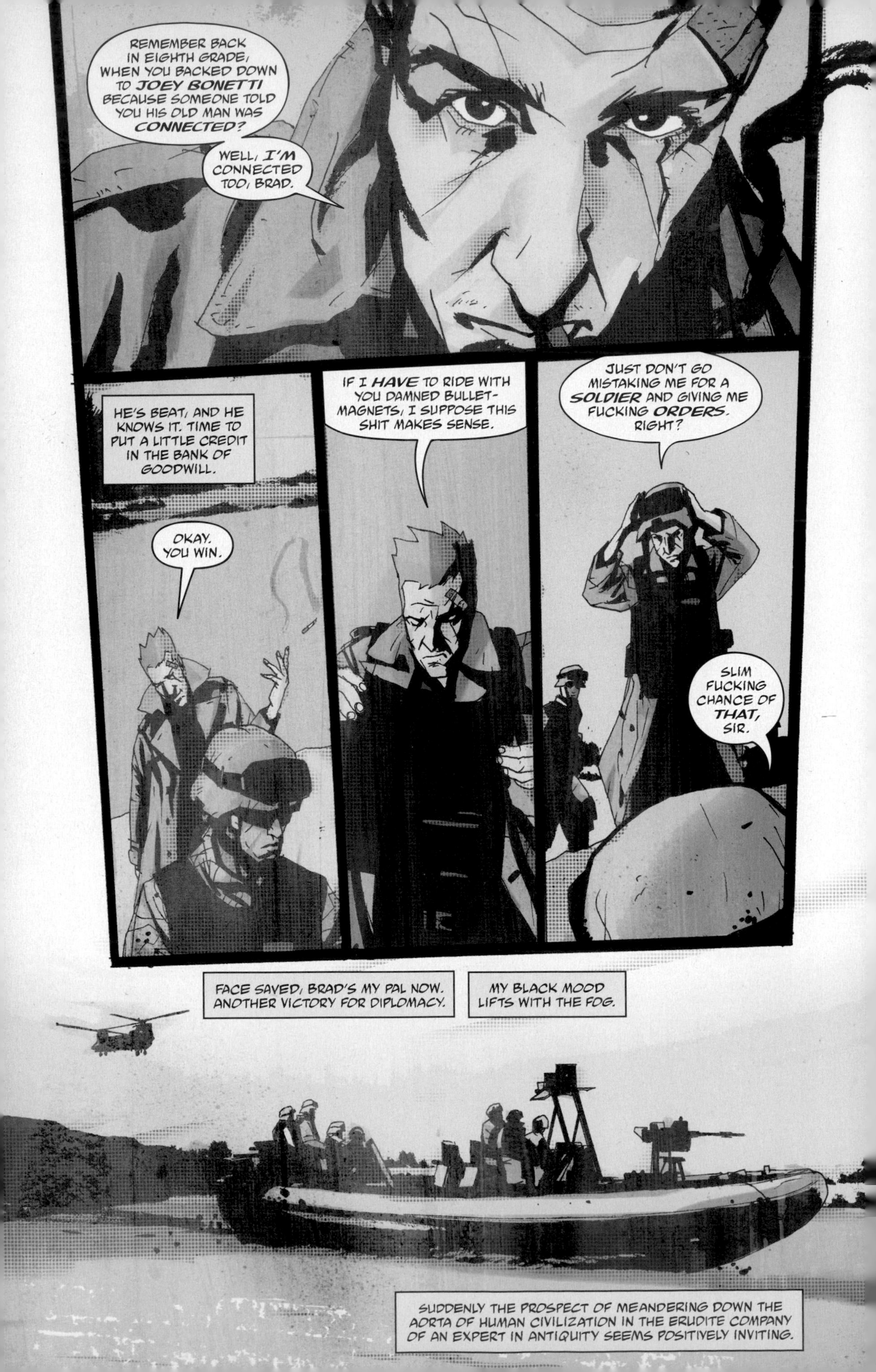

REMEMBER BACK IN EIGHTH GRADE, WHEN YOU BACKED DOWN TO JOEY BONETTI BECAUSE SOMEONE TOLD YOU HIS OLD MAN WAS CONNECTED?
WELL, I'M CONNECTED TOO, BRAD.
HE'S BEAT, AND HE KNOWS IT. TIME TO PUT A LITTLE CREDIT IN THE BANK OF GOODWILL.
OKAY. YOU WIN.
IF I HAVE TO RIDE WITH YOU DAMNED BULLET-MAGNETS, I SUPPOSE THIS SHIT MAKES SENSE.
JUST DON'T GO MISTAKING ME FOR A SOLDIER AND GIVING ME FUCKING ORDERS. RIGHT?
SLIM FUCKING CHANCE OF THAT, SIR.
FACE SAVED, BRAD'S MY PAL NOW. ANOTHER VICTORY FOR DIPLOMACY.
MY BLACK MOOD LIFTS WITH THE FOG.
SUDDENLY THE PROSPECT OF MEANDERING DOWN THE AORTA OF HUMAN CIVILIZATION IN THE ERUDITE COMPANY OF AN EXPERT IN ANTIQUITY SEEMS POSITIVELY INVITING.

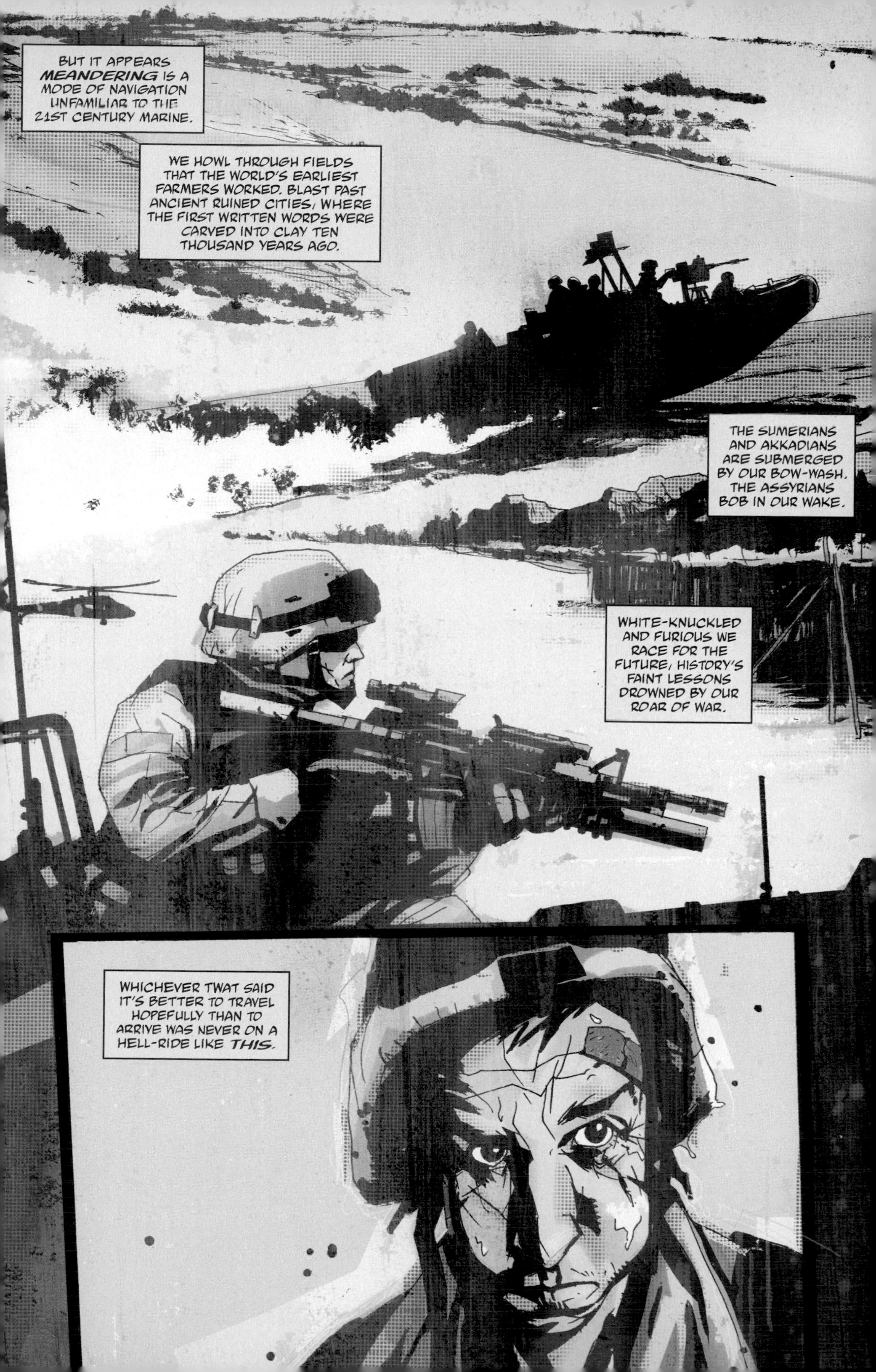

BUT IT APPEARS *MEANDERING* IS A MODE OF NAVIGATION UNFAMILIAR TO THE 21ST CENTURY MARINE.
WE HOWL THROUGH FIELDS THAT THE WORLD'S EARLIEST FARMERS WORKED. BLAST PAST ANCIENT RUINED CITIES, WHERE THE FIRST WRITTEN WORDS WERE CARVED INTO CLAY TEN THOUSAND YEARS AGO.
THE SUMERIANS AND AKKADIANS ARE SUBMERGED BY OUR BOW-WASH. THE ASSYRIANS BOB IN OUR WAKE.
WHITE-KNUCKLED AND FURIOUS WE RACE FOR THE FUTURE, HISTORY'S FAINT LESSONS DROWNED BY OUR ROAR OF WAR.
WHICHEVER TWAT SAID IT'S BETTER TO TRAVEL HOPEFULLY THAN TO ARRIVE WAS NEVER ON A HELL-RIDE LIKE *THIS*.

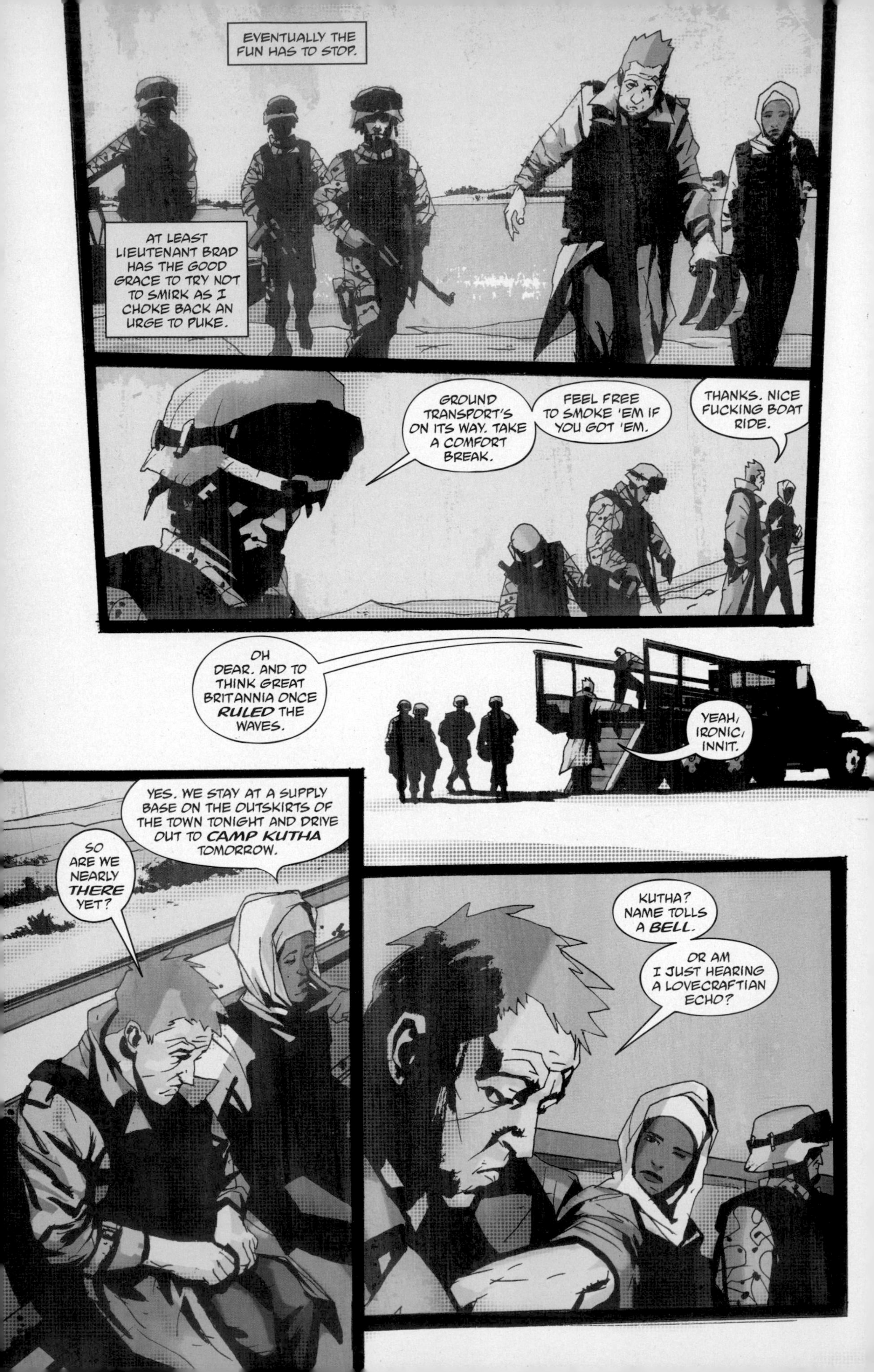
EVENTUALLY THE FUN HAS TO STOP.
AT LEAST LIEUTENANT BRAD HAS THE GOOD GRACE TO TRY NOT TO SMIRK AS I CHOKE BACK AN URGE TO PUKE.
GROUND TRANSPORT'S ON ITS WAY. TAKE A COMFORT BREAK.
FEEL FREE TO SMOKE 'EM IF YOU GOT 'EM.
THANKS. NICE FUCKING BOAT RIDE.
OH DEAR. AND TO THINK GREAT BRITANNIA ONCE RULED THE WAVES.
YEAH, IRONIC, INNIT.
SO ARE WE NEARLY THERE YET?
YES. WE STAY AT A SUPPLY BASE ON THE OUTSKIRTS OF THE TOWN TONIGHT AND DRIVE OUT TO CAMP KUTHA TOMORROW.
KUTHA? NAME TOLLS A BELL.
OR AM I JUST HEARING A LOVECRAFTIAN ECHO?

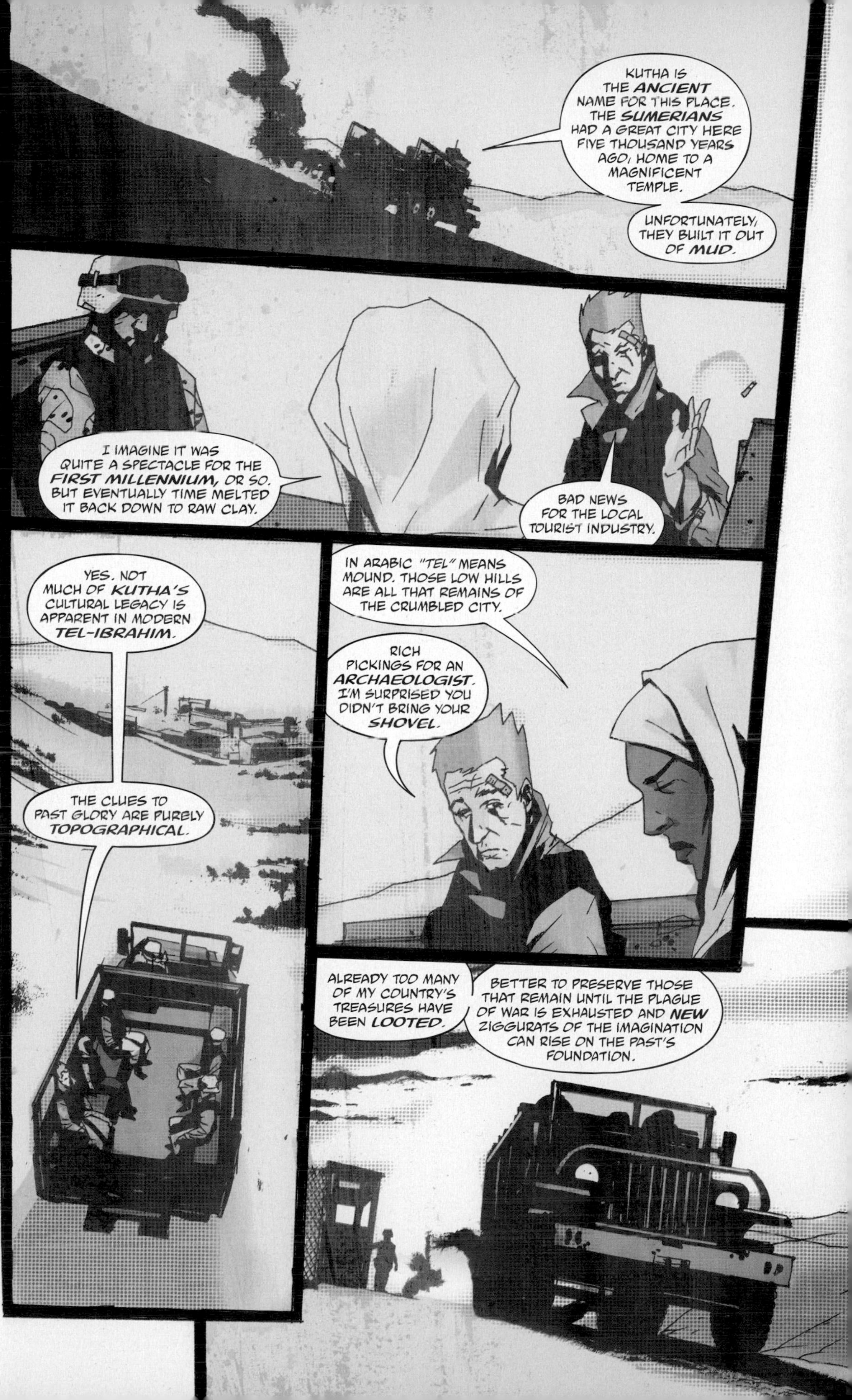
KUTHA IS THE ANCIENT NAME FOR THIS PLACE. THE SUMERIANS HAD A GREAT CITY HERE FIVE THOUSAND YEARS AGO, HOME TO A MAGNIFICENT TEMPLE.
UNFORTUNATELY, THEY BUILT IT OUT OF MUD.
I IMAGINE IT WAS QUITE A SPECTACLE FOR THE FIRST MILLENNIUM, OR SO. BUT EVENTUALLY TIME MELTED IT BACK DOWN TO RAW CLAY.
BAD NEWS FOR THE LOCAL TOURIST INDUSTRY.
YES. NOT MUCH OF KUTHA'S CULTURAL LEGACY IS APPARENT IN MODERN TEL-IBRAHIM.
THE CLUES TO PAST GLORY ARE PURELY TOPOGRAPHICAL.
IN ARABIC "TEL" MEANS MOUND. THOSE LOW HILLS ARE ALL THAT REMAINS OF THE CRUMBLED CITY.
RICH PICKINGS FOR AN ARCHAEOLOGIST. I'M SURPRISED YOU DIDN'T BRING YOUR SHOVEL.
ALREADY TOO MANY OF MY COUNTRY'S TREASURES HAVE BEEN LOOTED.
BETTER TO PRESERVE THOSE THAT REMAIN UNTIL THE PLAGUE OF WAR IS EXHAUSTED AND NEW ZIGGURATS OF THE IMAGINATION CAN RISE ON THE PAST'S FOUNDATION.

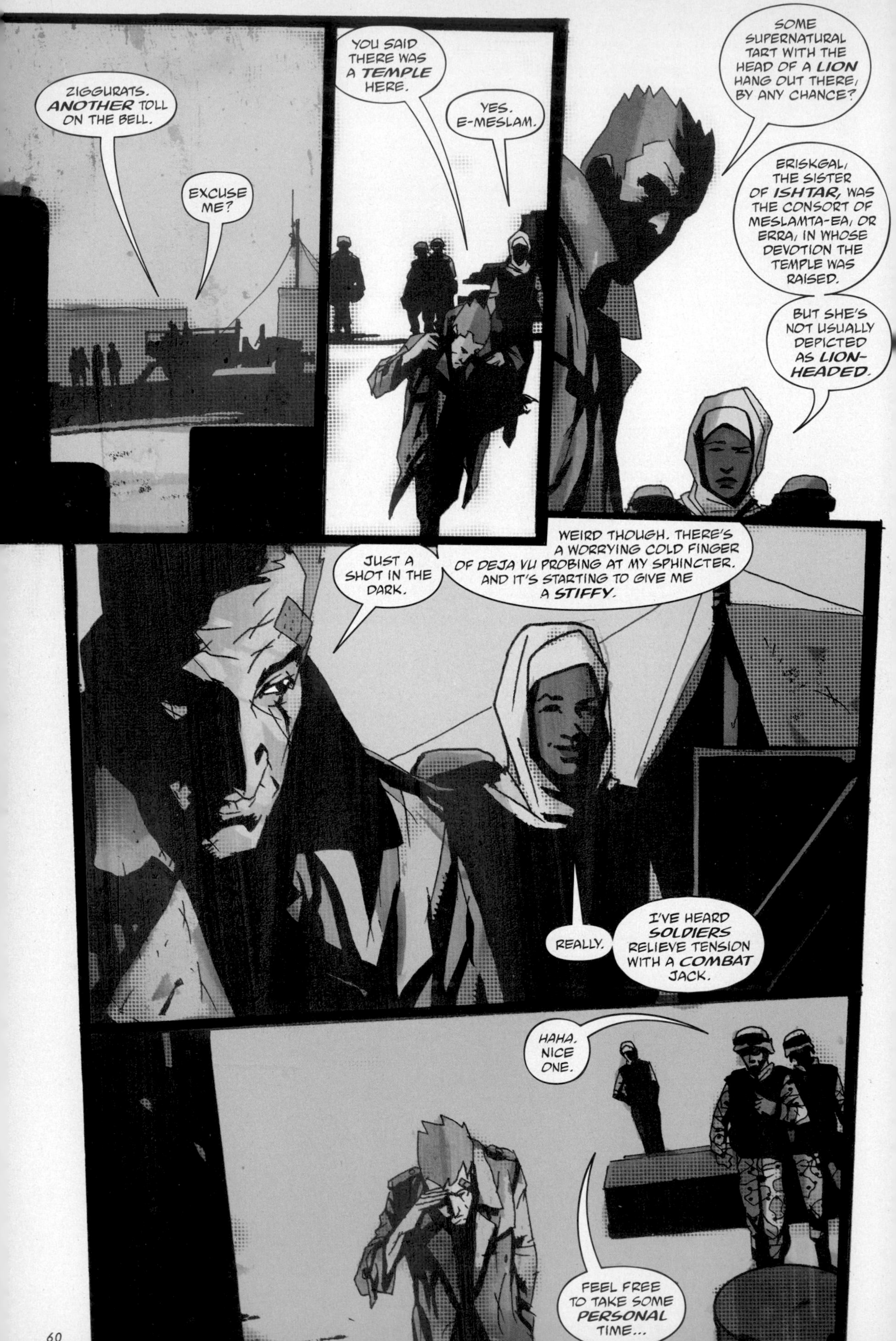
ZIGGURATS. ANOTHER TOLL ON THE BELL.
EXCUSE ME?
YOU SAID THERE WAS A TEMPLE HERE.
YES. E-MESLAM.
SOME SUPERNATURAL TART WITH THE HEAD OF A LION HANG OUT THERE, BY ANY CHANCE?
ERISKGAL, THE SISTER OF ISHTAR, WAS THE CONSORT OF MESLAMTA-EA, OR ERRA, IN WHOSE DEVOTION THE TEMPLE WAS RAISED.
BUT SHE'S NOT USUALLY DEPICTED AS LION-HEADED.
JUST A SHOT IN THE DARK.
WEIRD THOUGH. THERE'S A WORRYING COLD FINGER OF DEJA VU PROBING AT MY SPHINCTER. AND IT'S STARTING TO GIVE ME A STIFFY.
REALLY.
I'VE HEARD SOLDIERS RELIEVE TENSION WITH A COMBAT JACK.
HAHA. NICE ONE.
FEEL FREE TO TAKE SOME PERSONAL TIME...

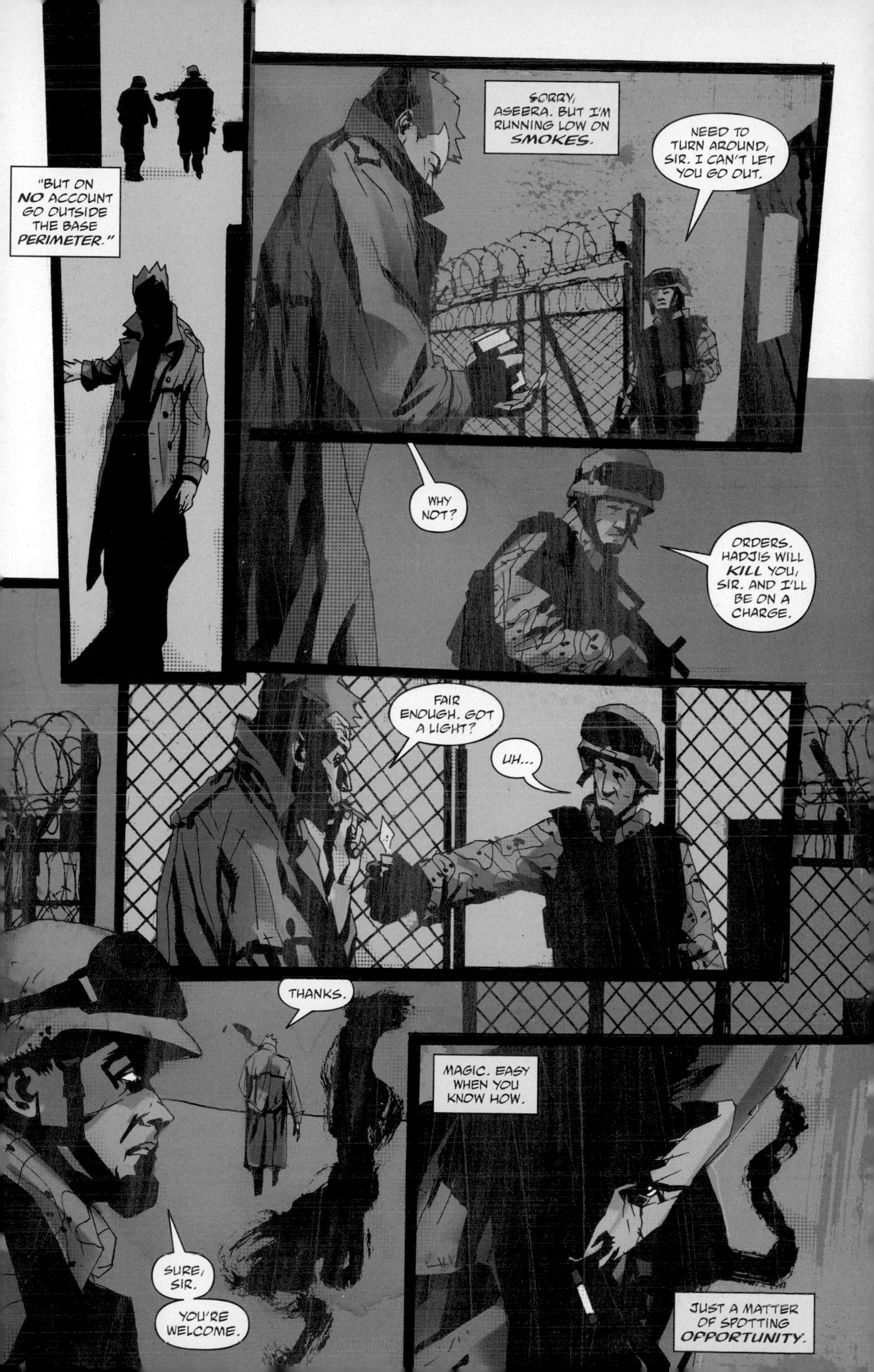
"BUT ON NO ACCOUNT GO OUTSIDE THE BASE PERIMETER."
SORRY, ASEERA. BUT I'M RUNNING LOW ON SMOKES.
NEED TO TURN AROUND, SIR. I CAN'T LET YOU GO OUT.
WHY NOT?
ORDERS. HADJIS WILL KILL YOU, SIR. AND I'LL BE ON A CHARGE.
FAIR ENOUGH. GOT A LIGHT?
UH...
THANKS.
SURE, SIR.
YOU'RE WELCOME.
MAGIC. EASY WHEN YOU KNOW HOW.
JUST A MATTER OF SPOTTING OPPORTUNITY.

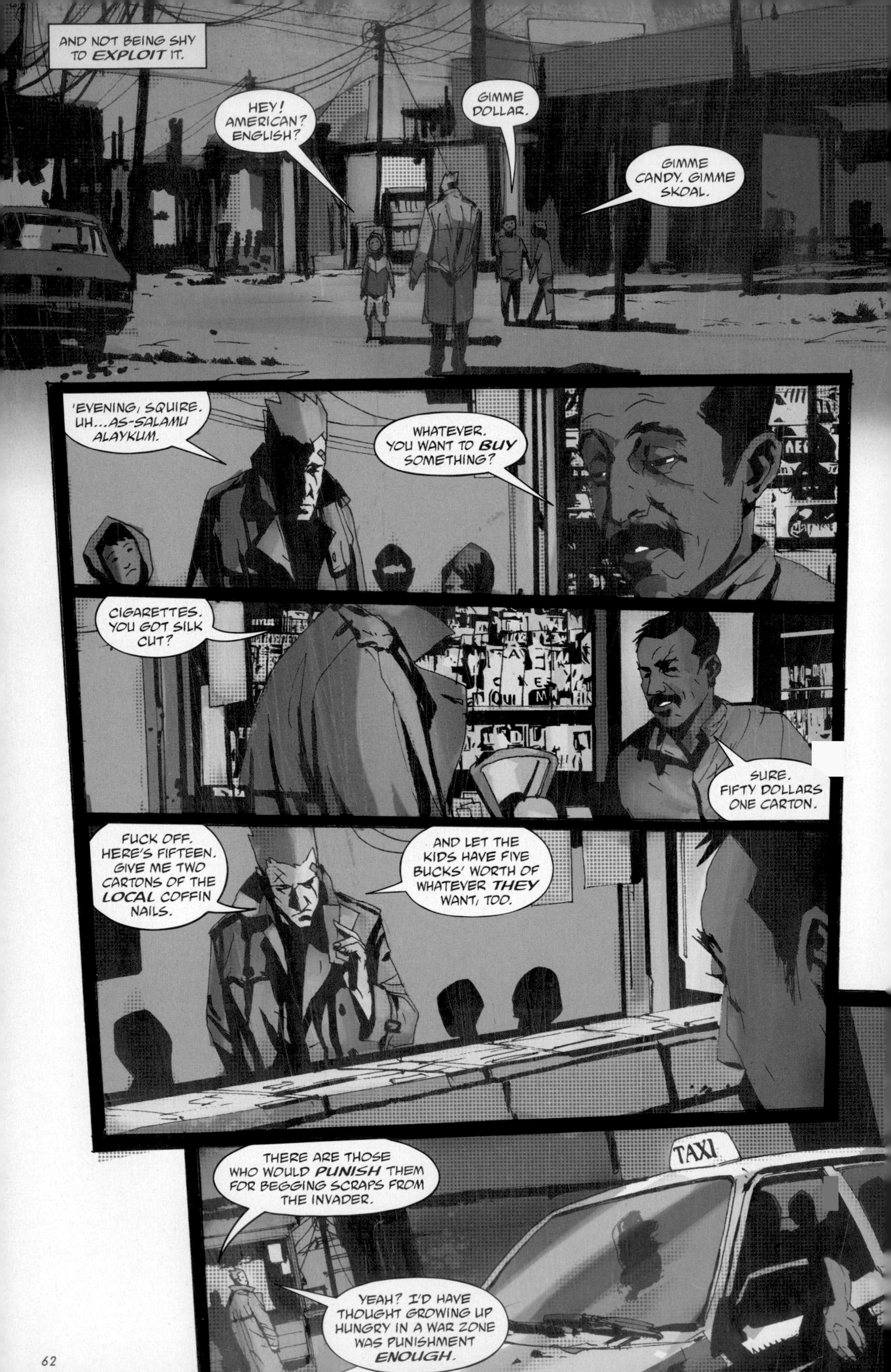
AND NOT BEING SHY TO EXPLOIT IT.
HEY! AMERICAN? ENGLISH?
GIMME DOLLAR.
GIMME CANDY. GIMME SKOAL.
'EVENING, SQUIRE. UH...AS-SALAMU ALAYKUM.
WHATEVER. YOU WANT TO BUY SOMETHING?
CIGARETTES. YOU GOT SILK CUT?
SURE. FIFTY DOLLARS ONE CARTON.
FUCK OFF. HERE'S FIFTEEN. GIVE ME TWO CARTONS OF THE LOCAL COFFIN NAILS.
AND LET THE KIDS HAVE FIVE BUCKS' WORTH OF WHATEVER THEY WANT, TOO.
TAXI
THERE ARE THOSE WHO WOULD PUNISH THEM FOR BEGGING SCRAPS FROM THE INVADER.
YEAH? I'D HAVE THOUGHT GROWING UP HUNGRY IN A WAR ZONE WAS PUNISHMENT ENOUGH.

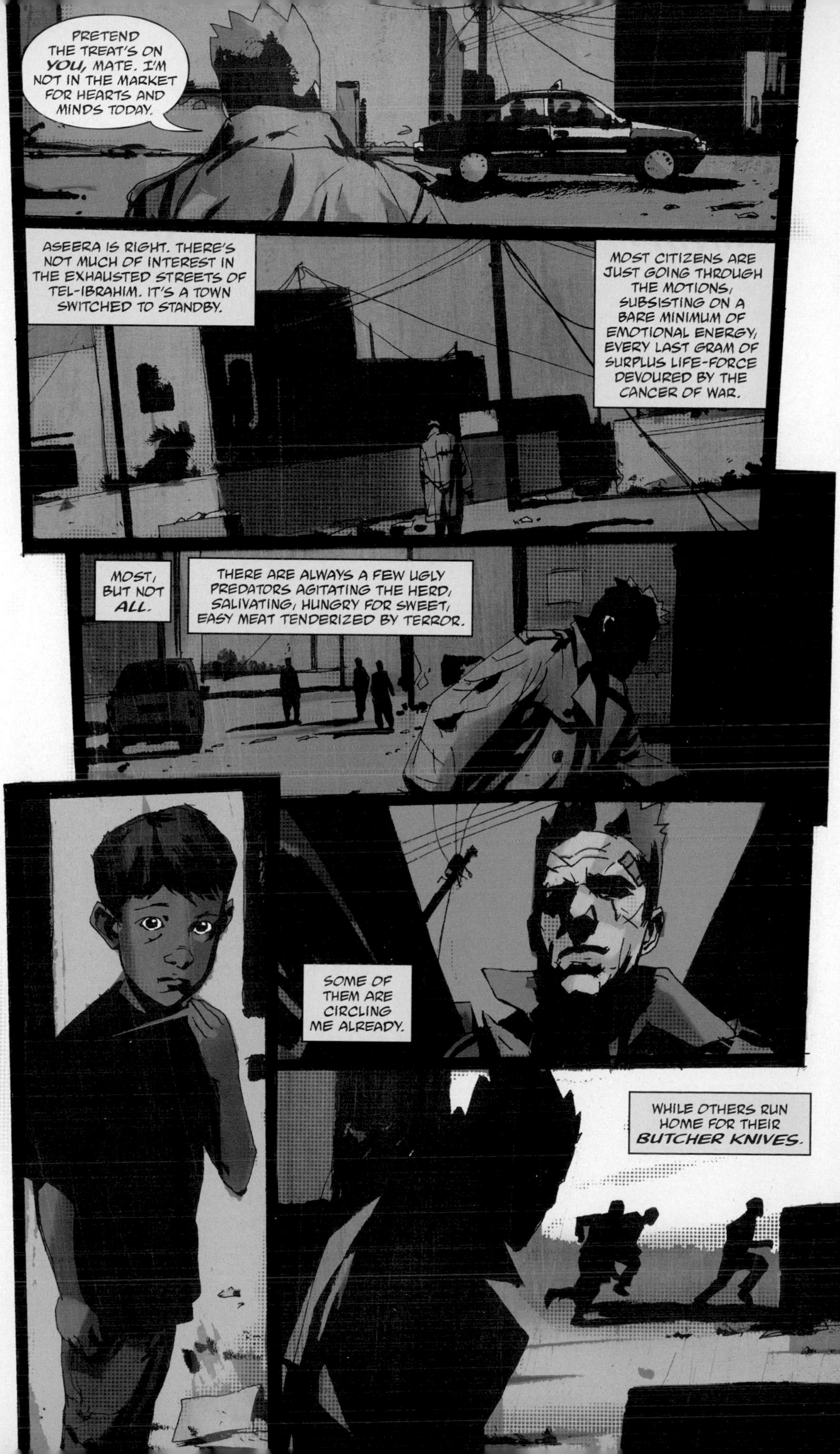
PRETEND THE TREAT'S ON YOU, MATE. I'M NOT IN THE MARKET FOR HEARTS AND MINDS TODAY.
ASEERA IS RIGHT. THERE'S NOT MUCH OF INTEREST IN THE EXHAUSTED STREETS OF TEL-IBRAHIM. IT'S A TOWN SWITCHED TO STANDBY.
MOST CITIZENS ARE JUST GOING THROUGH THE MOTIONS, SUBSISTING ON A BARE MINIMUM OF EMOTIONAL ENERGY, EVERY LAST GRAM OF SURPLUS LIFE-FORCE DEVOURED BY THE CANCER OF WAR.
MOST, BUT NOT ALL.
THERE ARE ALWAYS A FEW UGLY PREDATORS AGITATING THE HERD, SALIVATING, HUNGRY FOR SWEET, EASY MEAT TENDERIZED BY TERROR.
SOME OF THEM ARE CIRCLING ME ALREADY.
WHILE OTHERS RUN HOME FOR THEIR BUTCHER KNIVES.

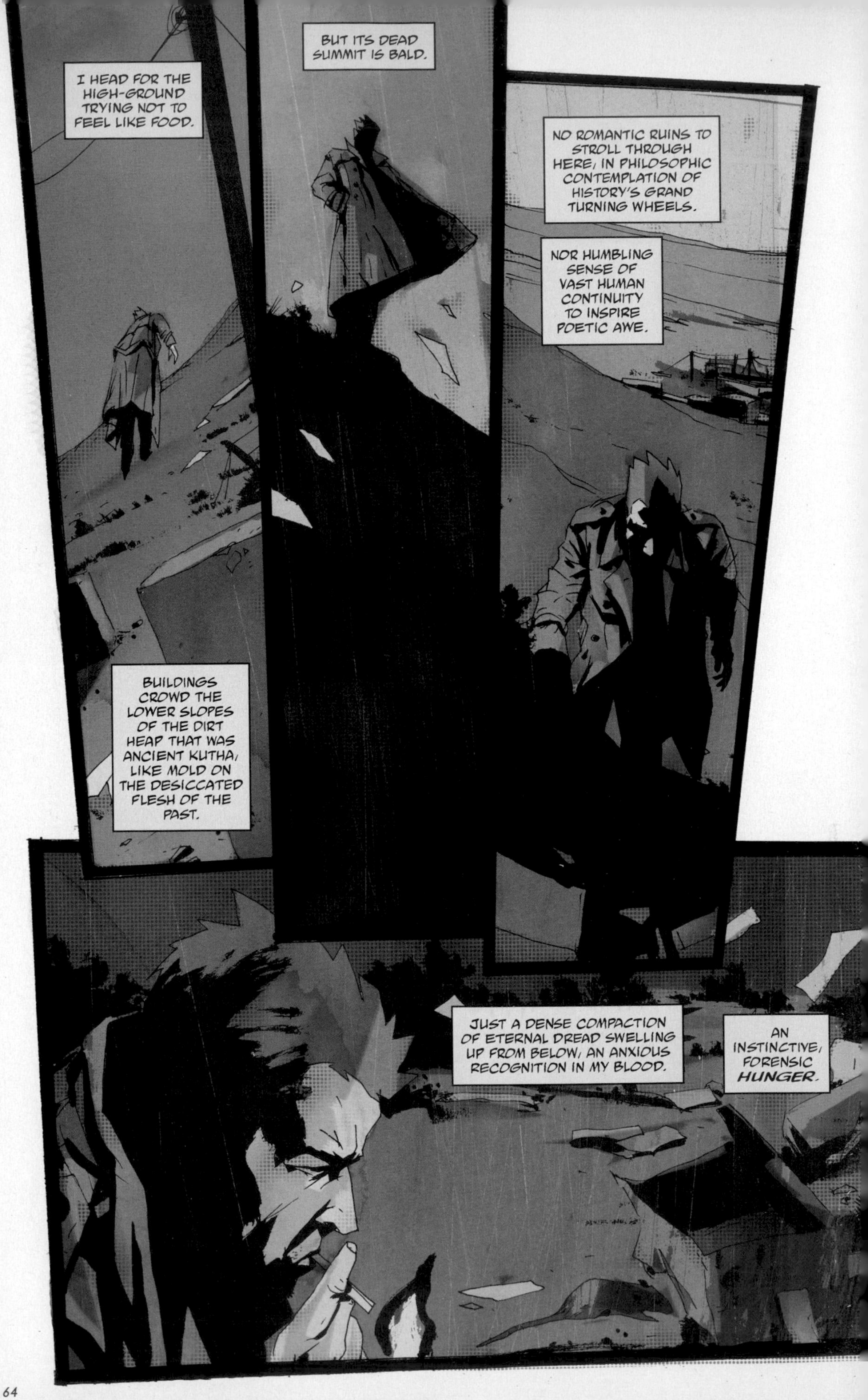
I HEAD FOR THE HIGH-GROUND TRYING NOT TO FEEL LIKE FOOD.
BUT ITS DEAD SUMMIT IS BALD.
NO ROMANTIC RUINS TO STROLL THROUGH HERE, IN PHILOSOPHIC CONTEMPLATION OF HISTORY'S GRAND TURNING WHEELS.
NOR HUMBLING SENSE OF VAST HUMAN CONTINUITY TO INSPIRE POETIC AWE.
BUILDINGS CROWD THE LOWER SLOPES OF THE DIRT HEAP THAT WAS ANCIENT KUTHA, LIKE MOLD ON THE DESICCATED FLESH OF THE PAST.
JUST A DENSE COMPACTION OF ETERNAL DREAD SWELLING UP FROM BELOW, AN ANXIOUS RECOGNITION IN MY BLOOD.
AN INSTINCTIVE, FORENSIC HUNGER.

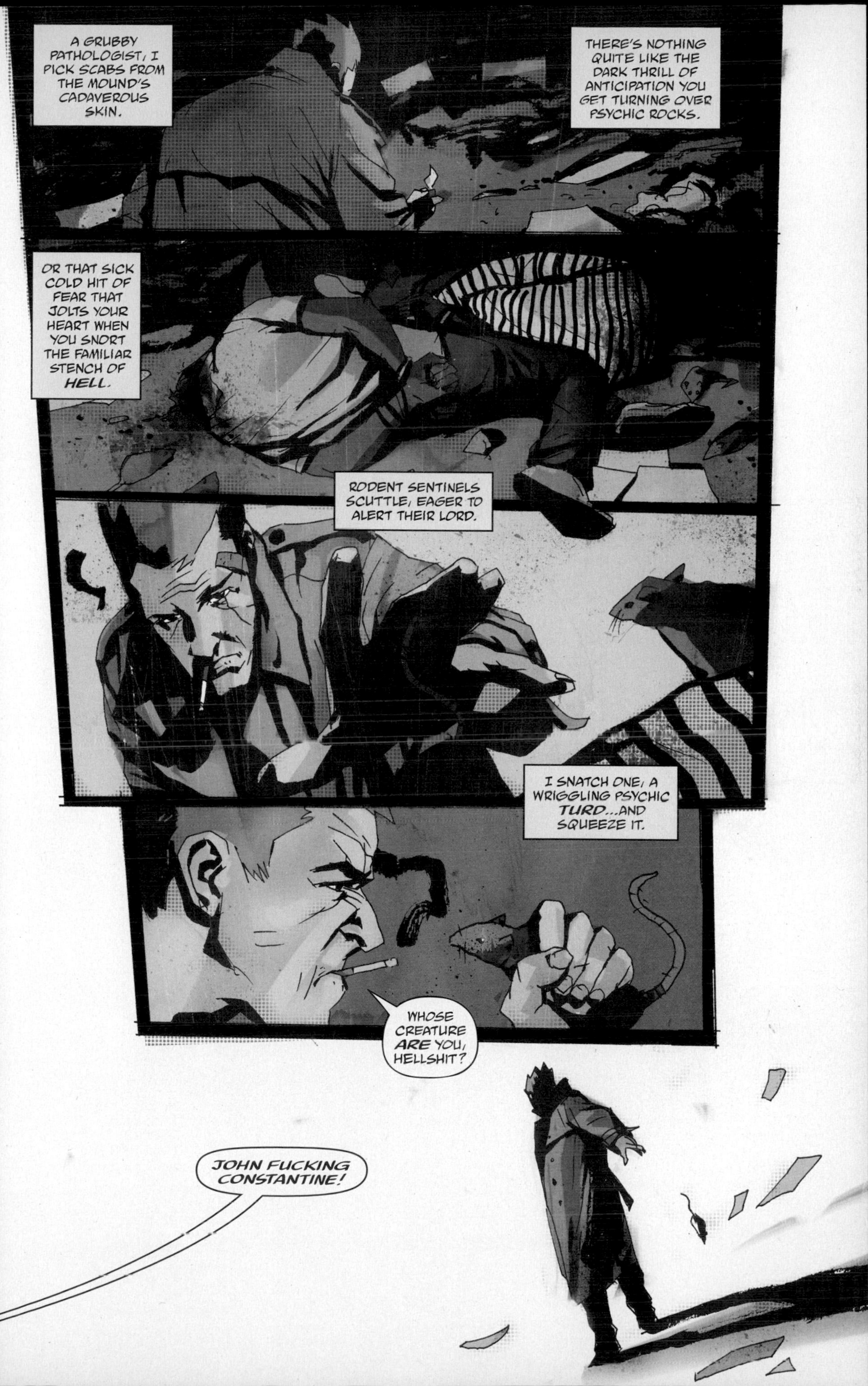
A GRUBBY PATHOLOGIST, I PICK SCABS FROM THE MOUND'S CADAVEROUS SKIN.
THERE'S NOTHING QUITE LIKE THE DARK THRILL OF ANTICIPATION YOU GET TURNING OVER PSYCHIC ROCKS.
OR THAT SICK COLD HIT OF FEAR THAT JOLTS YOUR HEART WHEN YOU SNORT THE FAMILIAR STENCH OF HELL.
RODENT SENTINELS SCUTTLE, EAGER TO ALERT THEIR LORD.
I SNATCH ONE, A WRIGGLING PSYCHIC TURD...AND SQUEEZE IT.
WHOSE CREATURE ARE YOU, HELLSHIT?
JOHN FUCKING CONSTANTINE!

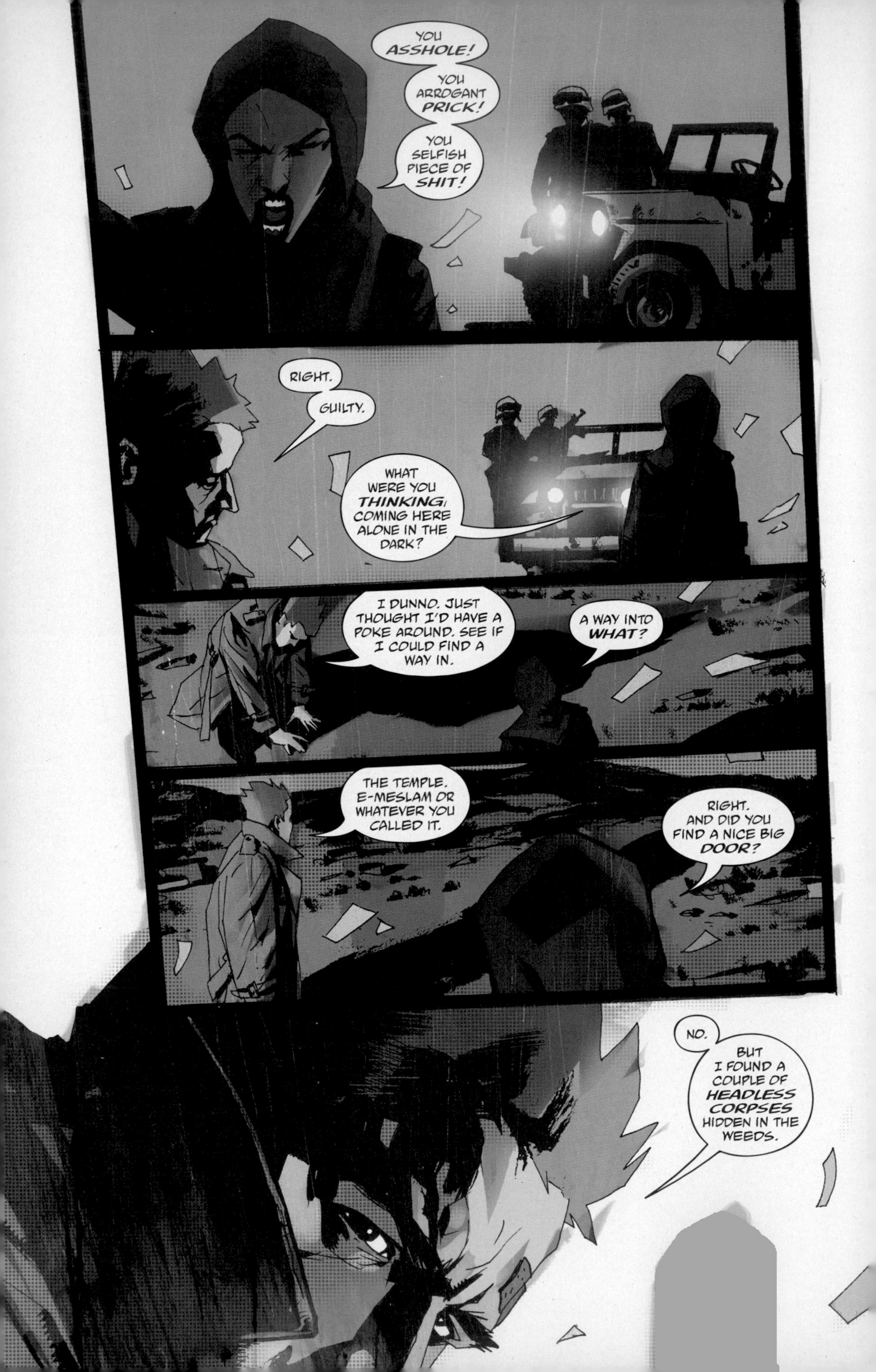
YOU ASSHOLE!
YOU ARROGANT PRICK!
YOU SELFISH PIECE OF SHIT!
RIGHT.
GUILTY.
WHAT WERE YOU THINKING, COMING HERE ALONE IN THE DARK?
I DUNNO. JUST THOUGHT I'D HAVE A POKE AROUND. SEE IF I COULD FIND A WAY IN.
A WAY INTO WHAT?
THE TEMPLE. E-MESLAM OR WHATEVER YOU CALLED IT.
RIGHT. AND DID YOU FIND A NICE BIG DOOR?
NO.
BUT I FOUND A COUPLE OF HEADLESS CORPSES HIDDEN IN THE WEEDS.

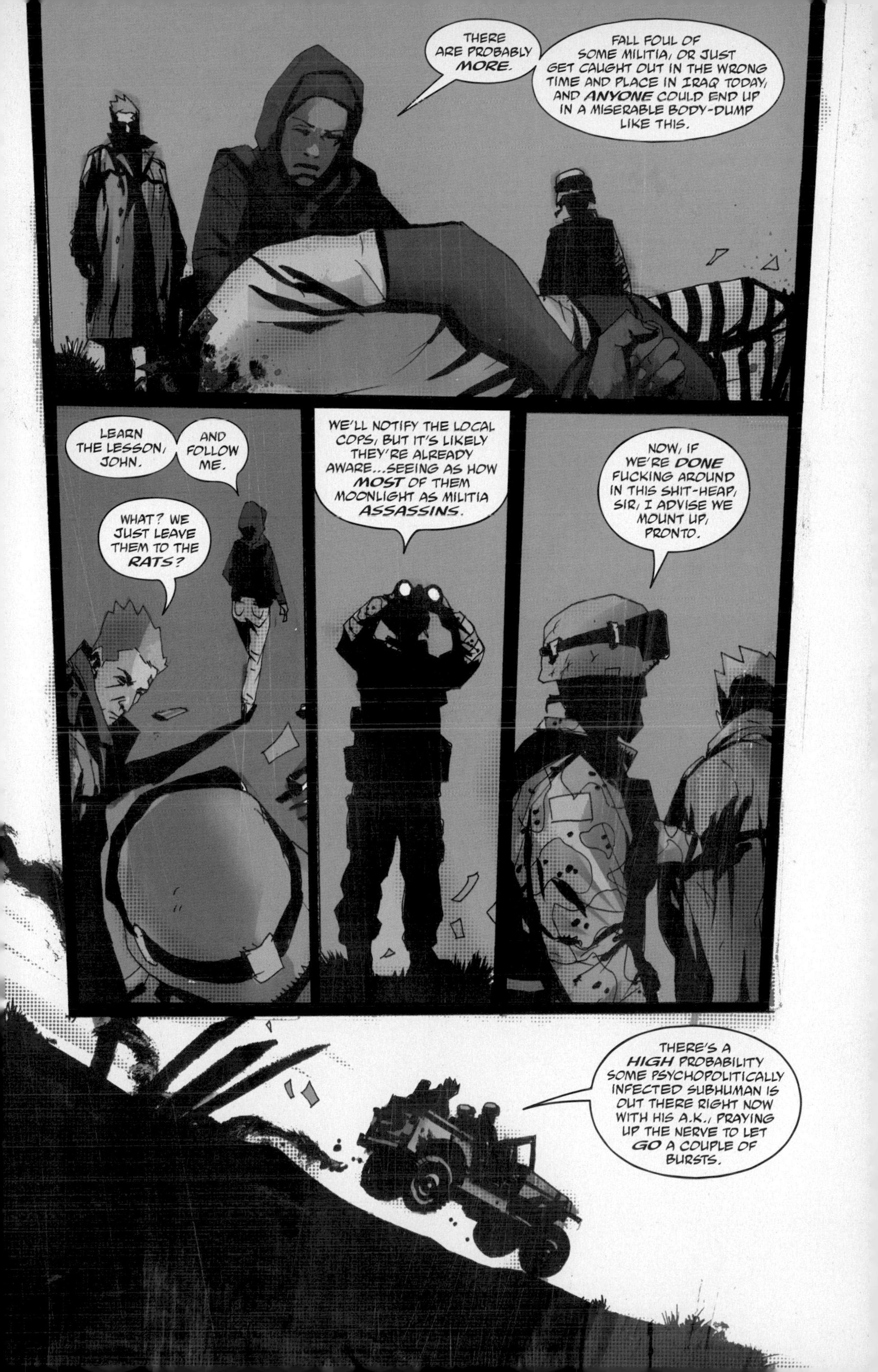
THERE ARE PROBABLY MORE.
FALL FOUL OF SOME MILITIA, OR JUST GET CAUGHT OUT IN THE WRONG TIME AND PLACE IN IRAQ TODAY, AND ANYONE COULD END UP IN A MISERABLE BODY-DUMP LIKE THIS.
LEARN THE LESSON, JOHN.
AND FOLLOW ME.
WHAT? WE JUST LEAVE THEM TO THE RATS?
WE'LL NOTIFY THE LOCAL COPS, BUT IT'S LIKELY THEY'RE ALREADY AWARE...SEEING AS HOW MOST OF THEM MOONLIGHT AS MILITIA ASSASSINS.
NOW, IF WE'RE DONE FUCKING AROUND IN THIS SHIT-HEAP, SIR, I ADVISE WE MOUNT UP, PRONTO.
THERE'S A HIGH PROBABILITY SOME PSYCHOPOLITICALLY INFECTED SUBHUMAN IS OUT THERE RIGHT NOW WITH HIS A.K., PRAYING UP THE NERVE TO LET GO A COUPLE OF BURSTS.

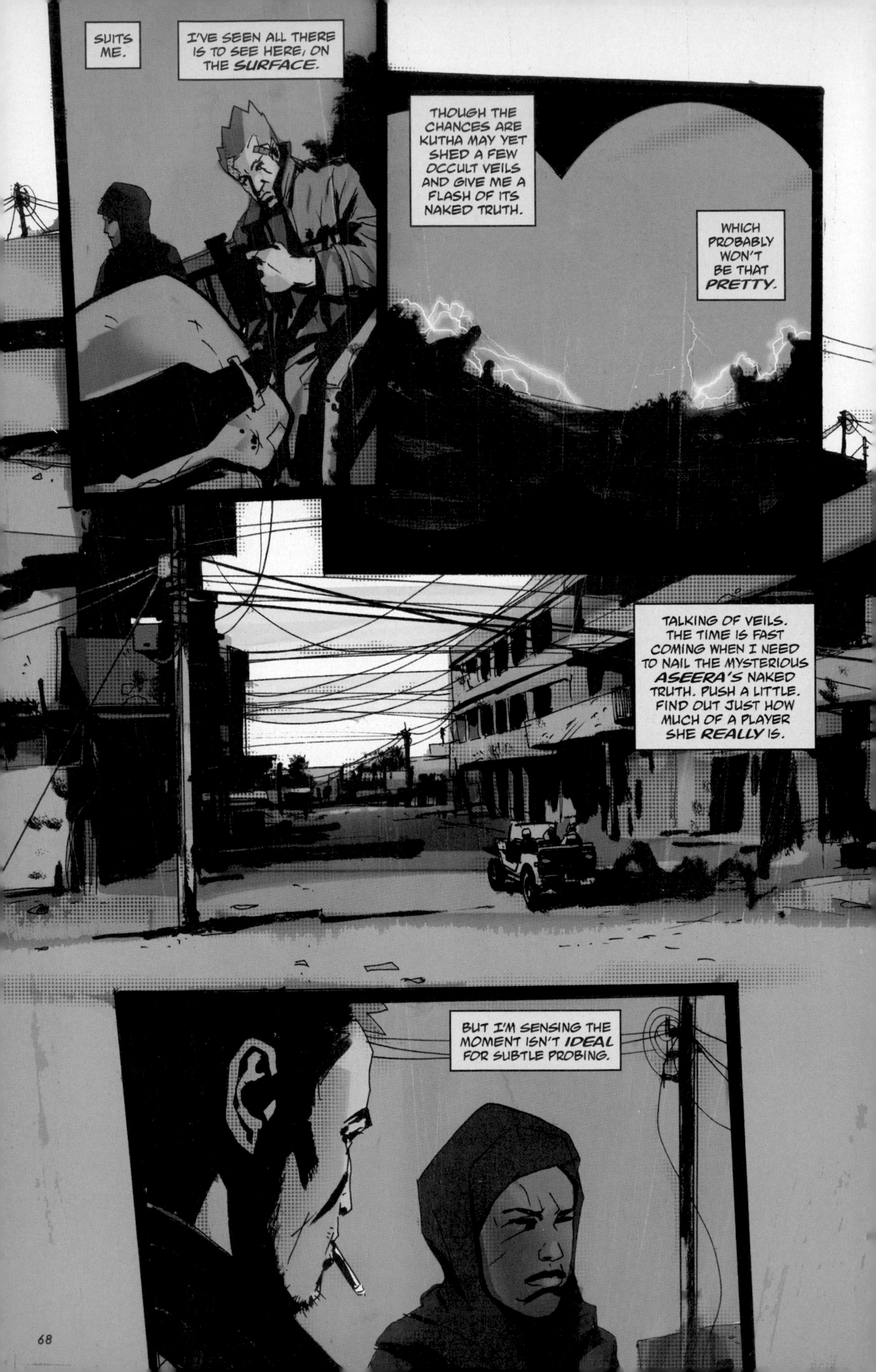
SUITS ME.
I'VE SEEN ALL THERE IS TO SEE HERE, ON THE SURFACE.
THOUGH THE CHANCES ARE KUTHA MAY YET SHED A FEW OCCULT VEILS AND GIVE ME A FLASH OF ITS NAKED TRUTH.
WHICH PROBABLY WON'T BE THAT PRETTY.
TALKING OF VEILS. THE TIME IS FAST COMING WHEN I NEED TO NAIL THE MYSTERIOUS ASEERA'S NAKED TRUTH. PUSH A LITTLE. FIND OUT JUST HOW MUCH OF A PLAYER SHE REALLY IS.
BUT I'M SENSING THE MOMENT ISN'T IDEAL FOR SUBTLE PROBING.

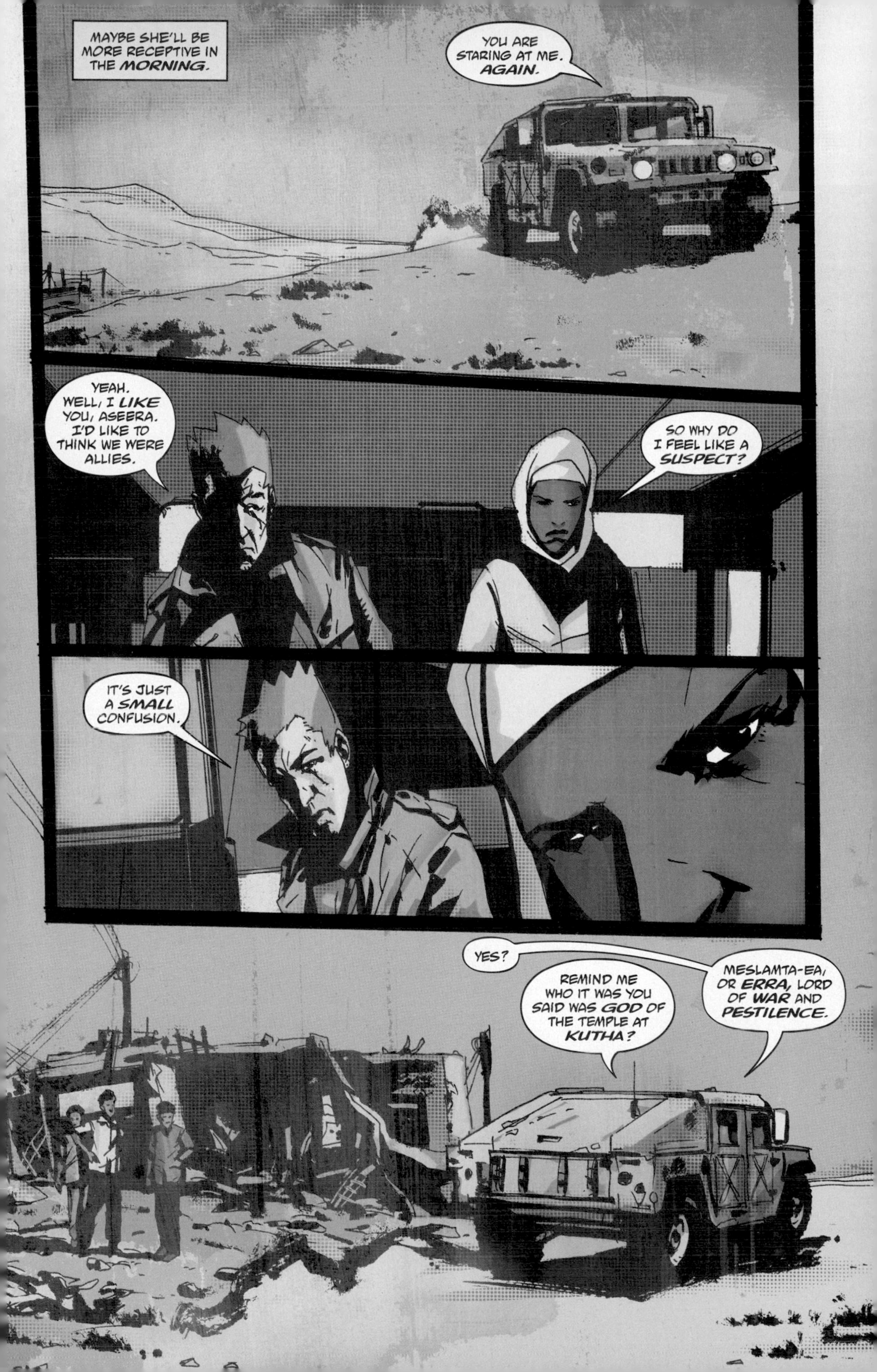
MAYBE SHE'LL BE MORE RECEPTIVE IN THE MORNING.
YOU ARE STARING AT ME. AGAIN.
YEAH. WELL, I LIKE YOU, ASEERA. I'D LIKE TO THINK WE WERE ALLIES.
SO WHY DO I FEEL LIKE A SUSPECT?
IT'S JUST A SMALL CONFUSION.
REMIND ME WHO IT WAS YOU SAID WAS GOD OF THE TEMPLE AT KUTHA?
MESLAMTA-EA, OR ERRA, LORD OF WAR AND PESTILENCE.
YES?

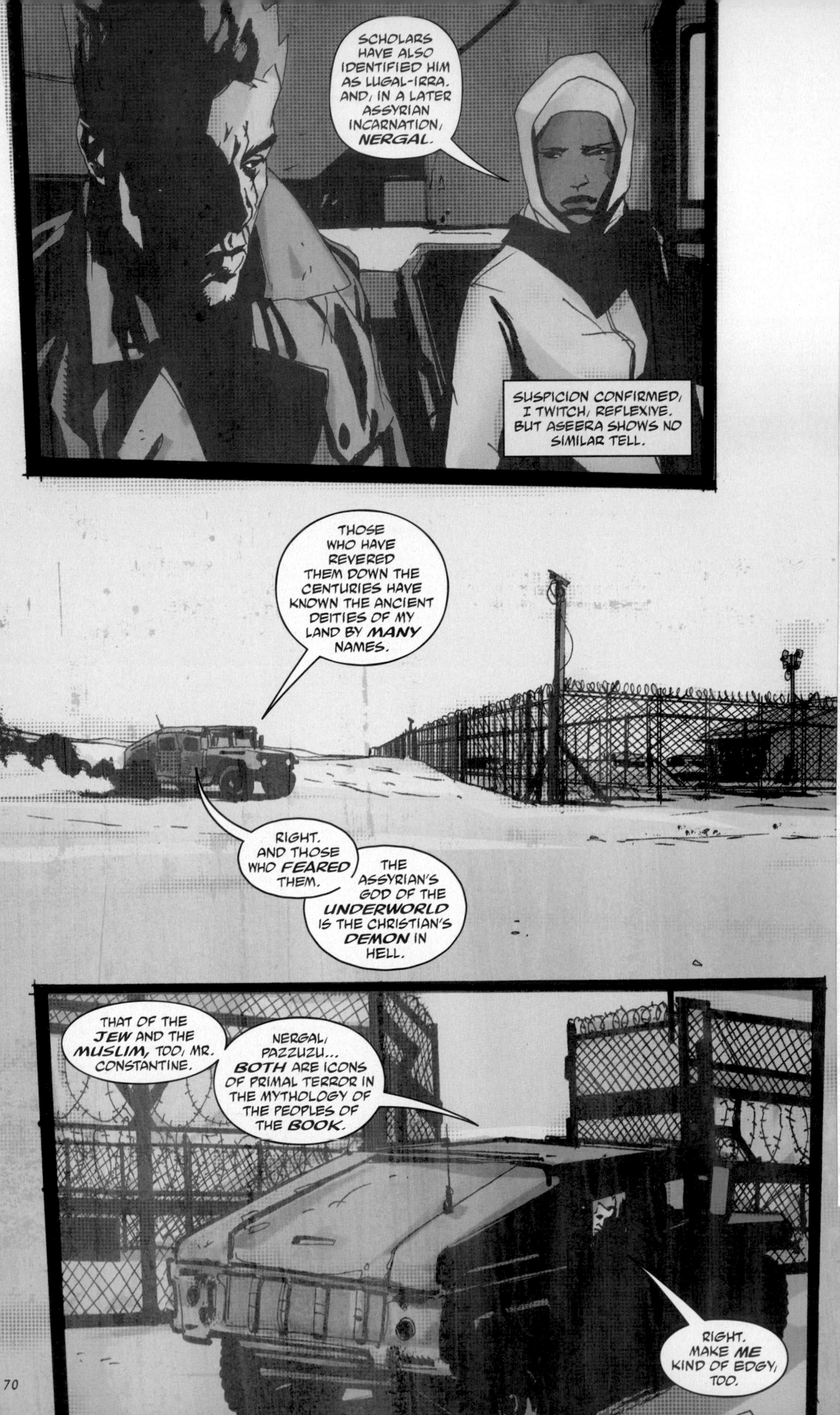
SCHOLARS HAVE ALSO IDENTIFIED HIM AS LUGAL-IRRA. AND, IN A LATER ASSYRIAN INCARNATION, NERGAL.
SUSPICION CONFIRMED, I TWITCH, REFLEXIVE. BUT ASEERA SHOWS NO SIMILAR TELL.
THOSE WHO HAVE REVERED THEM DOWN THE CENTURIES HAVE KNOWN THE ANCIENT DEITIES OF MY LAND BY MANY NAMES.
RIGHT. AND THOSE WHO FEARED THEM.
THE ASSYRIAN'S GOD OF THE UNDERWORLD IS THE CHRISTIAN'S DEMON IN HELL.
THAT OF THE JEW AND THE MUSLIM, TOO, MR. CONSTANTINE.
NERGAL, PAZZUZU... BOTH ARE ICONS OF PRIMAL TERROR IN THE MYTHOLOGY OF THE PEOPLES OF THE BOOK.
RIGHT. MAKE ME KIND OF EDGY, TOO.

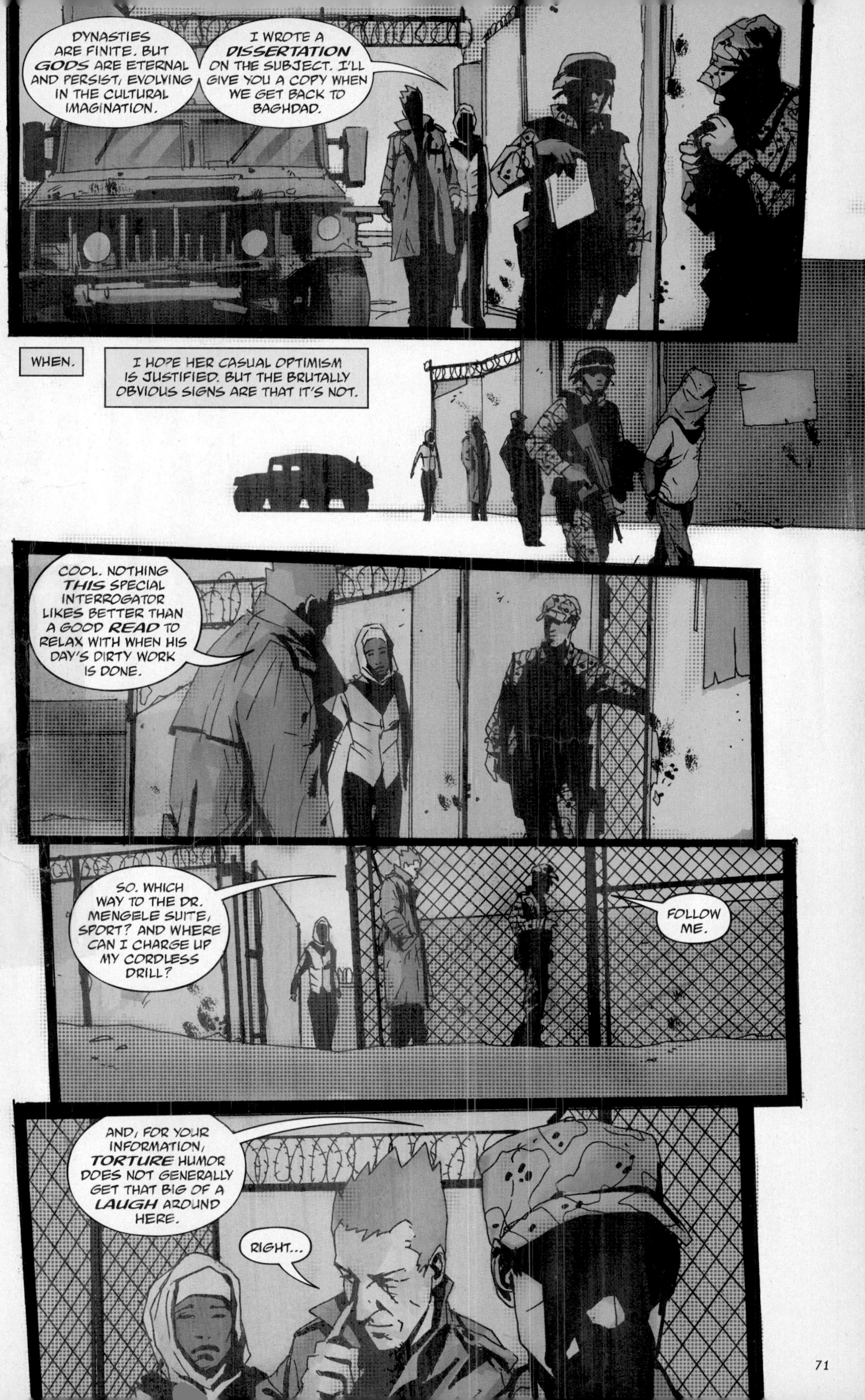
DYNASTIES ARE FINITE. BUT GODS ARE ETERNAL AND PERSIST, EVOLVING IN THE CULTURAL IMAGINATION.
I WROTE A DISSERTATION ON THE SUBJECT. I'LL GIVE YOU A COPY WHEN WE GET BACK TO BAGHDAD.
WHEN.
I HOPE HER CASUAL OPTIMISM IS JUSTIFIED. BUT THE BRUTALLY OBVIOUS SIGNS ARE THAT IT'S NOT.
COOL. NOTHING THIS SPECIAL INTERROGATOR LIKES BETTER THAN A GOOD READ TO RELAX WITH WHEN HIS DAY'S DIRTY WORK IS DONE.
SO. WHICH WAY TO THE DR. MENGELE SUITE, SPORT? AND WHERE CAN I CHARGE UP MY CORDLESS DRILL?
FOLLOW ME.
AND, FOR YOUR INFORMATION, TORTURE HUMOR DOES NOT GENERALLY GET THAT BIG OF A LAUGH AROUND HERE.
RIGHT...

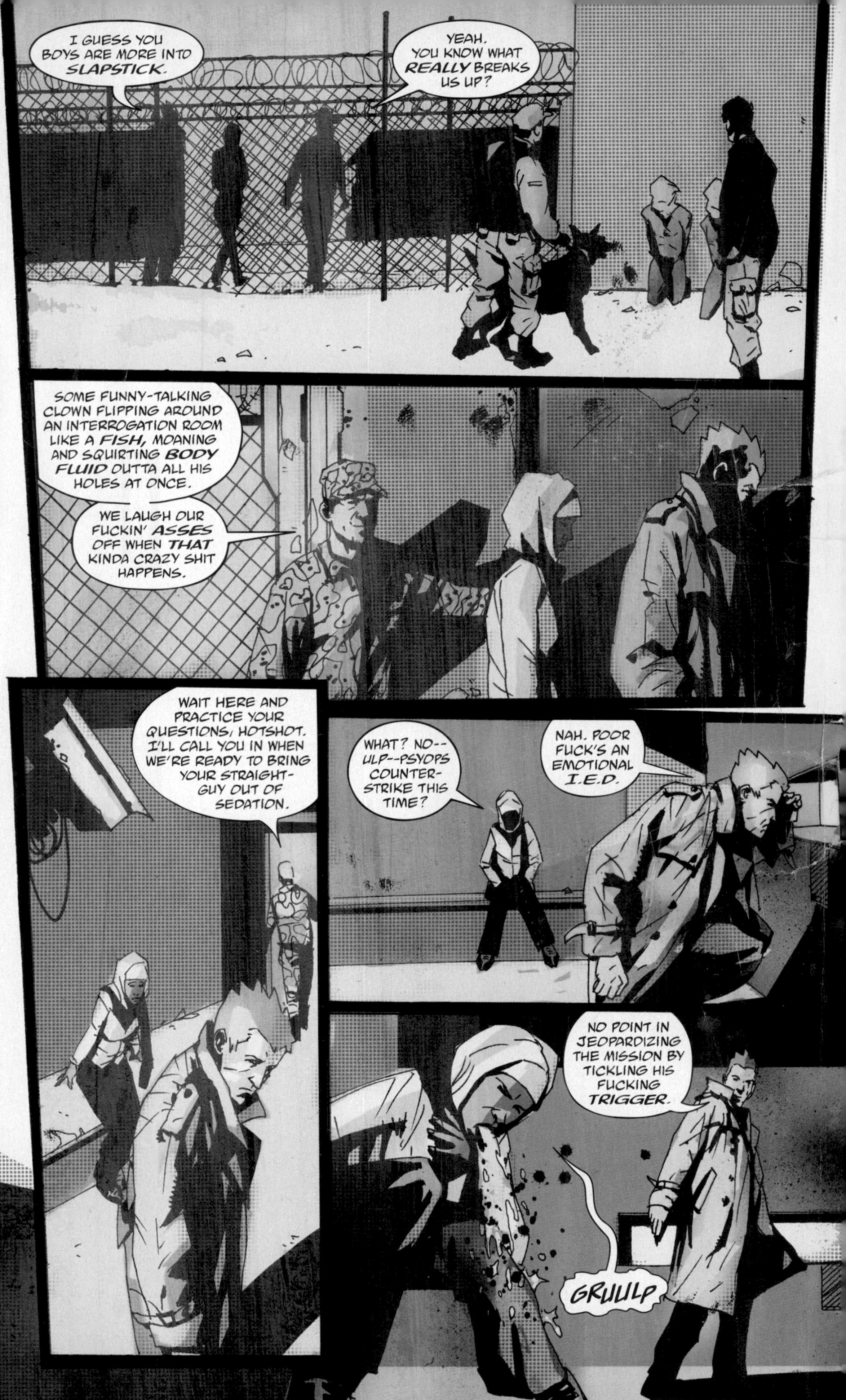
I GUESS YOU BOYS ARE MORE INTO SLAPSTICK.
YEAH. YOU KNOW WHAT REALLY BREAKS US UP?
SOME FUNNY-TALKING CLOWN FLIPPING AROUND AN INTERROGATION ROOM LIKE A FISH, MOANING AND SQUIRTING BODY FLUID OUTTA ALL HIS HOLES AT ONCE.
WE LAUGH OUR FUCKIN' ASSES OFF WHEN THAT KINDA CRAZY SHIT HAPPENS.
WAIT HERE AND PRACTICE YOUR QUESTIONS, HOTSHOT. I'LL CALL YOU IN WHEN WE'RE READY TO BRING YOUR STRAIGHT-GUY OUT OF SEDATION.
WHAT? NO--ULP--PSYOPS COUNTER-STRIKE THIS TIME?
NAH. POOR FUCK'S AN EMOTIONAL I.E.D.
NO POINT IN JEOPARDIZING THE MISSION BY TICKLING HIS FUCKING TRIGGER.
GRUULP

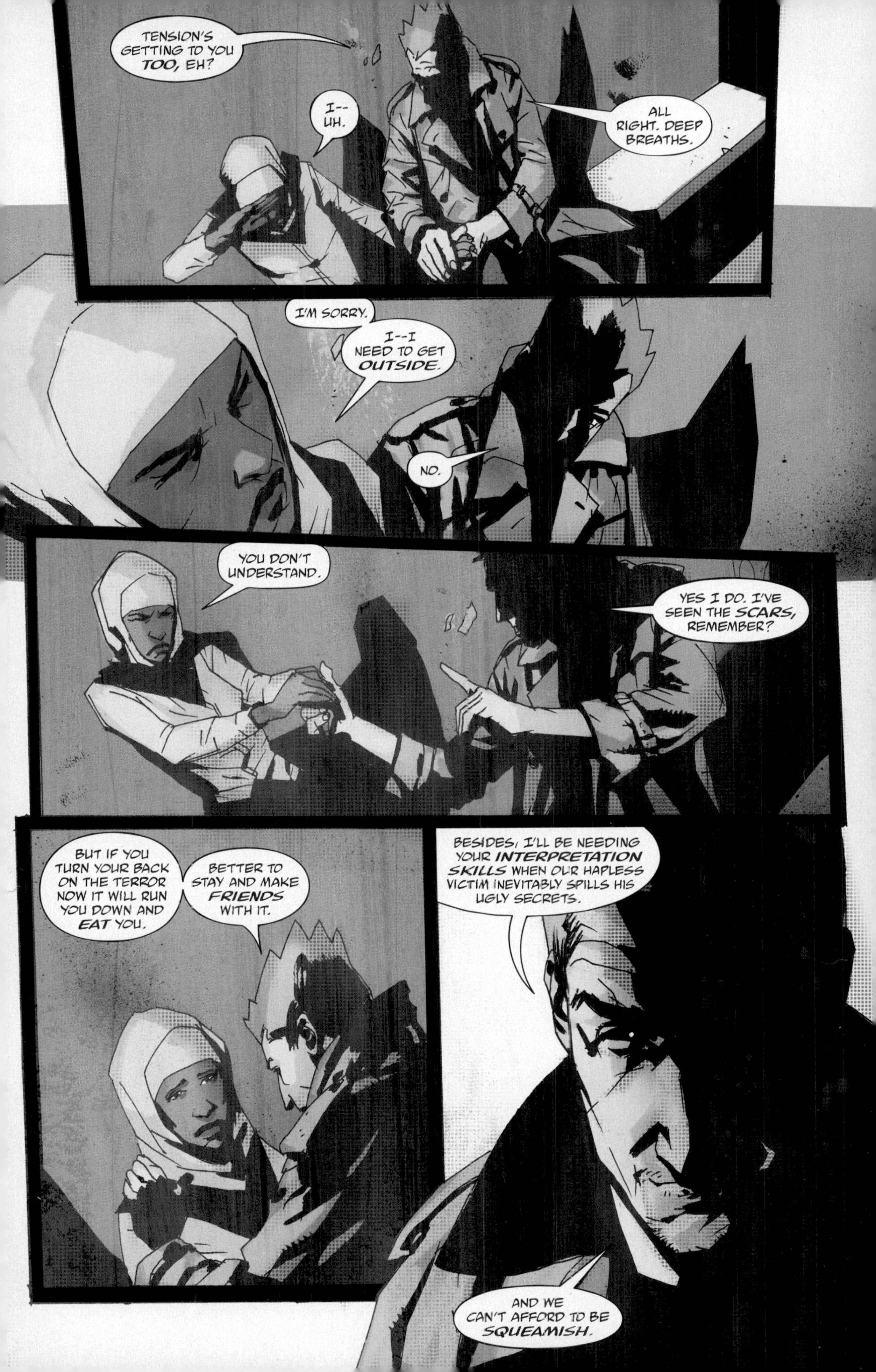
TENSION'S GETTING TO YOU TOO, EH?
I-- UH.
ALL RIGHT. DEEP BREATHS.
I'M SORRY.
I--I NEED TO GET OUTSIDE.
NO.
YOU DON'T UNDERSTAND.
YES I DO. I'VE SEEN THE SCARS, REMEMBER?
BUT IF YOU TURN YOUR BACK ON THE TERROR NOW IT WILL RUN YOU DOWN AND EAT YOU.
BETTER TO STAY AND MAKE FRIENDS WITH IT.
BESIDES, I'LL BE NEEDING YOUR INTERPRETATION SKILLS WHEN OUR HAPLESS VICTIM INEVITABLY SPILLS HIS UGLY SECRETS.
AND WE CAN'T AFFORD TO BE SQUEAMISH.

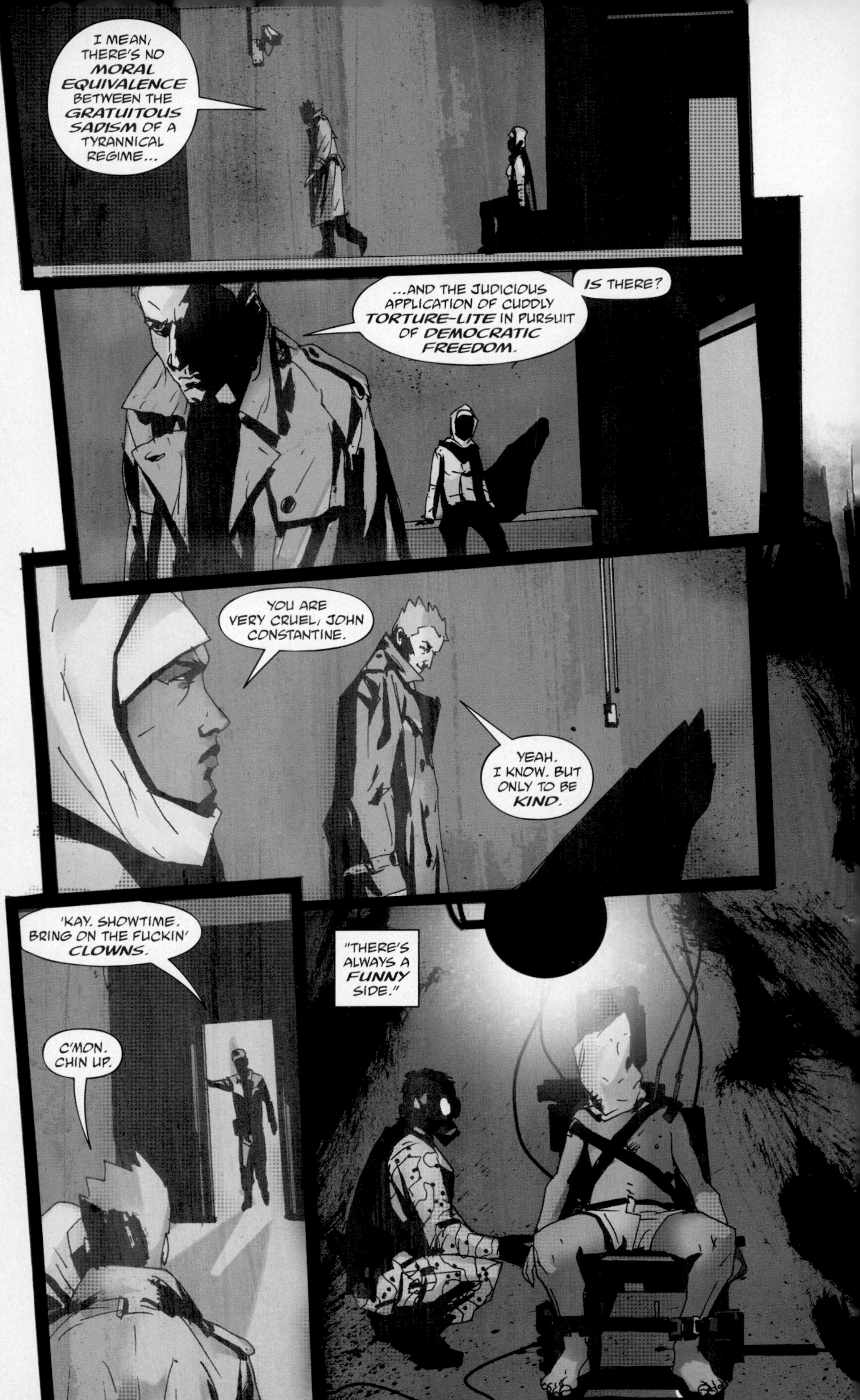

I MEAN, THERE'S NO MORAL EQUIVALENCE BETWEEN THE GRATUITOUS SADISM OF A TYRANNICAL REGIME...
...AND THE JUDICIOUS APPLICATION OF CUDDLY TORTURE-LITE IN PURSUIT OF DEMOCRATIC FREEDOM.
IS THERE?
YOU ARE VERY CRUEL, JOHN CONSTANTINE.
YEAH. I KNOW. BUT ONLY TO BE KIND.
'KAY. SHOWTIME. BRING ON THE FUCKIN' CLOWNS.
C'MON. CHIN UP.
"THERE'S ALWAYS A FUNNY SIDE."

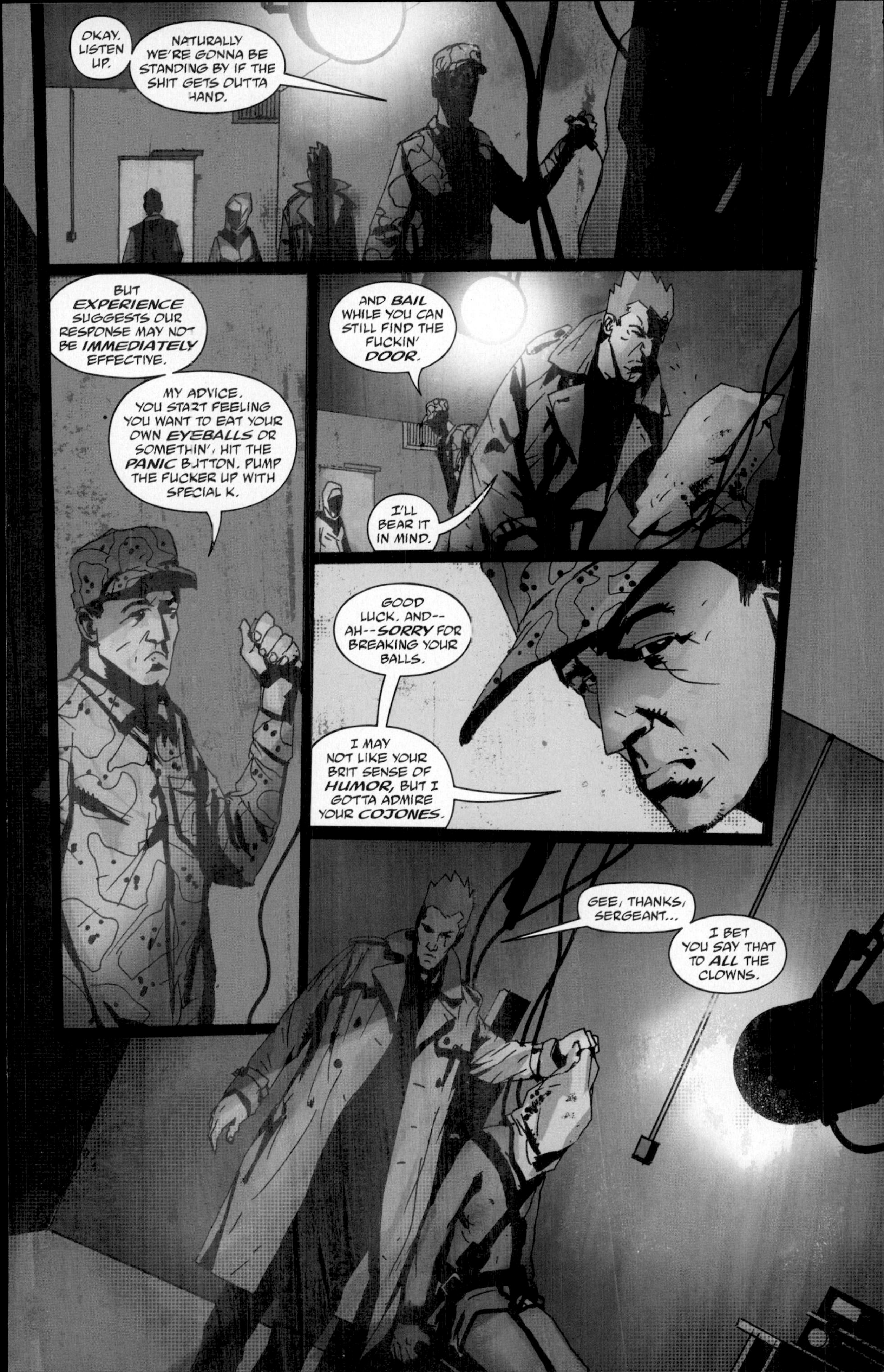
OKAY. LISTEN UP.
NATURALLY WE'RE GONNA BE STANDING BY IF THE SHIT GETS OUTTA HAND.
BUT EXPERIENCE SUGGESTS OUR RESPONSE MAY NOT BE IMMEDIATELY EFFECTIVE.
MY ADVICE. YOU START FEELING YOU WANT TO EAT YOUR OWN EYEBALLS OR SOMETHIN', HIT THE PANIC BUTTON. PUMP THE FUCKER UP WITH SPECIAL K.
AND BAIL WHILE YOU CAN STILL FIND THE FUCKIN' DOOR.
I'LL BEAR IT IN MIND.
GOOD LUCK. AND--AH--SORRY FOR BREAKING YOUR BALLS.
I MAY NOT LIKE YOUR BRIT SENSE OF HUMOR, BUT I GOTTA ADMIRE YOUR COJONES.
GEE, THANKS, SERGEANT...
I BET YOU SAY THAT TO ALL THE CLOWNS.

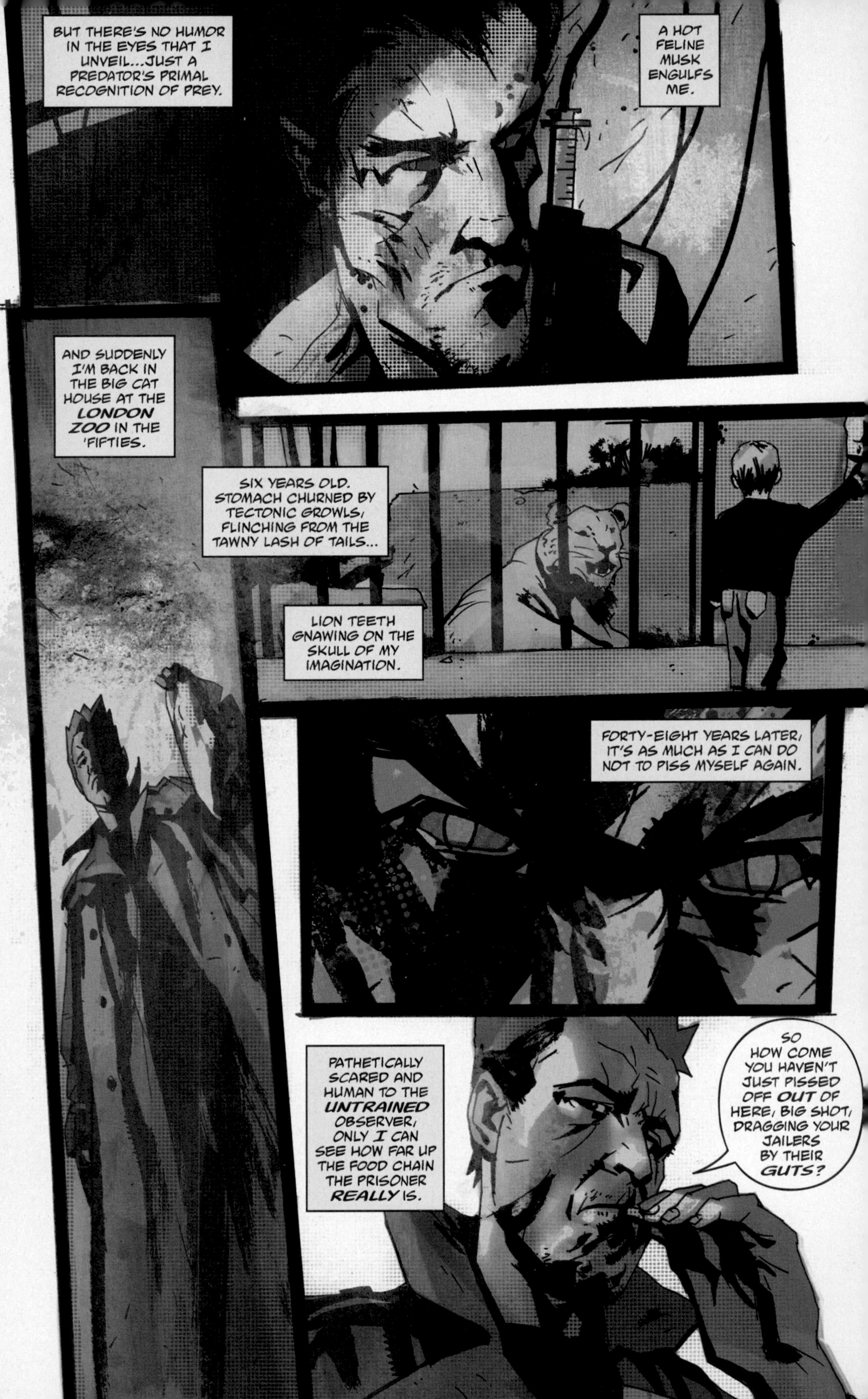
BUT THERE'S NO HUMOR IN THE EYES THAT I UNVEIL...JUST A PREDATOR'S PRIMAL RECOGNITION OF PREY.
A HOT FELINE MUSK ENGULFS ME.
AND SUDDENLY I'M BACK IN THE BIG CAT HOUSE AT THE LONDON ZOO IN THE 'FIFTIES.
SIX YEARS OLD. STOMACH CHURNED BY TECTONIC GROWLS, FLINCHING FROM THE TAWNY LASH OF TAILS...
LION TEETH GNAWING ON THE SKULL OF MY IMAGINATION.
FORTY-EIGHT YEARS LATER, IT'S AS MUCH AS I CAN DO NOT TO PISS MYSELF AGAIN.
PATHETICALLY SCARED AND HUMAN TO THE UNTRAINED OBSERVER, ONLY I CAN SEE HOW FAR UP THE FOOD CHAIN THE PRISONER REALLY IS.
SO HOW COME YOU HAVEN'T JUST PISSED OFF OUT OF HERE, BIG SHOT, DRAGGING YOUR JAILERS BY THEIR GUTS?

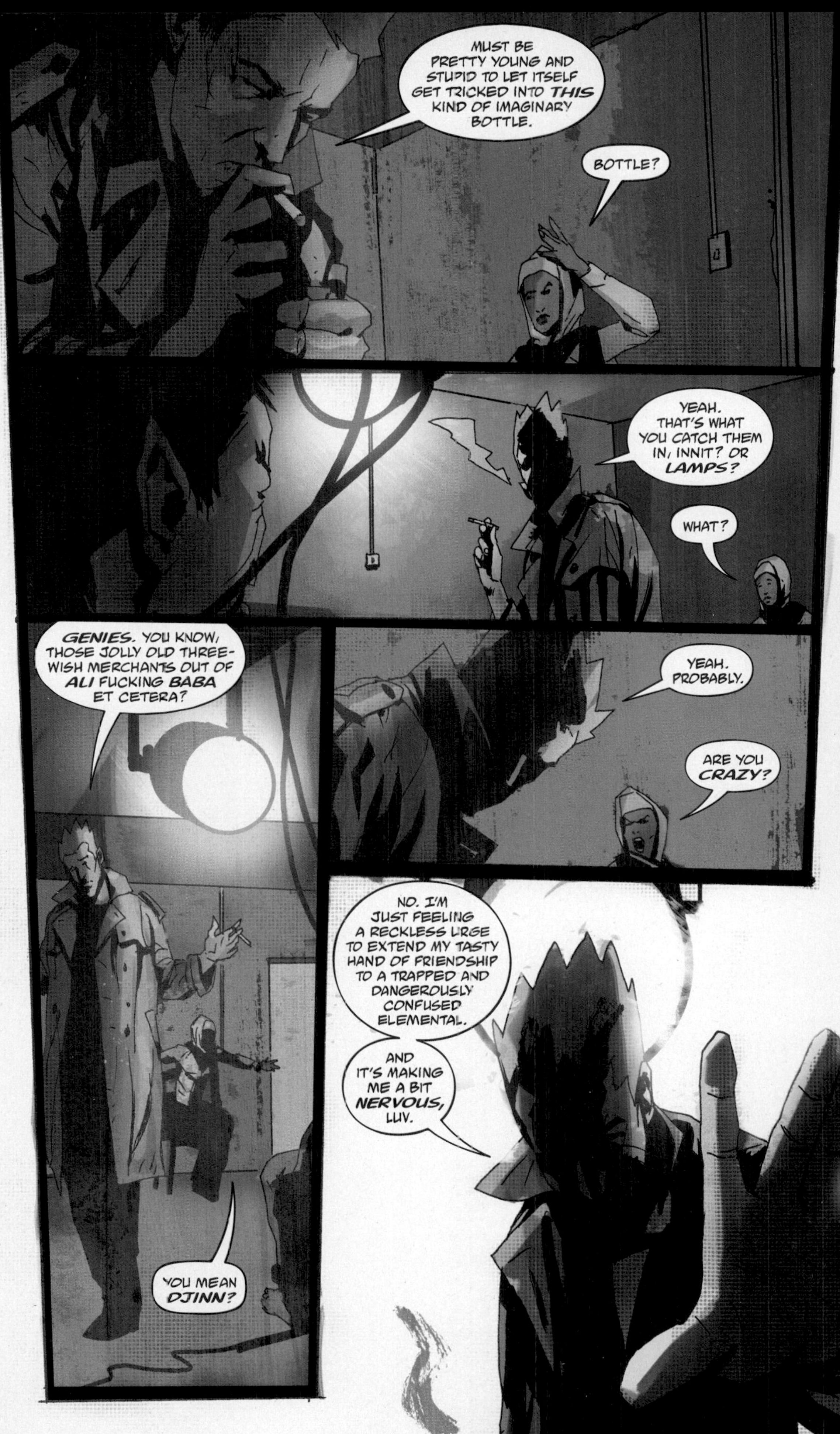
MUST BE PRETTY YOUNG AND STUPID TO LET ITSELF GET TRICKED INTO THIS KIND OF IMAGINARY BOTTLE.
BOTTLE?
YEAH. THAT'S WHAT YOU CATCH THEM IN, INNIT? OR LAMPS?
WHAT?
GENIES. YOU KNOW, THOSE JOLLY OLD THREE-WISH MERCHANTS OUT OF ALI FUCKING BABA ET CETERA?
YOU MEAN DJINN?
YEAH. PROBABLY.
ARE YOU CRAZY?
NO. I'M JUST FEELING A RECKLESS URGE TO EXTEND MY TASTY HAND OF FRIENDSHIP TO A TRAPPED AND DANGEROUSLY CONFUSED ELEMENTAL.
AND IT'S MAKING ME A BIT NERVOUS, LUV.

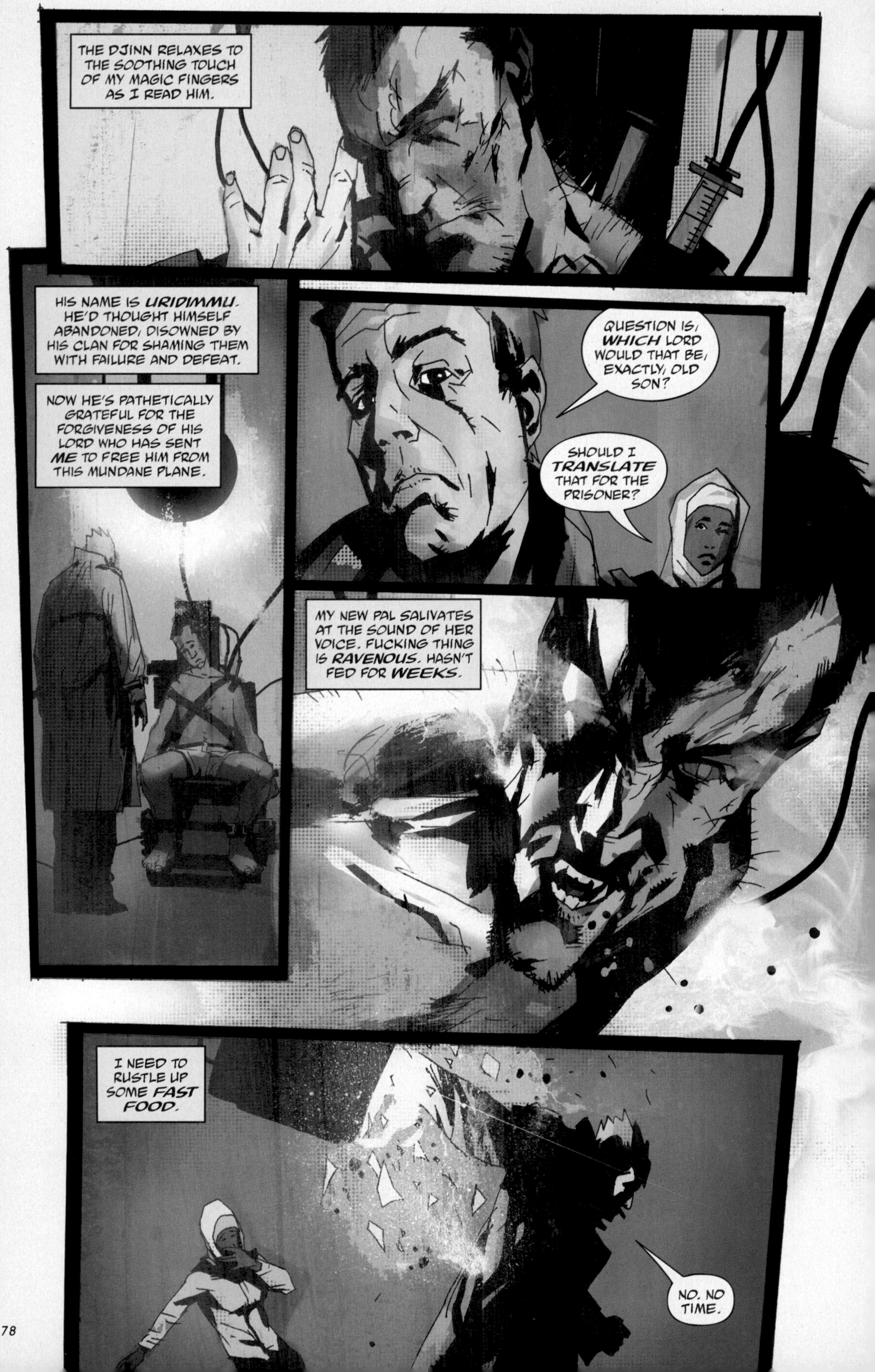
THE DJINN RELAXES TO THE SOOTHING TOUCH OF MY MAGIC FINGERS AS I READ HIM.
HIS NAME IS URIDIMMU. HE'D THOUGHT HIMSELF ABANDONED, DISOWNED BY HIS CLAN FOR SHAMING THEM WITH FAILURE AND DEFEAT.
NOW HE'S PATHETICALLY GRATEFUL FOR THE FORGIVENESS OF HIS LORD WHO HAS SENT ME TO FREE HIM FROM THIS MUNDANE PLANE.
QUESTION IS, WHICH LORD WOULD THAT BE, EXACTLY, OLD SON?
SHOULD I TRANSLATE THAT FOR THE PRISONER?
MY NEW PAL SALIVATES AT THE SOUND OF HER VOICE. FUCKING THING IS RAVENOUS. HASN'T FED FOR WEEKS.
I NEED TO RUSTLE UP SOME FAST FOOD.
NO. NO TIME.

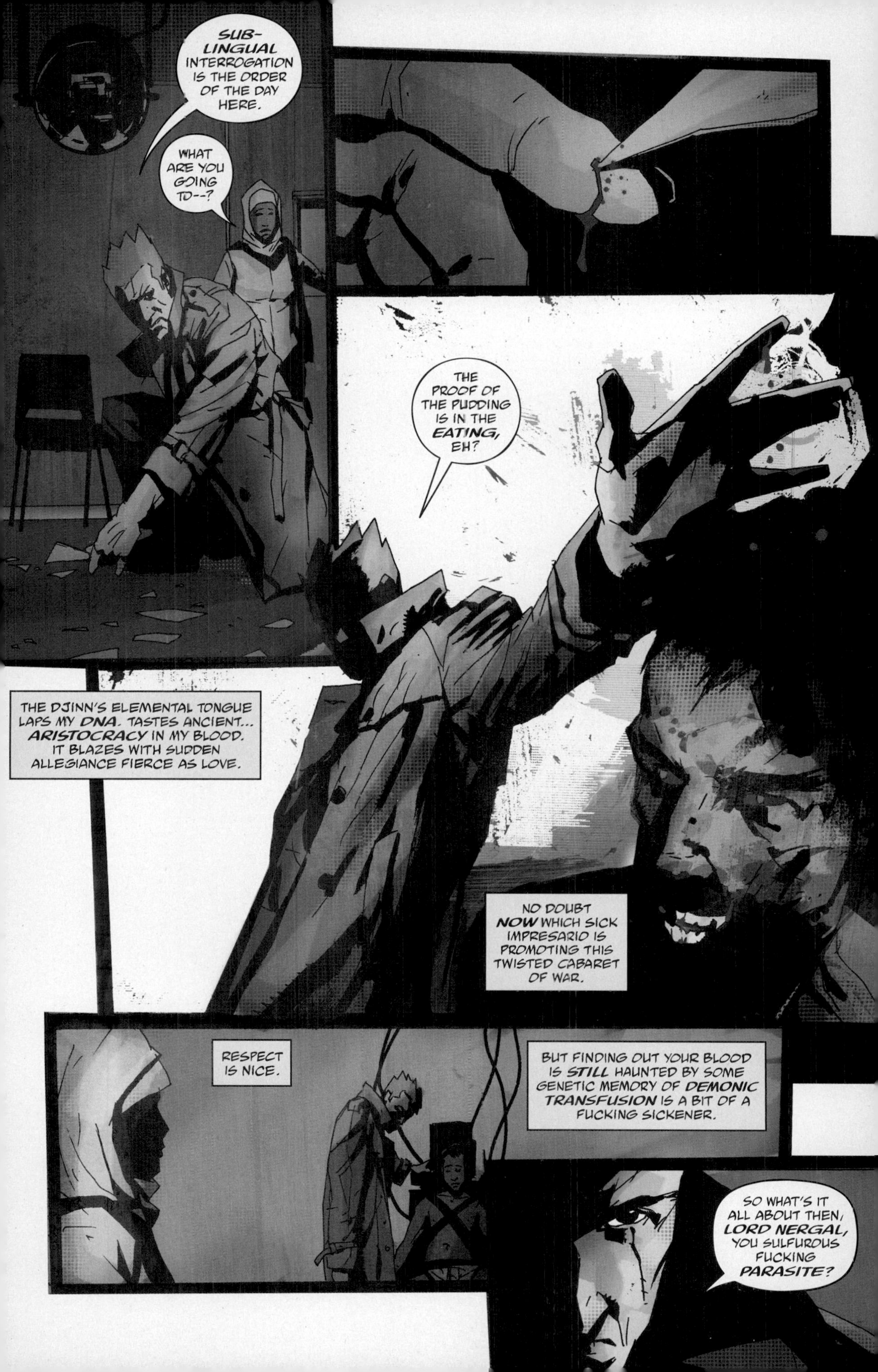
SUB-LINGUAL INTERROGATION IS THE ORDER OF THE DAY HERE.
WHAT ARE YOU GOING TO--?
THE PROOF OF THE PUDDING IS IN THE EATING, EH?
THE DJINN'S ELEMENTAL TONGUE LAPS MY DNA. TASTES ANCIENT... ARISTOCRACY IN MY BLOOD. IT BLAZES WITH SUDDEN ALLEGIANCE FIERCE AS LOVE.
NO DOUBT NOW WHICH SICK IMPRESARIO IS PROMOTING THIS TWISTED CABARET OF WAR.
RESPECT IS NICE.
BUT FINDING OUT YOUR BLOOD IS STILL HAUNTED BY SOME GENETIC MEMORY OF DEMONIC TRANSFUSION IS A BIT OF A FUCKING SICKENER.
SO WHAT'S IT ALL ABOUT THEN, LORD NERGAL, YOU SULFUROUS FUCKING PARASITE?

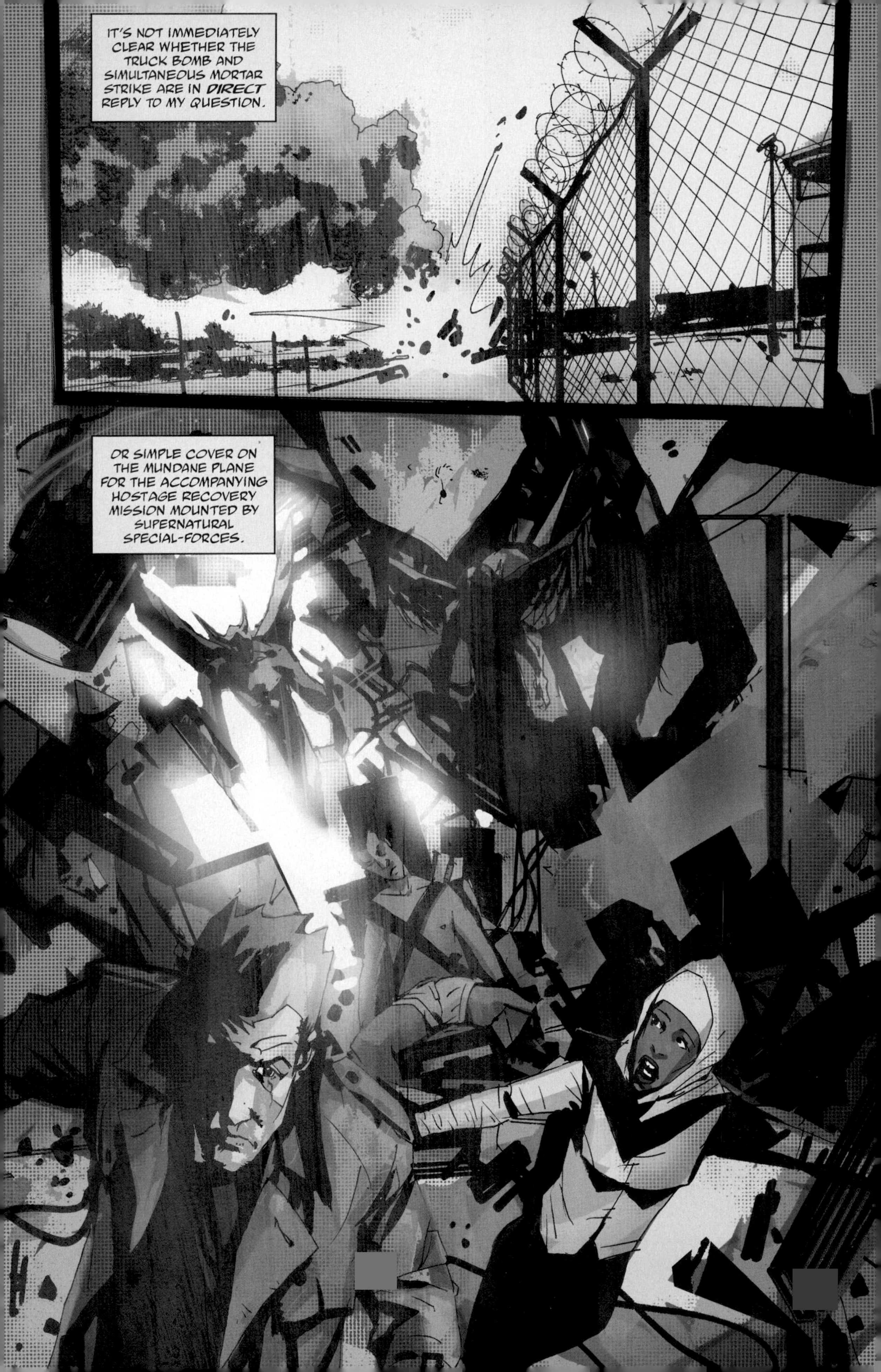
IT'S NOT IMMEDIATELY CLEAR WHETHER THE TRUCK BOMB AND SIMULTANEOUS MORTAR STRIKE ARE IN *DIRECT* REPLY TO MY QUESTION.
OR SIMPLE COVER ON THE MUNDANE PLANE FOR THE ACCOMPANYING HOSTAGE RECOVERY MISSION MOUNTED BY SUPERNATURAL SPECIAL-FORCES.

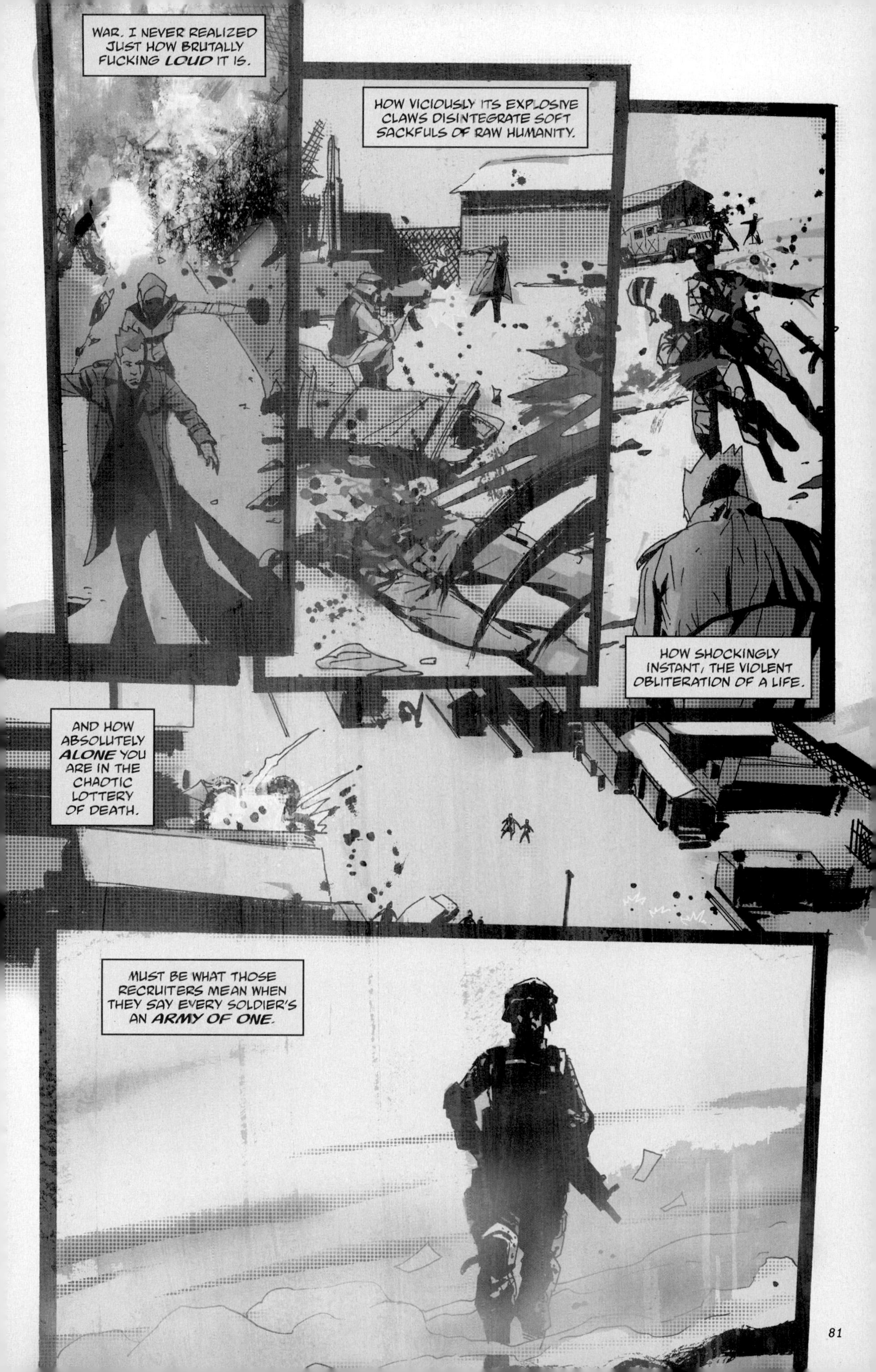
WAR. I NEVER REALIZED JUST HOW BRUTALLY FUCKING LOUD IT IS.
HOW VICIOUSLY ITS EXPLOSIVE CLAWS DISINTEGRATE SOFT SACKFULS OF RAW HUMANITY.
HOW SHOCKINGLY INSTANT, THE VIOLENT OBLITERATION OF A LIFE.
AND HOW ABSOLUTELY ALONE YOU ARE IN THE CHAOTIC LOTTERY OF DEATH.
MUST BE WHAT THOSE RECRUITERS MEAN WHEN THEY SAY EVERY SOLDIER'S AN ARMY OF ONE.

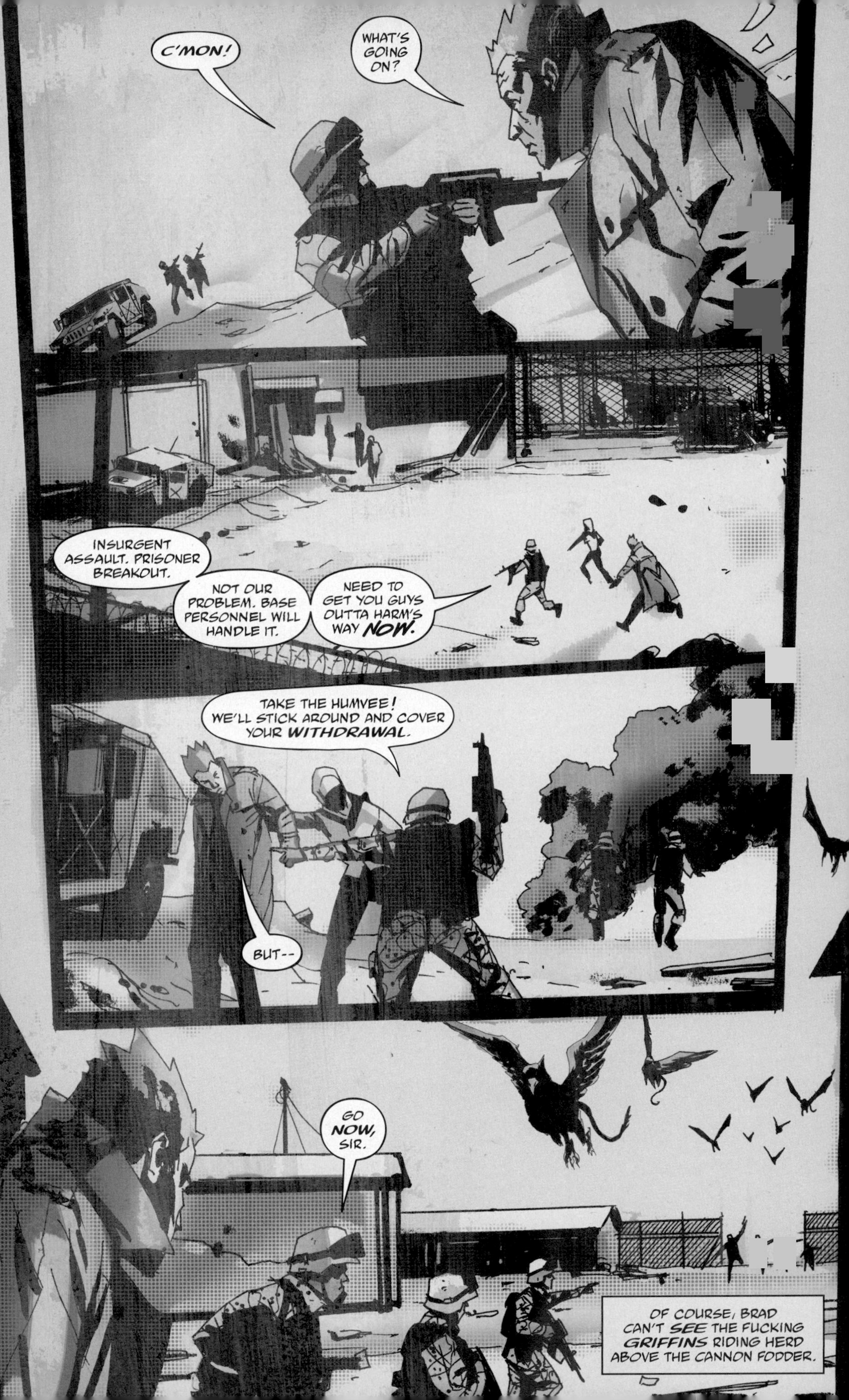
C'MON!
WHAT'S GOING ON?
INSURGENT ASSAULT. PRISONER BREAKOUT.
NOT OUR PROBLEM. BASE PERSONNEL WILL HANDLE IT.
NEED TO GET YOU GUYS OUTTA HARM'S WAY NOW.
TAKE THE HUMVEE! WE'LL STICK AROUND AND COVER YOUR WITHDRAWAL.
BUT--
GO NOW, SIR.
OF COURSE, BRAD CAN'T SEE THE FUCKING GRIFFINS RIDING HERD ABOVE THE CANNON FODDER.

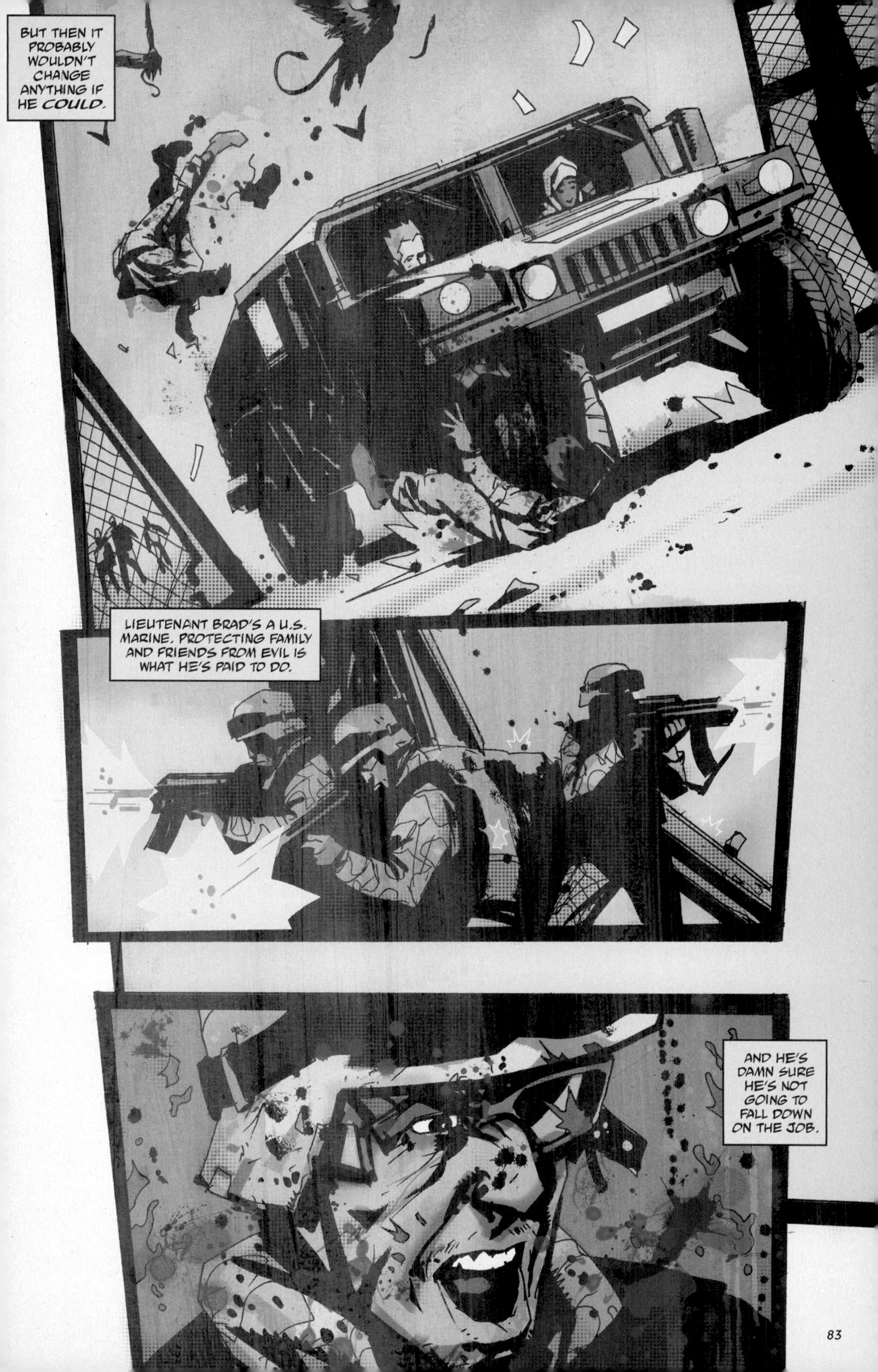
BUT THEN IT PROBABLY WOULDN'T CHANGE ANYTHING IF HE COULD.
LIEUTENANT BRAD'S A U.S. MARINE. PROTECTING FAMILY AND FRIENDS FROM EVIL IS WHAT HE'S PAID TO DO.
AND HE'S DAMN SURE HE'S NOT GOING TO FALL DOWN ON THE JOB.

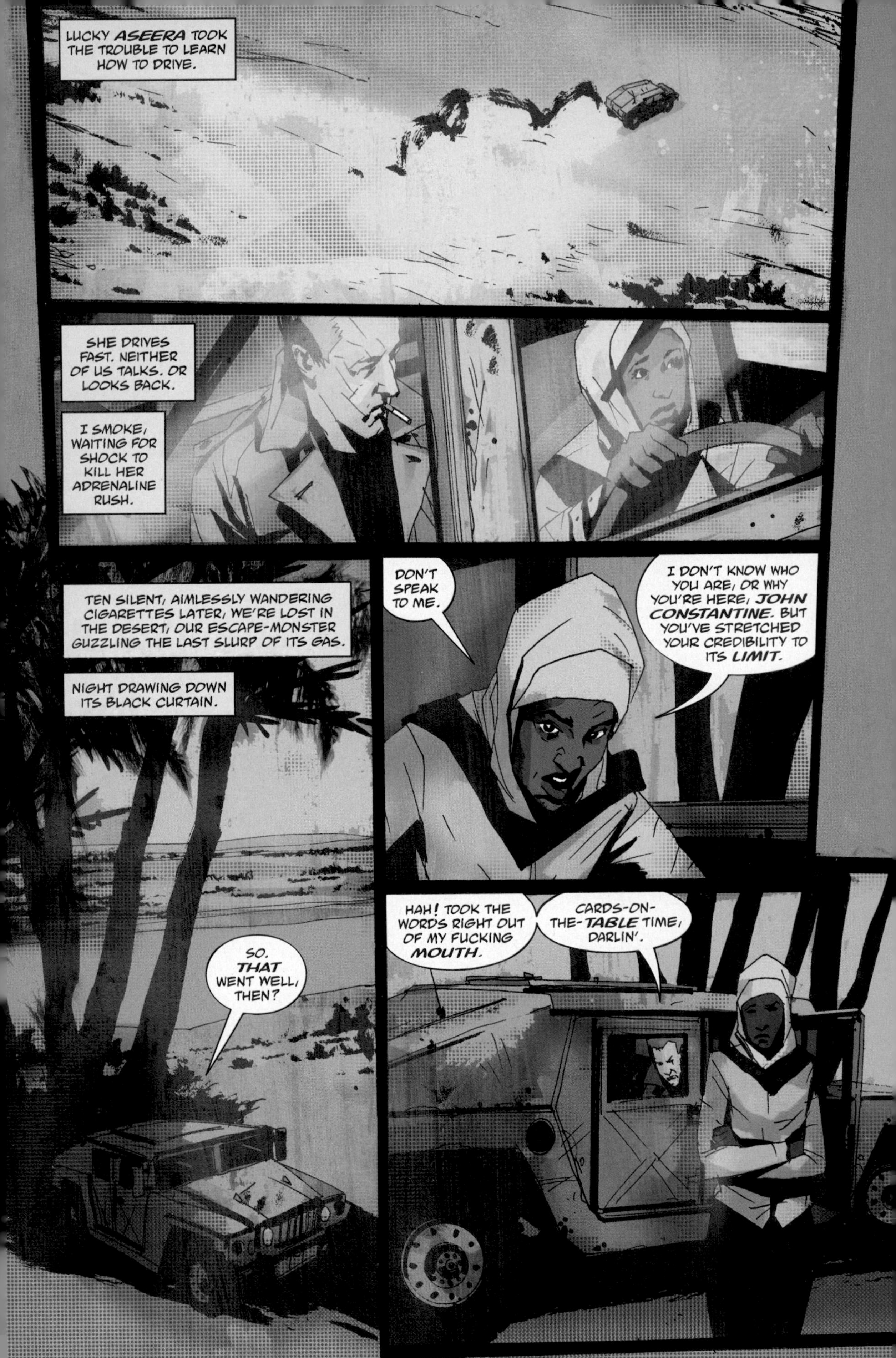
LUCKY ASEERA TOOK THE TROUBLE TO LEARN HOW TO DRIVE.
SHE DRIVES FAST. NEITHER OF US TALKS. OR LOOKS BACK.
I SMOKE, WAITING FOR SHOCK TO KILL HER ADRENALINE RUSH.
TEN SILENT, AIMLESSLY WANDERING CIGARETTES LATER, WE'RE LOST IN THE DESERT, OUR ESCAPE-MONSTER GUZZLING THE LAST SLURP OF ITS GAS.
NIGHT DRAWING DOWN ITS BLACK CURTAIN.
SO. THAT WENT WELL, THEN?
DON'T SPEAK TO ME.
I DON'T KNOW WHO YOU ARE, OR WHY YOU'RE HERE, JOHN CONSTANTINE. BUT YOU'VE STRETCHED YOUR CREDIBILITY TO ITS LIMIT.
HAH! TOOK THE WORDS RIGHT OUT OF MY FUCKING MOUTH.
CARDS-ON-THE-TABLE TIME, DARLIN'.

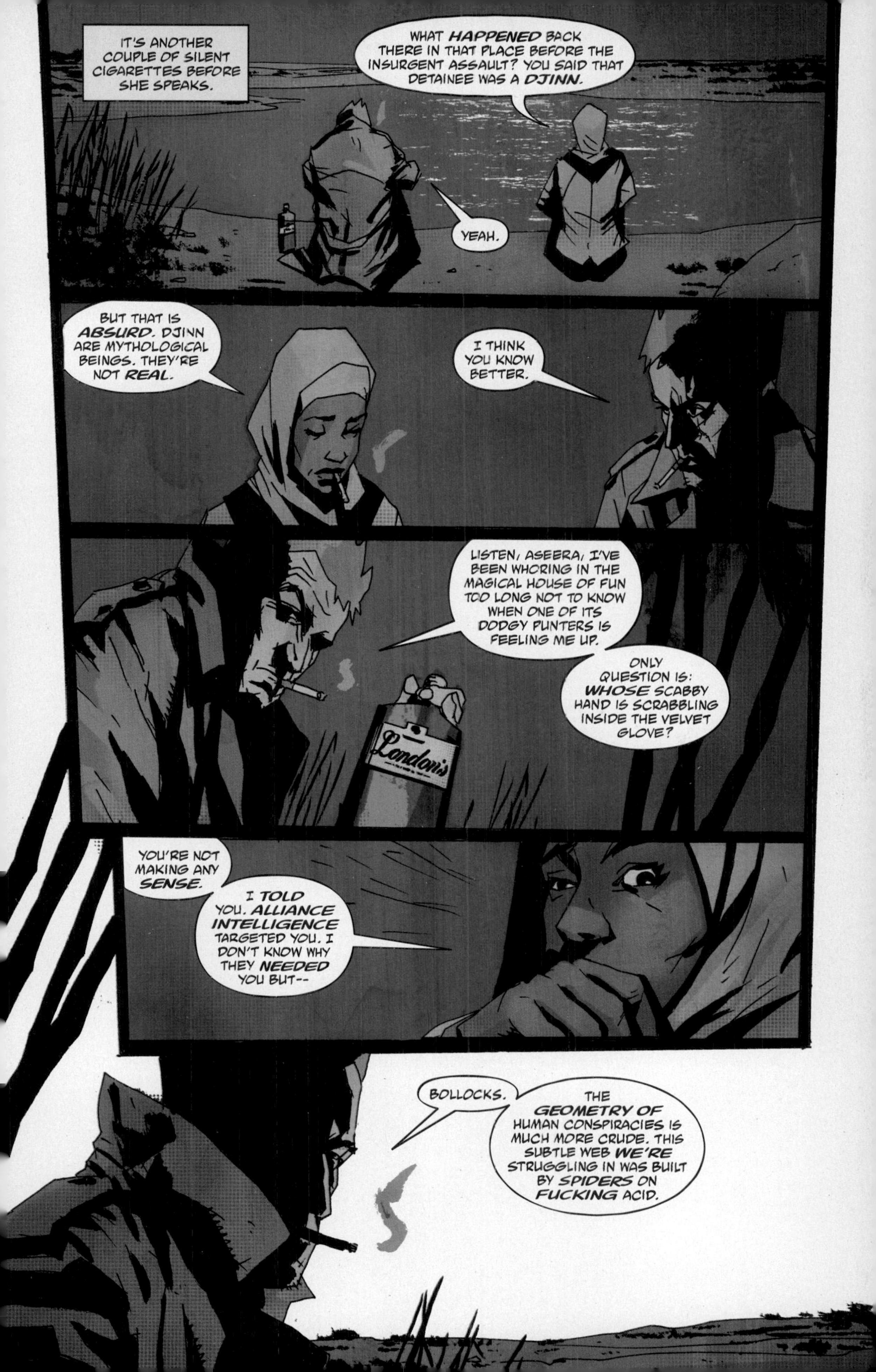
IT'S ANOTHER COUPLE OF SILENT CIGARETTES BEFORE SHE SPEAKS.
WHAT HAPPENED BACK THERE IN THAT PLACE BEFORE THE INSURGENT ASSAULT? YOU SAID THAT DETAINEE WAS A DJINN.
YEAH.
BUT THAT IS ABSURD. DJINN ARE MYTHOLOGICAL BEINGS. THEY'RE NOT REAL.
I THINK YOU KNOW BETTER.
LISTEN, ASEERA, I'VE BEEN WHORING IN THE MAGICAL HOUSE OF FUN TOO LONG NOT TO KNOW WHEN ONE OF ITS DODGY PUNTERS IS FEELING ME UP.
ONLY QUESTION IS: WHOSE SCABBY HAND IS SCRABBLING INSIDE THE VELVET GLOVE?
London's
YOU'RE NOT MAKING ANY SENSE.
I TOLD YOU. ALLIANCE INTELLIGENCE TARGETED YOU. I DON'T KNOW WHY THEY NEEDED YOU BUT--
BOLLOCKS.
THE GEOMETRY OF HUMAN CONSPIRACIES IS MUCH MORE CRUDE. THIS SUBTLE WEB WE'RE STRUGGLING IN WAS BUILT BY SPIDERS ON FUCKING ACID.

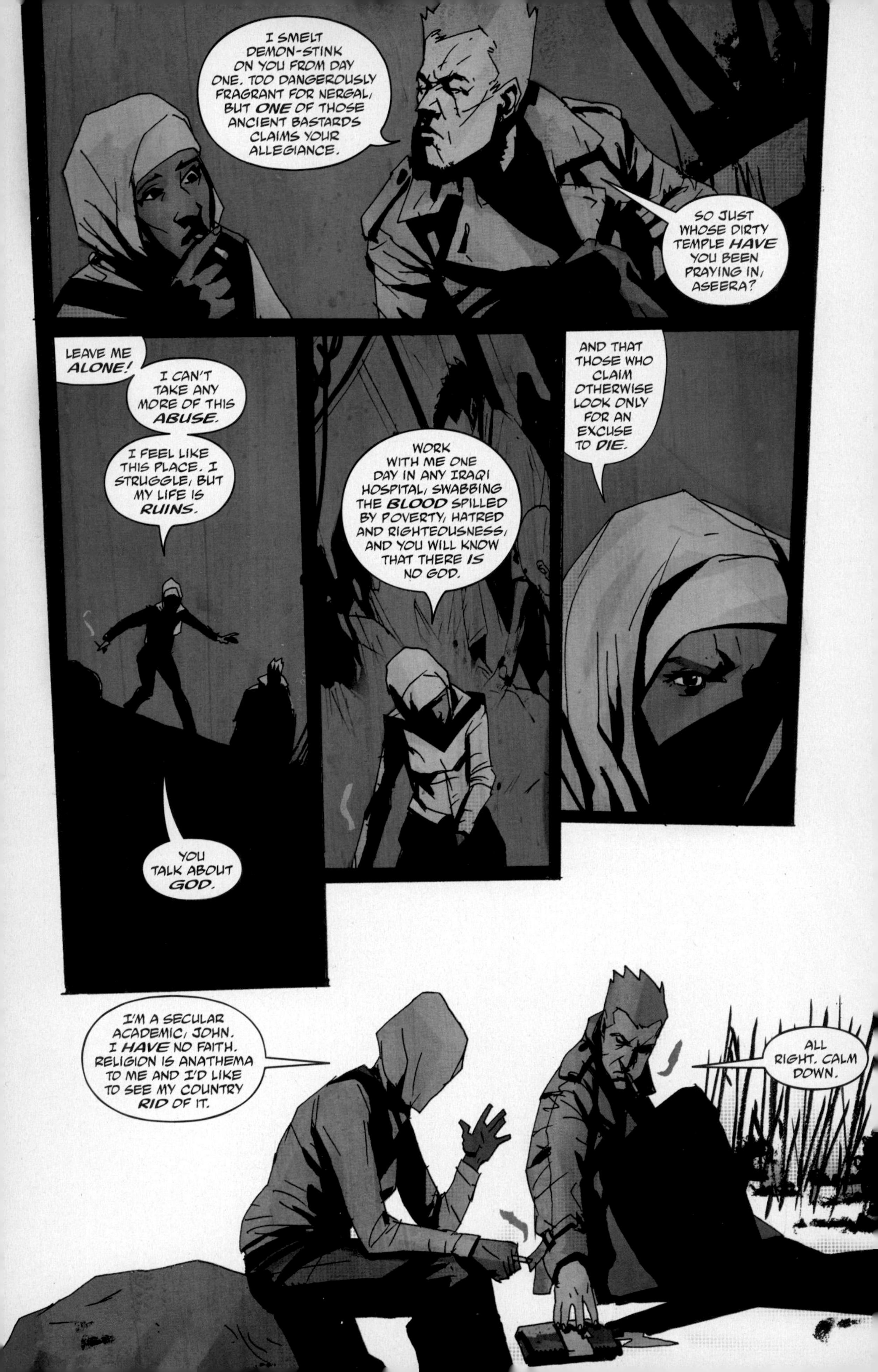
I SMELT DEMON-STINK ON YOU FROM DAY ONE. TOO DANGEROUSLY FRAGRANT FOR NERGAL, BUT ONE OF THOSE ANCIENT BASTARDS CLAIMS YOUR ALLEGIANCE.
SO JUST WHOSE DIRTY TEMPLE HAVE YOU BEEN PRAYING IN, ASEERA?
LEAVE ME ALONE!
I CAN'T TAKE ANY MORE OF THIS ABUSE.
I FEEL LIKE THIS PLACE. I STRUGGLE, BUT MY LIFE IS RUINS.
YOU TALK ABOUT GOD.
WORK WITH ME ONE DAY IN ANY IRAQI HOSPITAL, SWABBING THE BLOOD SPILLED BY POVERTY, HATRED AND RIGHTEOUSNESS, AND YOU WILL KNOW THAT THERE IS NO GOD.
AND THAT THOSE WHO CLAIM OTHERWISE LOOK ONLY FOR AN EXCUSE TO DIE.
I'M A SECULAR ACADEMIC, JOHN. I HAVE NO FAITH. RELIGION IS ANATHEMA TO ME AND I'D LIKE TO SEE MY COUNTRY RID OF IT.
ALL RIGHT. CALM DOWN.

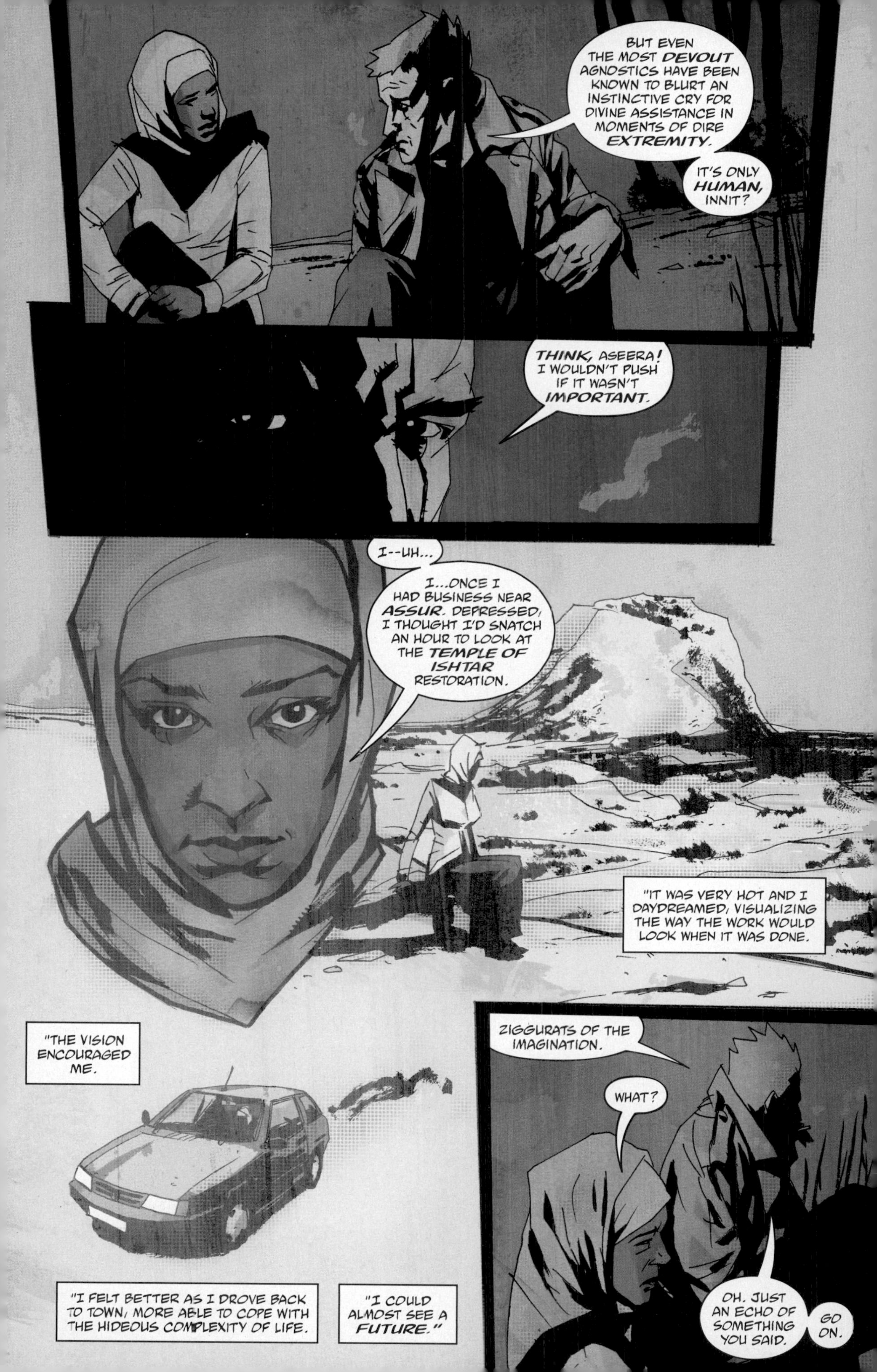
BUT EVEN THE MOST DEVOUT AGNOSTICS HAVE BEEN KNOWN TO BLURT AN INSTINCTIVE CRY FOR DIVINE ASSISTANCE IN MOMENTS OF DIRE EXTREMITY.
IT'S ONLY HUMAN, INNIT?
THINK, ASEERA! I WOULDN'T PUSH IF IT WASN'T IMPORTANT.
I--UH...
I...ONCE I HAD BUSINESS NEAR ASSUR. DEPRESSED, I THOUGHT I'D SNATCH AN HOUR TO LOOK AT THE TEMPLE OF ISHTAR RESTORATION.
"IT WAS VERY HOT AND I DAYDREAMED, VISUALIZING THE WAY THE WORK WOULD LOOK WHEN IT WAS DONE.
"THE VISION ENCOURAGED ME.
"I FELT BETTER AS I DROVE BACK TO TOWN, MORE ABLE TO COPE WITH THE HIDEOUS COMPLEXITY OF LIFE.
"I COULD ALMOST SEE A FUTURE."
ZIGGURATS OF THE IMAGINATION.
WHAT?
OH. JUST AN ECHO OF SOMETHING YOU SAID.
GO ON.

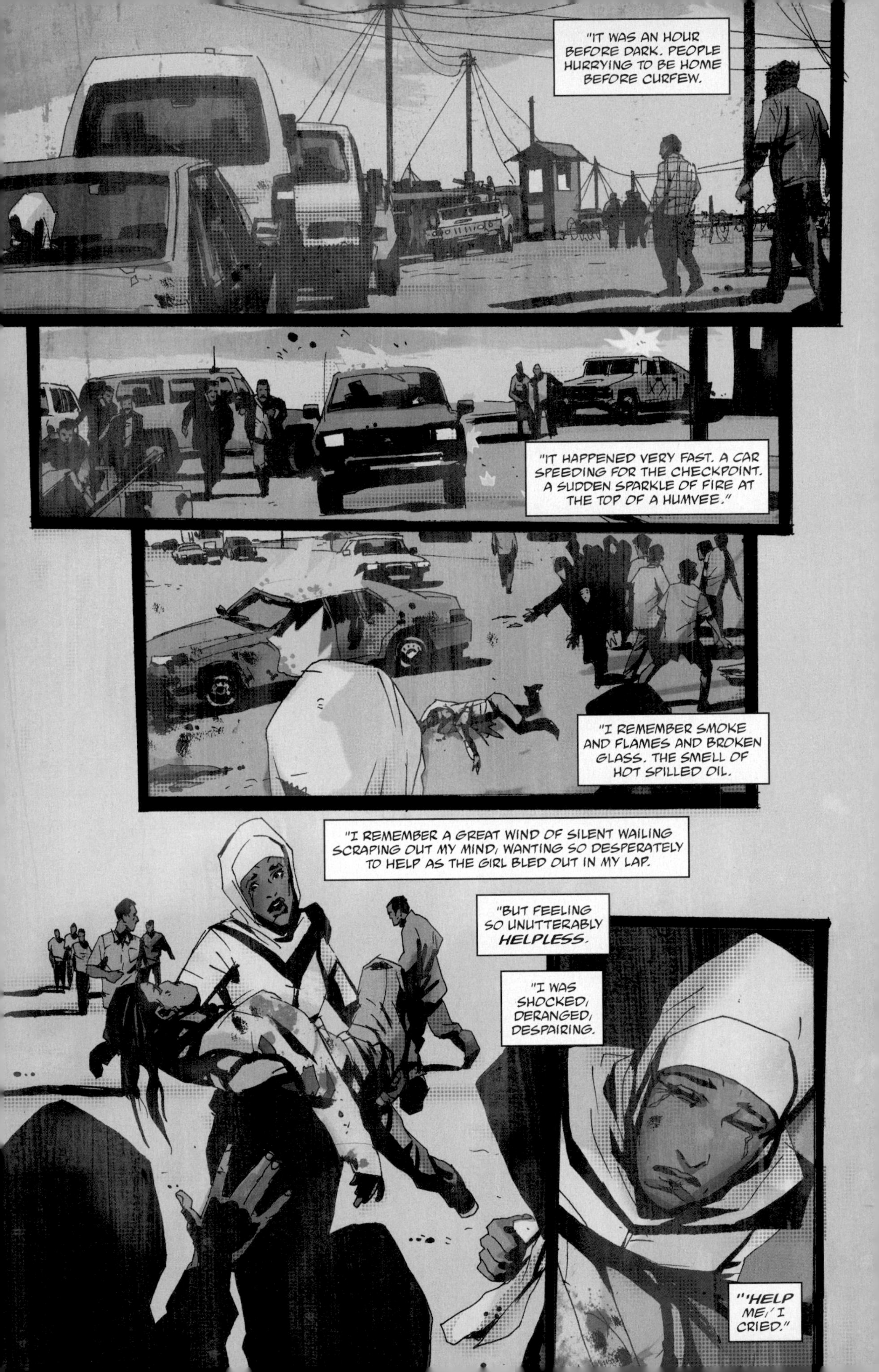
"IT WAS AN HOUR BEFORE DARK. PEOPLE HURRYING TO BE HOME BEFORE CURFEW.
"IT HAPPENED VERY FAST. A CAR SPEEDING FOR THE CHECKPOINT. A SUDDEN SPARKLE OF FIRE AT THE TOP OF A HUMVEE."
"I REMEMBER SMOKE AND FLAMES AND BROKEN GLASS. THE SMELL OF HOT SPILLED OIL.
"I REMEMBER A GREAT WIND OF SILENT WAILING SCRAPING OUT MY MIND, WANTING SO DESPERATELY TO HELP AS THE GIRL BLED OUT IN MY LAP.
"BUT FEELING SO UNUTTERABLY *HELPLESS*.
"I WAS SHOCKED, DERANGED, DESPAIRING.
"'*HELP ME*,' I CRIED."

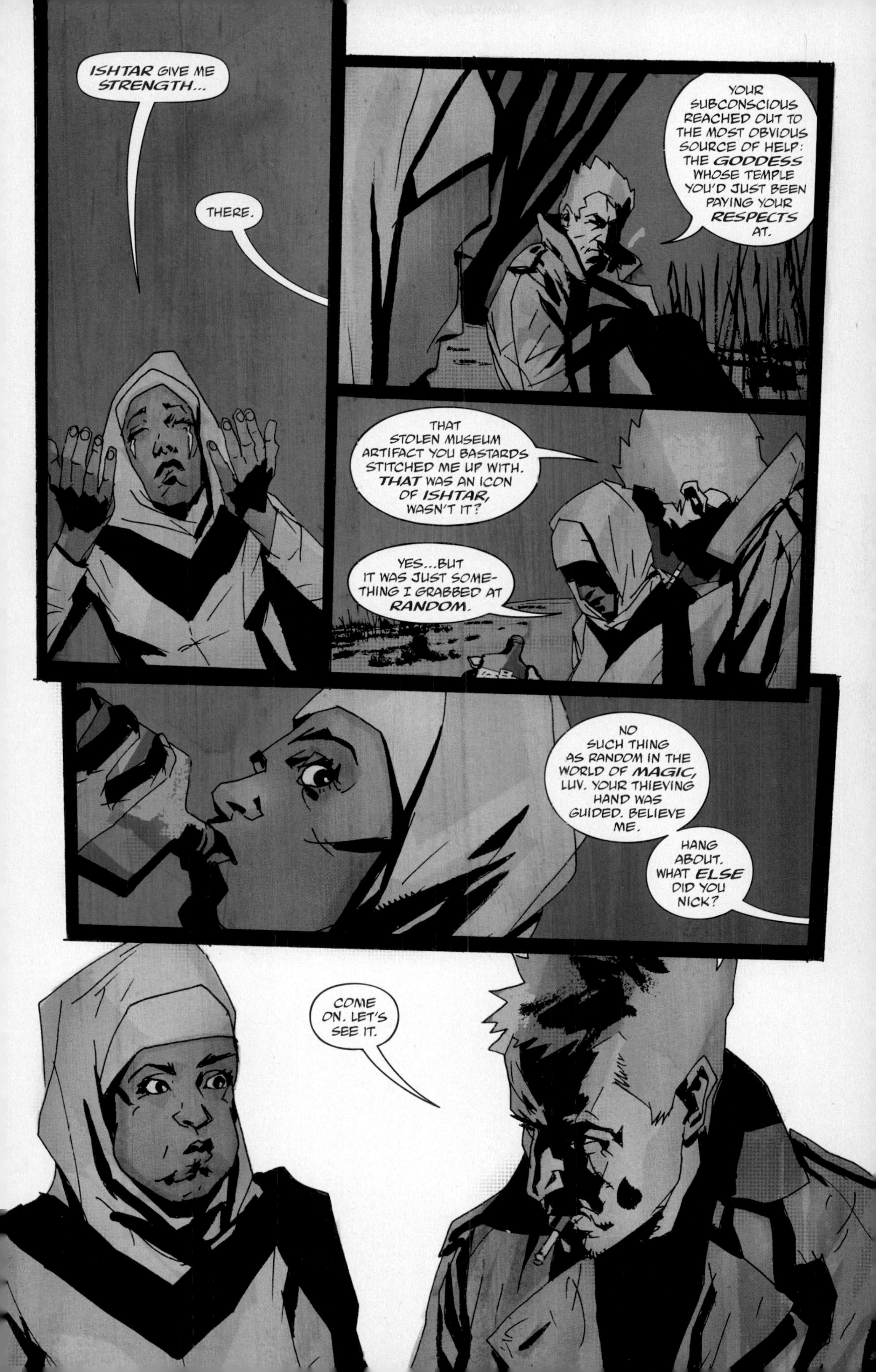
ISHTAR GIVE ME STRENGTH...
THERE.
YOUR SUBCONSCIOUS REACHED OUT TO THE MOST OBVIOUS SOURCE OF HELP: THE GODDESS WHOSE TEMPLE YOU'D JUST BEEN PAYING YOUR RESPECTS AT.
THAT STOLEN MUSEUM ARTIFACT YOU BASTARDS STITCHED ME UP WITH. THAT WAS AN ICON OF ISHTAR, WASN'T IT?
YES...BUT IT WAS JUST SOME-THING I GRABBED AT RANDOM.
NO SUCH THING AS RANDOM IN THE WORLD OF MAGIC, LUV. YOUR THIEVING HAND WAS GUIDED. BELIEVE ME.
HANG ABOUT. WHAT ELSE DID YOU NICK?
COME ON. LET'S SEE IT.

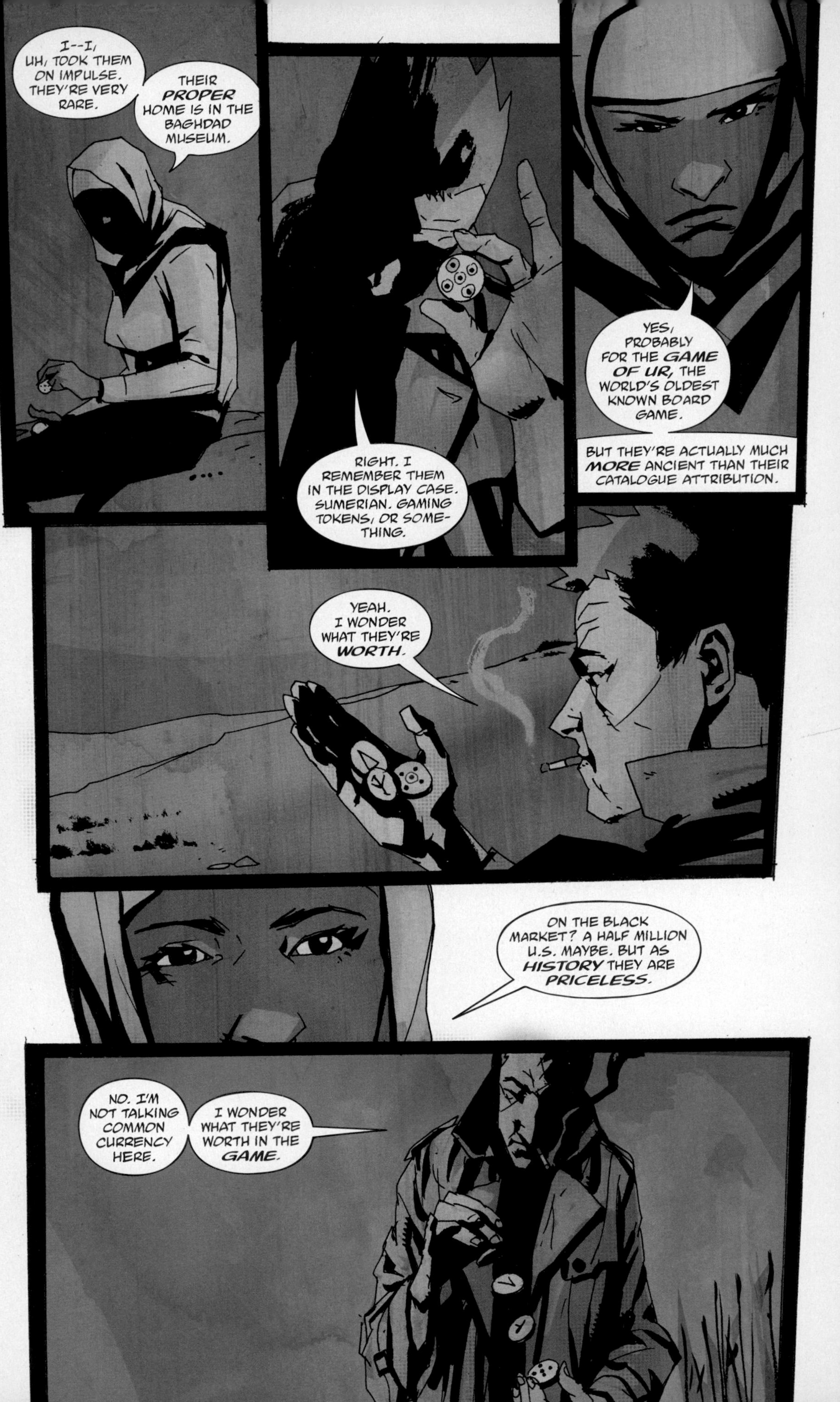
I--I, UH, TOOK THEM ON IMPULSE. THEY'RE VERY RARE.
THEIR PROPER HOME IS IN THE BAGHDAD MUSEUM.
RIGHT. I REMEMBER THEM IN THE DISPLAY CASE. SUMERIAN. GAMING TOKENS, OR SOME-THING.
YES, PROBABLY FOR THE GAME OF UR, THE WORLD'S OLDEST KNOWN BOARD GAME.
BUT THEY'RE ACTUALLY MUCH MORE ANCIENT THAN THEIR CATALOGUE ATTRIBUTION.
YEAH. I WONDER WHAT THEY'RE WORTH.
ON THE BLACK MARKET? A HALF MILLION U.S. MAYBE. BUT AS HISTORY THEY ARE PRICELESS.
NO. I'M NOT TALKING COMMON CURRENCY HERE.
I WONDER WHAT THEY'RE WORTH IN THE GAME.

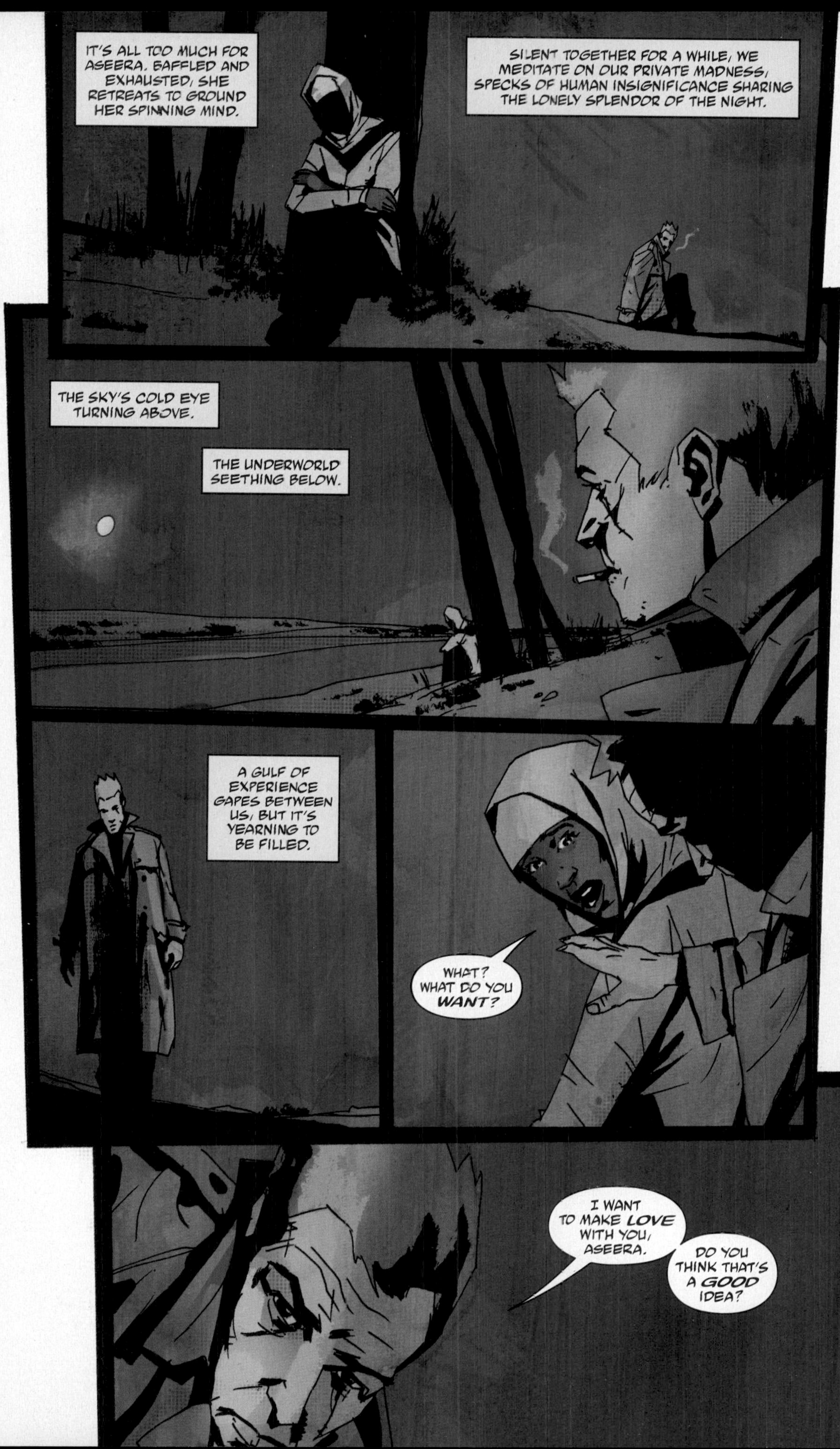
IT'S ALL TOO MUCH FOR ASEERA. BAFFLED AND EXHAUSTED, SHE RETREATS TO GROUND HER SPINNING MIND.
SILENT TOGETHER FOR A WHILE, WE MEDITATE ON OUR PRIVATE MADNESS, SPECKS OF HUMAN INSIGNIFICANCE SHARING THE LONELY SPLENDOR OF THE NIGHT.
THE SKY'S COLD EYE TURNING ABOVE.
THE UNDERWORLD SEETHING BELOW.
A GULF OF EXPERIENCE GAPES BETWEEN US, BUT IT'S YEARNING TO BE FILLED.
WHAT? WHAT DO YOU *WANT?*
I WANT TO MAKE *LOVE* WITH YOU, ASEERA.
DO YOU THINK THAT'S A *GOOD* IDEA?

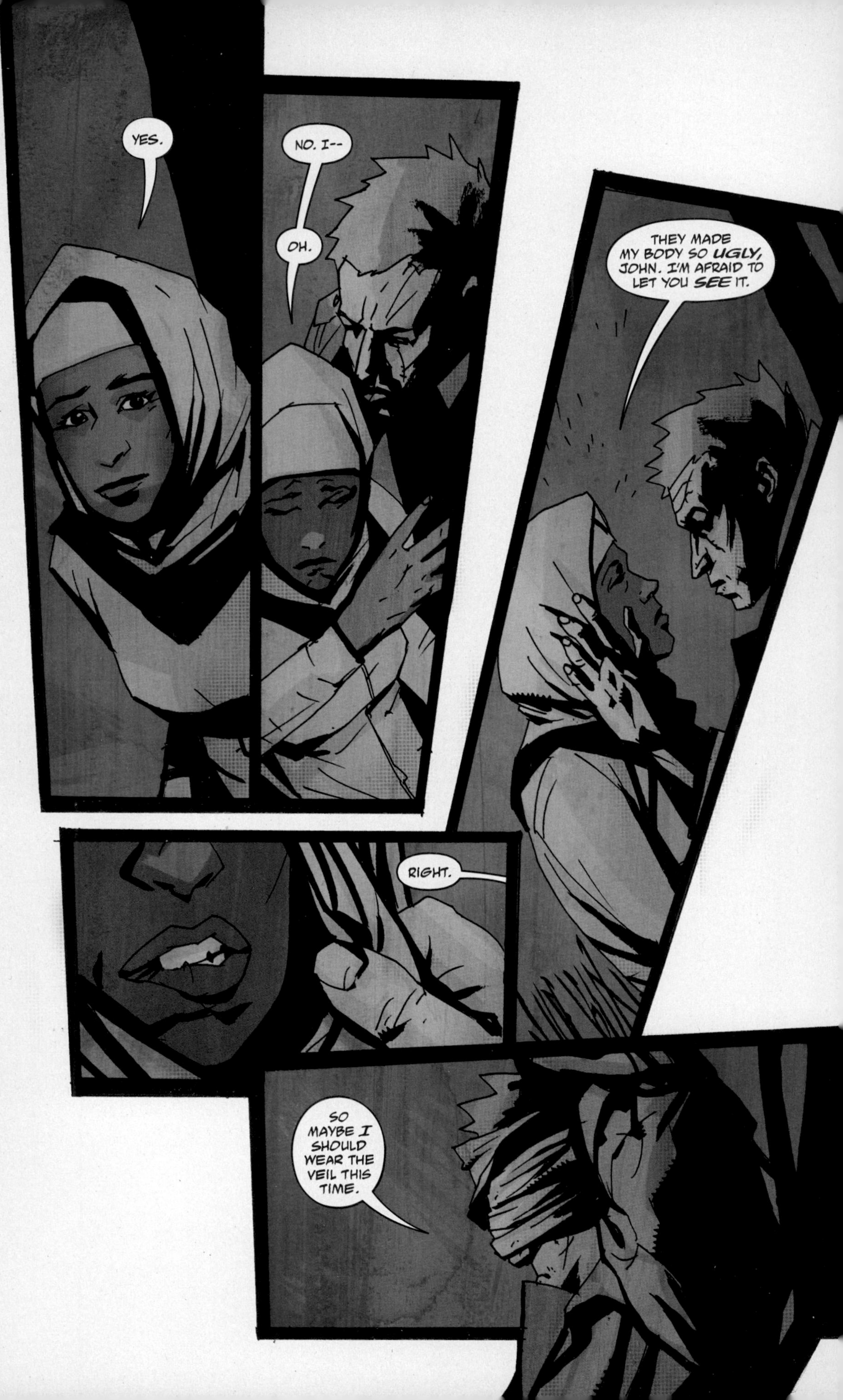
YES.
NO. I--
OH.
THEY MADE MY BODY SO UGLY, JOHN. I'M AFRAID TO LET YOU SEE IT.
RIGHT.
SO MAYBE I SHOULD WEAR THE VEIL THIS TIME.

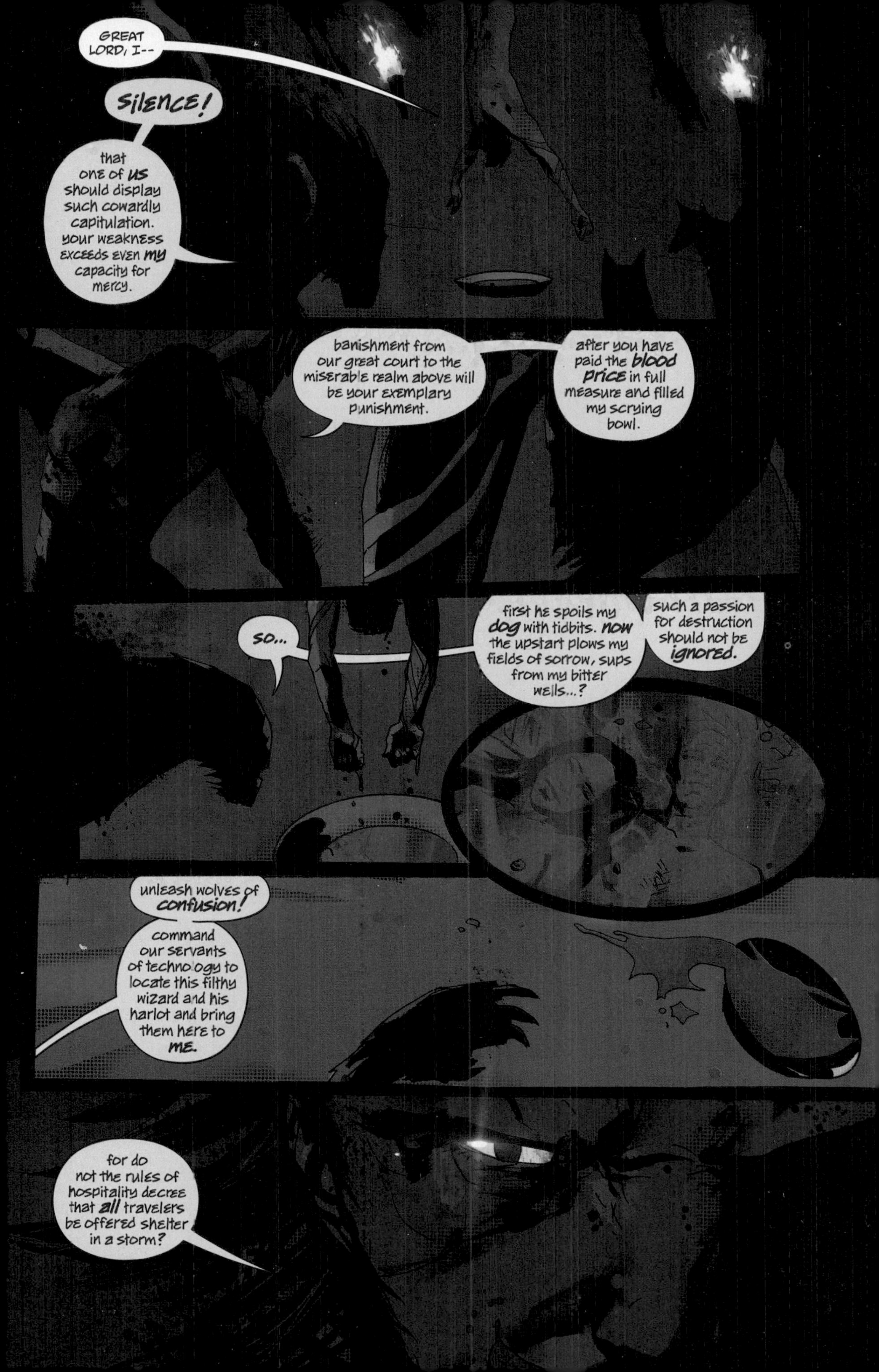
GREAT LORD, I--
SILENCE!
that one of us should display such cowardly capitulation. your weakness exceeds even my capacity for mercy.
banishment from our great court to the miserable realm above will be your exemplary punishment.
after you have paid the blood price in full measure and filled my scrying bowl.
so...
first he spoils my dog with tidbits. now the upstart plows my fields of sorrow, sups from my bitter wells...?
such a passion for destruction should not be ignored.
unleash wolves of confusion!
command our servants of technology to locate this filthy wizard and his harlot and bring them here to me.
for do not the rules of hospitality decree that all travelers be offered shelter in a storm?

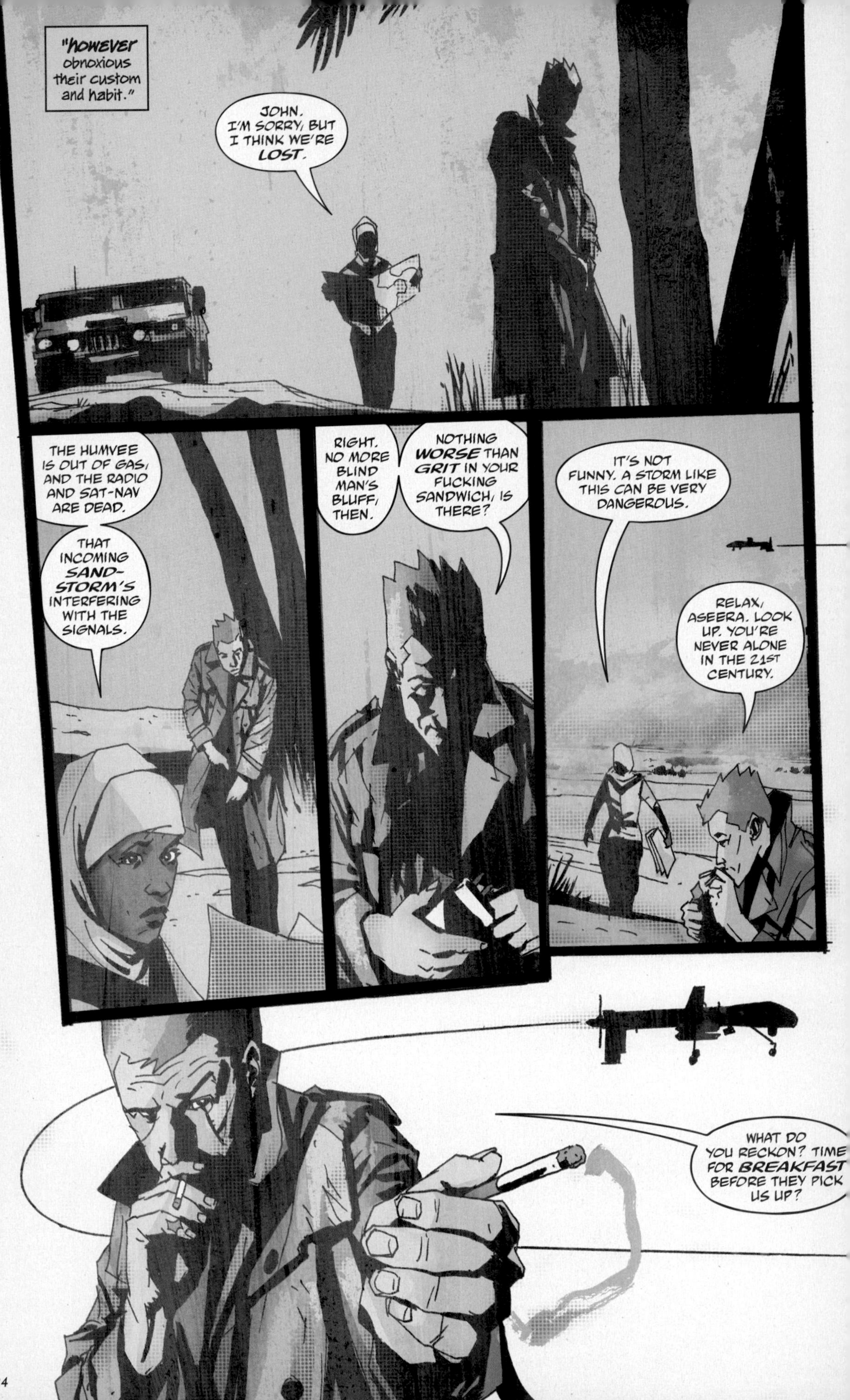
"however obnoxious their custom and habit."
JOHN. I'M SORRY, BUT I THINK WE'RE LOST.
THE HUMVEE IS OUT OF GAS, AND THE RADIO AND SAT-NAV ARE DEAD.
THAT INCOMING SAND-STORM'S INTERFERING WITH THE SIGNALS.
RIGHT. NO MORE BLIND MAN'S BLUFF, THEN.
NOTHING WORSE THAN GRIT IN YOUR FUCKING SANDWICH, IS THERE?
IT'S NOT FUNNY. A STORM LIKE THIS CAN BE VERY DANGEROUS.
RELAX, ASEERA. LOOK UP. YOU'RE NEVER ALONE IN THE 21ST CENTURY.
WHAT DO YOU RECKON? TIME FOR BREAKFAST BEFORE THEY PICK US UP?

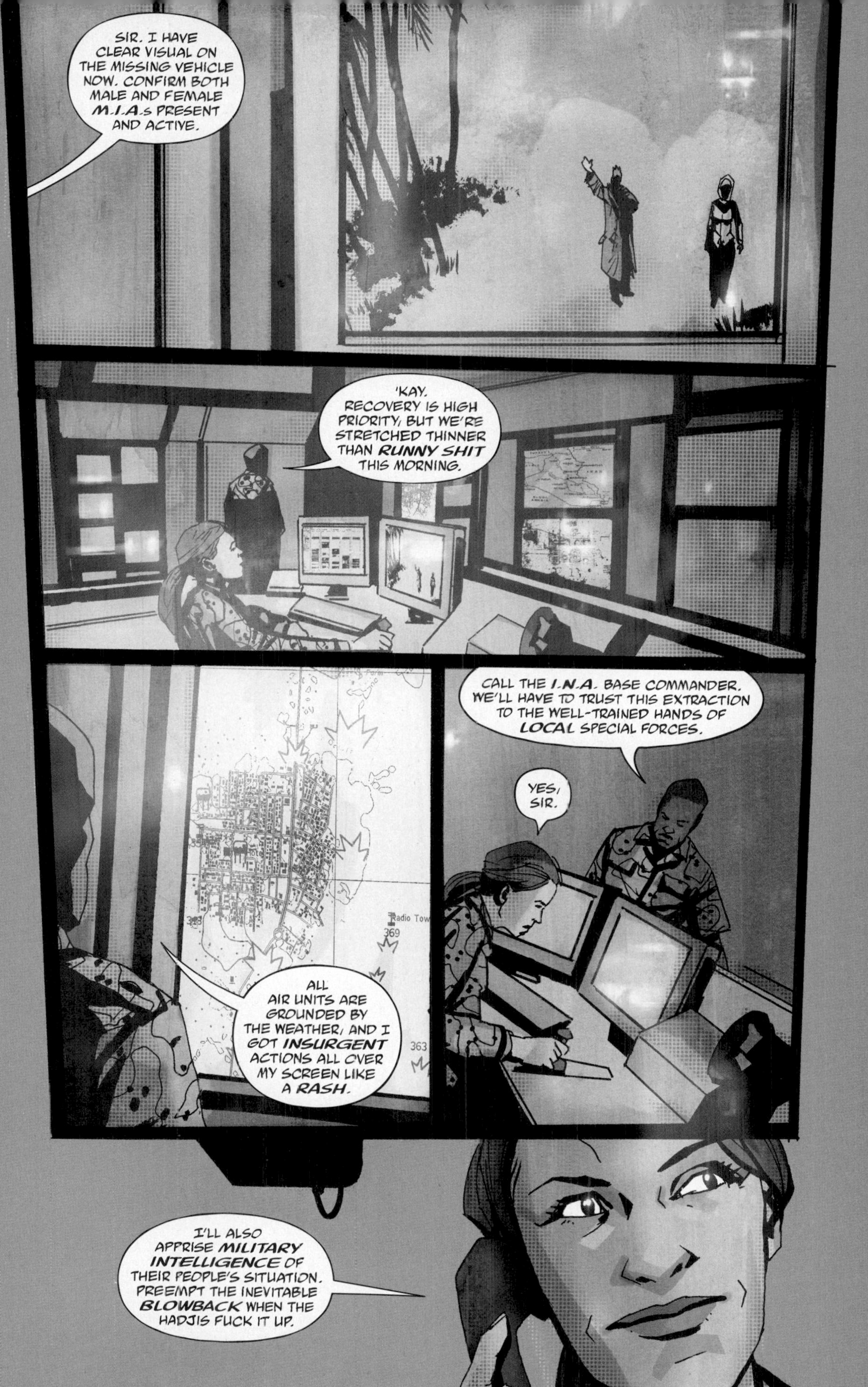
SIR. I HAVE CLEAR VISUAL ON THE MISSING VEHICLE NOW. CONFIRM BOTH MALE AND FEMALE M.I.A.S PRESENT AND ACTIVE.
'KAY. RECOVERY IS HIGH PRIORITY, BUT WE'RE STRETCHED THINNER THAN RUNNY SHIT THIS MORNING.
ALL AIR UNITS ARE GROUNDED BY THE WEATHER, AND I GOT INSURGENT ACTIONS ALL OVER MY SCREEN LIKE A RASH.
CALL THE I.N.A. BASE COMMANDER. WE'LL HAVE TO TRUST THIS EXTRACTION TO THE WELL-TRAINED HANDS OF LOCAL SPECIAL FORCES.
YES, SIR.
I'LL ALSO APPRISE MILITARY INTELLIGENCE OF THEIR PEOPLE'S SITUATION. PREEMPT THE INEVITABLE BLOWBACK WHEN THE HADJIS FUCK IT UP.

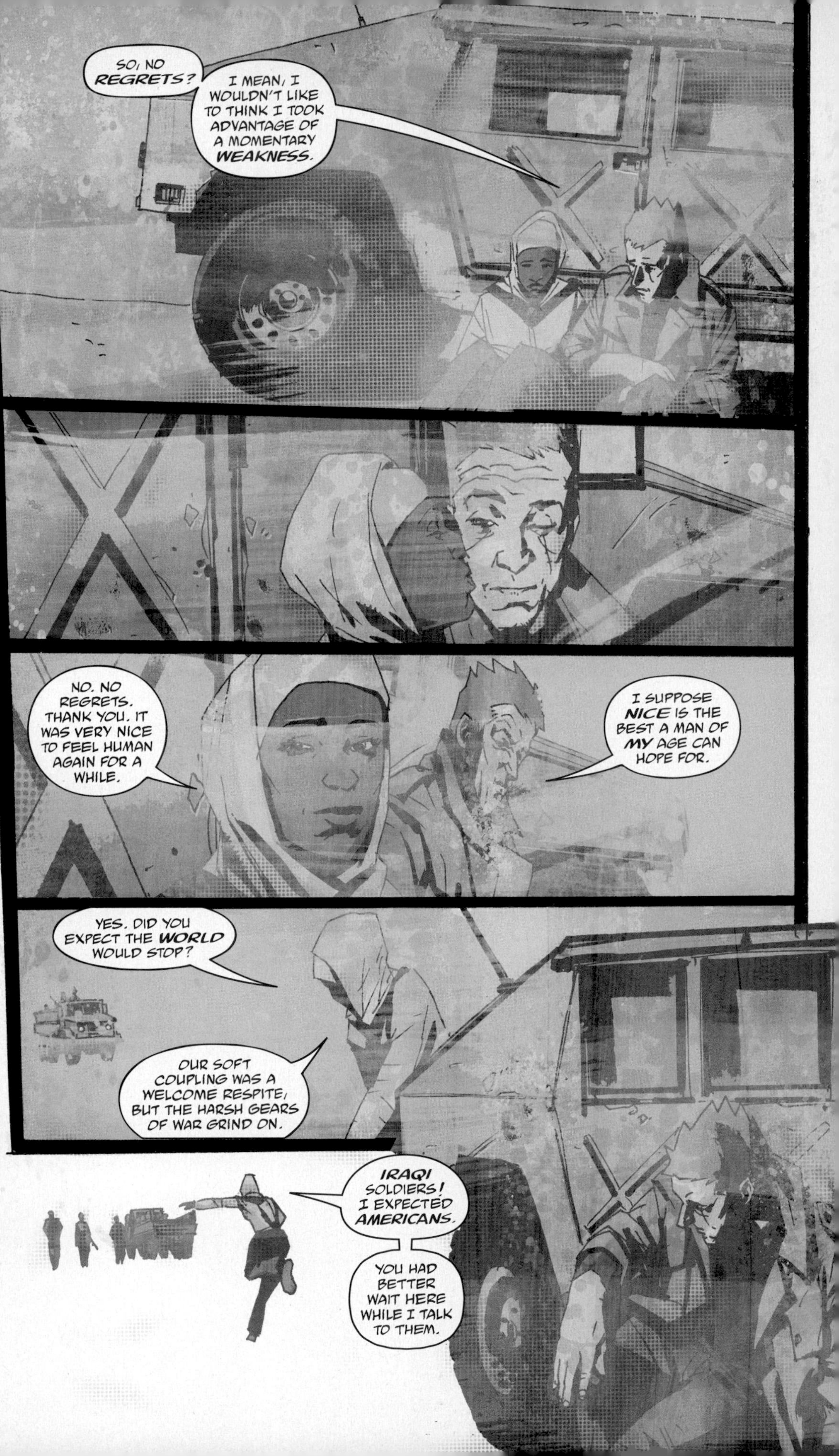
SO, NO REGRETS?
I MEAN, I WOULDN'T LIKE TO THINK I TOOK ADVANTAGE OF A MOMENTARY WEAKNESS.
NO. NO REGRETS. THANK YOU. IT WAS VERY NICE TO FEEL HUMAN AGAIN FOR A WHILE.
I SUPPOSE NICE IS THE BEST A MAN OF MY AGE CAN HOPE FOR.
YES. DID YOU EXPECT THE WORLD WOULD STOP?
OUR SOFT COUPLING WAS A WELCOME RESPITE, BUT THE HARSH GEARS OF WAR GRIND ON.
IRAQI SOLDIERS! I EXPECTED AMERICANS.
YOU HAD BETTER WAIT HERE WHILE I TALK TO THEM.

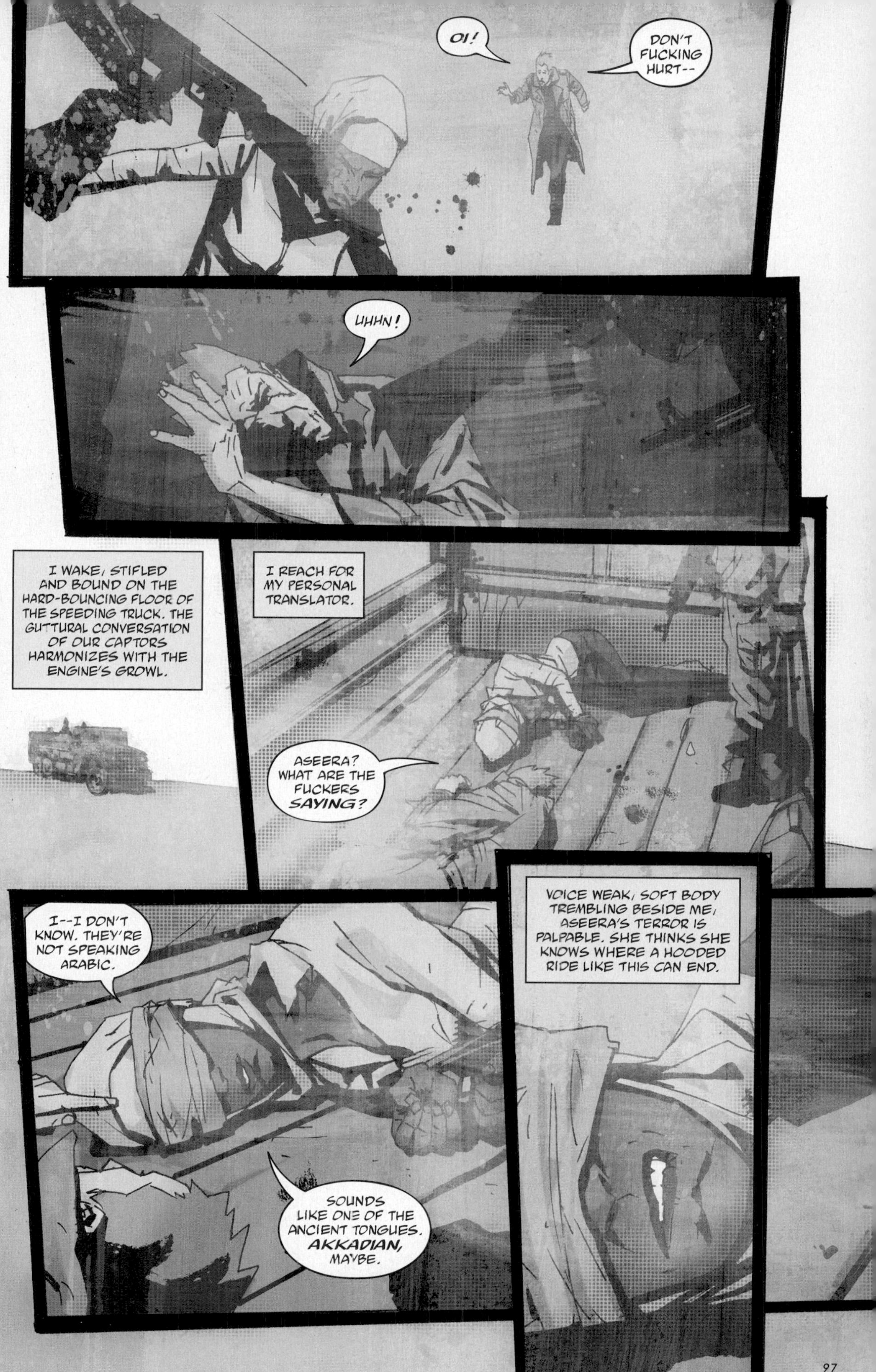
OI!
DON'T FUCKING HURT--
UHHN!
I WAKE, STIFLED AND BOUND ON THE HARD-BOUNCING FLOOR OF THE SPEEDING TRUCK. THE GUTTURAL CONVERSATION OF OUR CAPTORS HARMONIZES WITH THE ENGINE'S GROWL.
I REACH FOR MY PERSONAL TRANSLATOR.
ASEERA? WHAT ARE THE FUCKERS *SAYING?*
I--I DON'T KNOW. THEY'RE NOT SPEAKING ARABIC.
SOUNDS LIKE ONE OF THE ANCIENT TONGUES. ***AKKADIAN,*** MAYBE.
VOICE WEAK, SOFT BODY TREMBLING BESIDE ME, ASEERA'S TERROR IS PALPABLE. SHE THINKS SHE KNOWS WHERE A HOODED RIDE LIKE THIS CAN END.

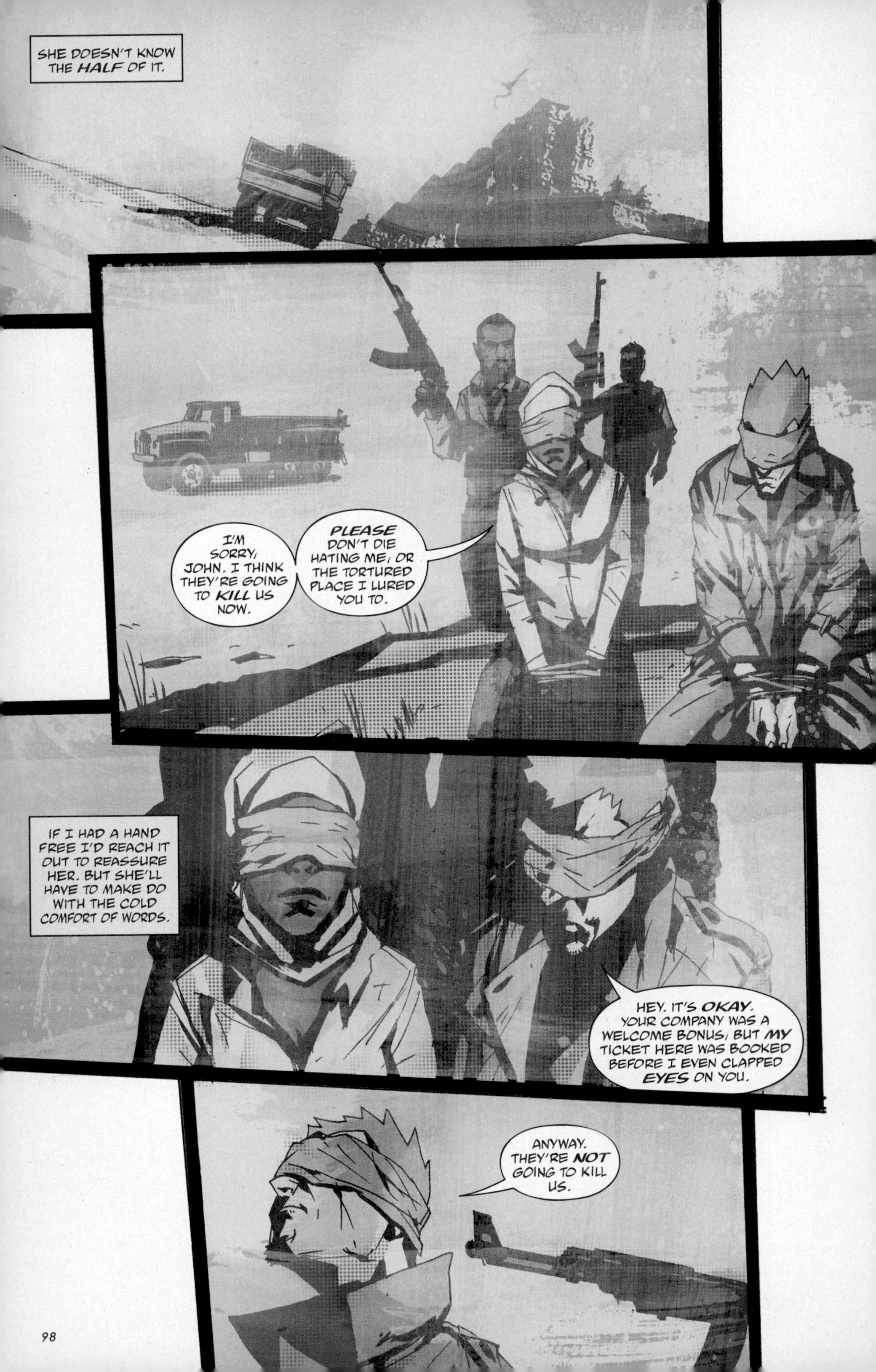
SHE DOESN'T KNOW THE HALF OF IT.
I'M SORRY, JOHN. I THINK THEY'RE GOING TO KILL US NOW.
PLEASE DON'T DIE HATING ME, OR THE TORTURED PLACE I LURED YOU TO.
IF I HAD A HAND FREE I'D REACH IT OUT TO REASSURE HER. BUT SHE'LL HAVE TO MAKE DO WITH THE COLD COMFORT OF WORDS.
HEY. IT'S OKAY. YOUR COMPANY WAS A WELCOME BONUS, BUT MY TICKET HERE WAS BOOKED BEFORE I EVEN CLAPPED EYES ON YOU.
ANYWAY. THEY'RE NOT GOING TO KILL US.

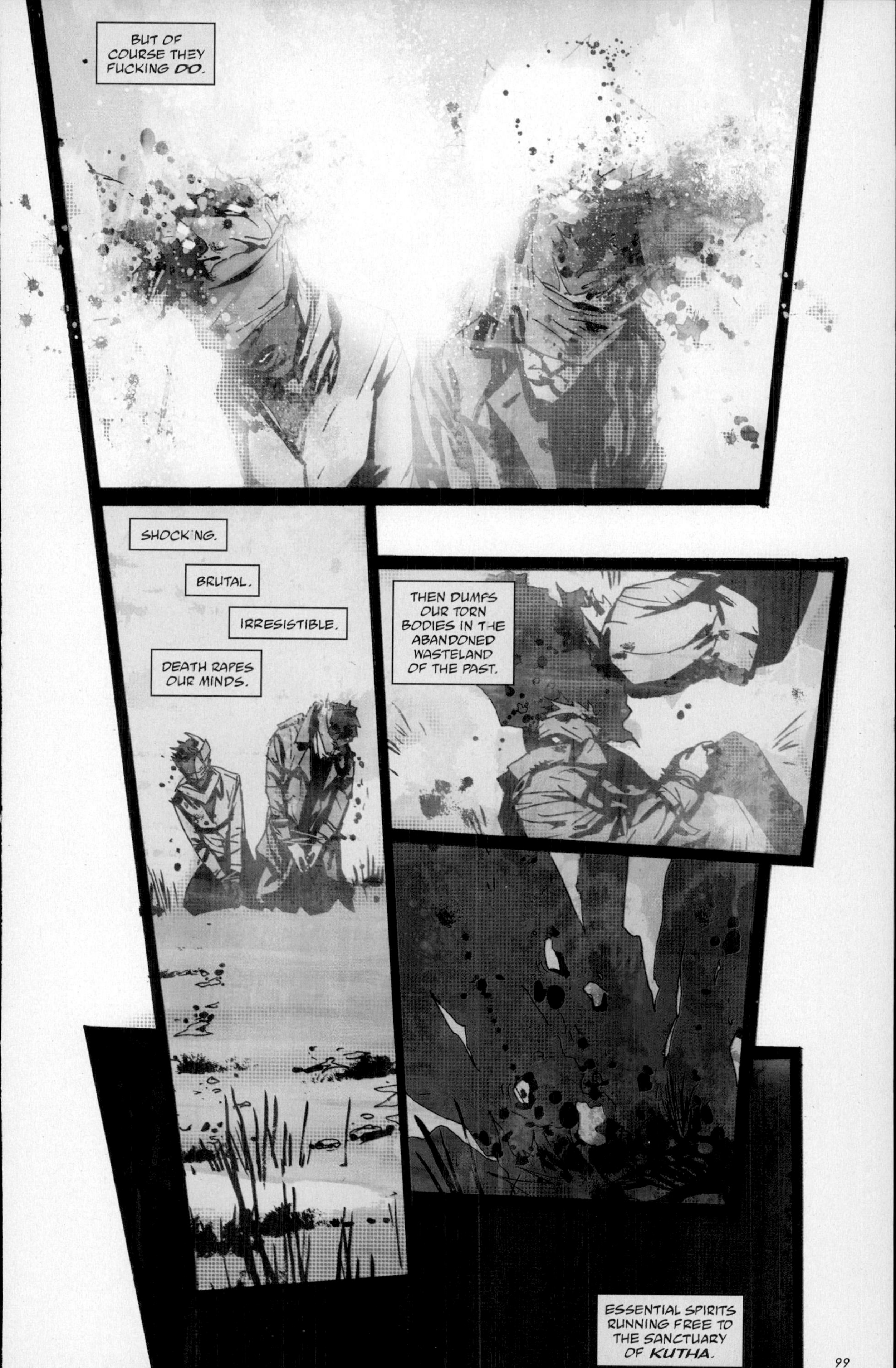
BUT OF COURSE THEY FUCKING DO.
SHOCKING.
BRUTAL.
IRRESISTIBLE.
DEATH RAPES OUR MINDS.
THEN DUMPS OUR TORN BODIES IN THE ABANDONED WASTELAND OF THE PAST.
ESSENTIAL SPIRITS RUNNING FREE TO THE SANCTUARY OF KUTHA.

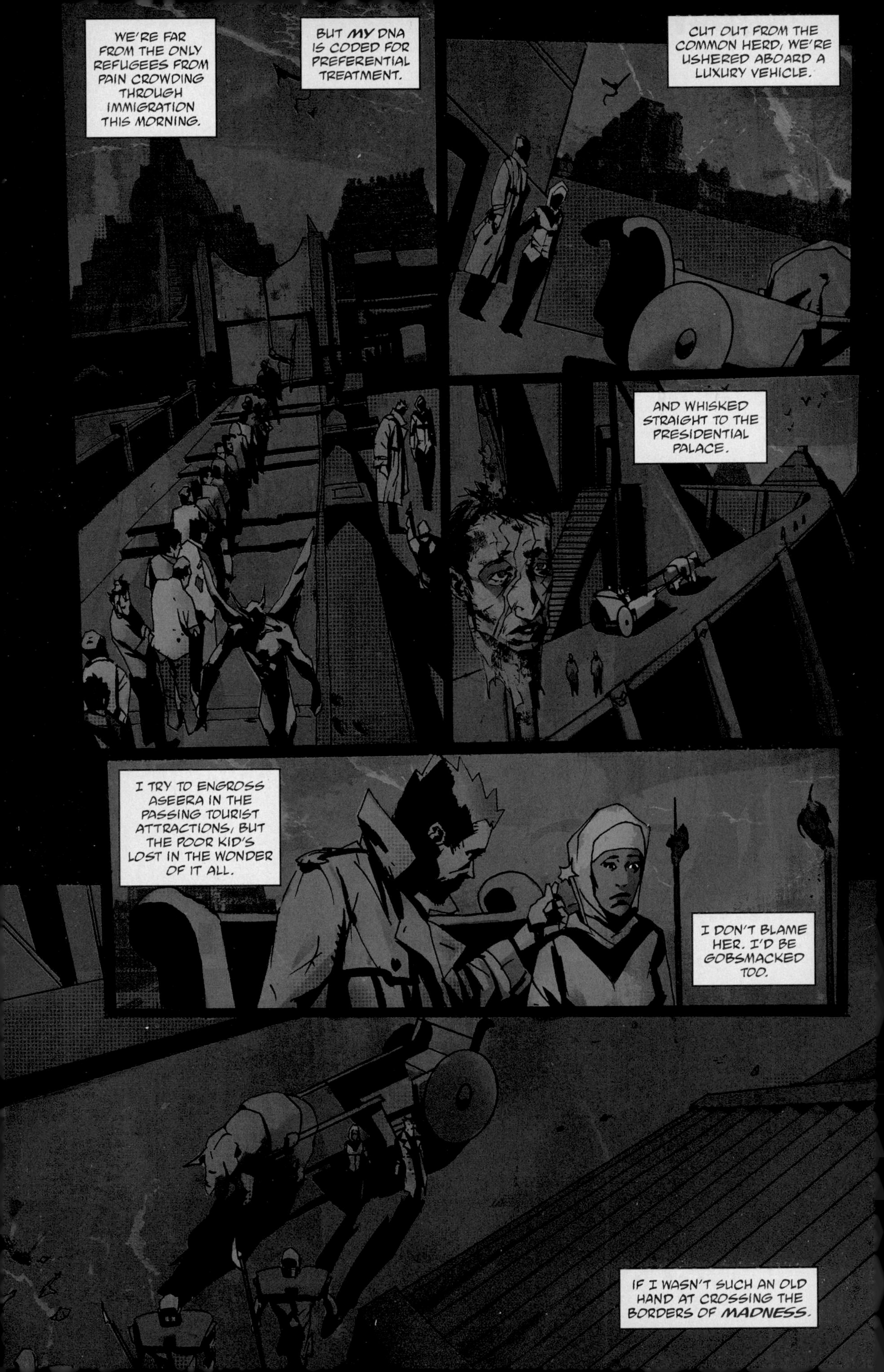
WE'RE FAR FROM THE ONLY REFUGEES FROM PAIN CROWDING THROUGH IMMIGRATION THIS MORNING.
BUT MY DNA IS CODED FOR PREFERENTIAL TREATMENT.
CUT OUT FROM THE COMMON HERD, WE'RE USHERED ABOARD A LUXURY VEHICLE.
AND WHISKED STRAIGHT TO THE PRESIDENTIAL PALACE.
I TRY TO ENGROSS ASEERA IN THE PASSING TOURIST ATTRACTIONS, BUT THE POOR KID'S LOST IN THE WONDER OF IT ALL.
I DON'T BLAME HER. I'D BE GOBSMACKED TOO.
IF I WASN'T SUCH AN OLD HAND AT CROSSING THE BORDERS OF MADNESS.

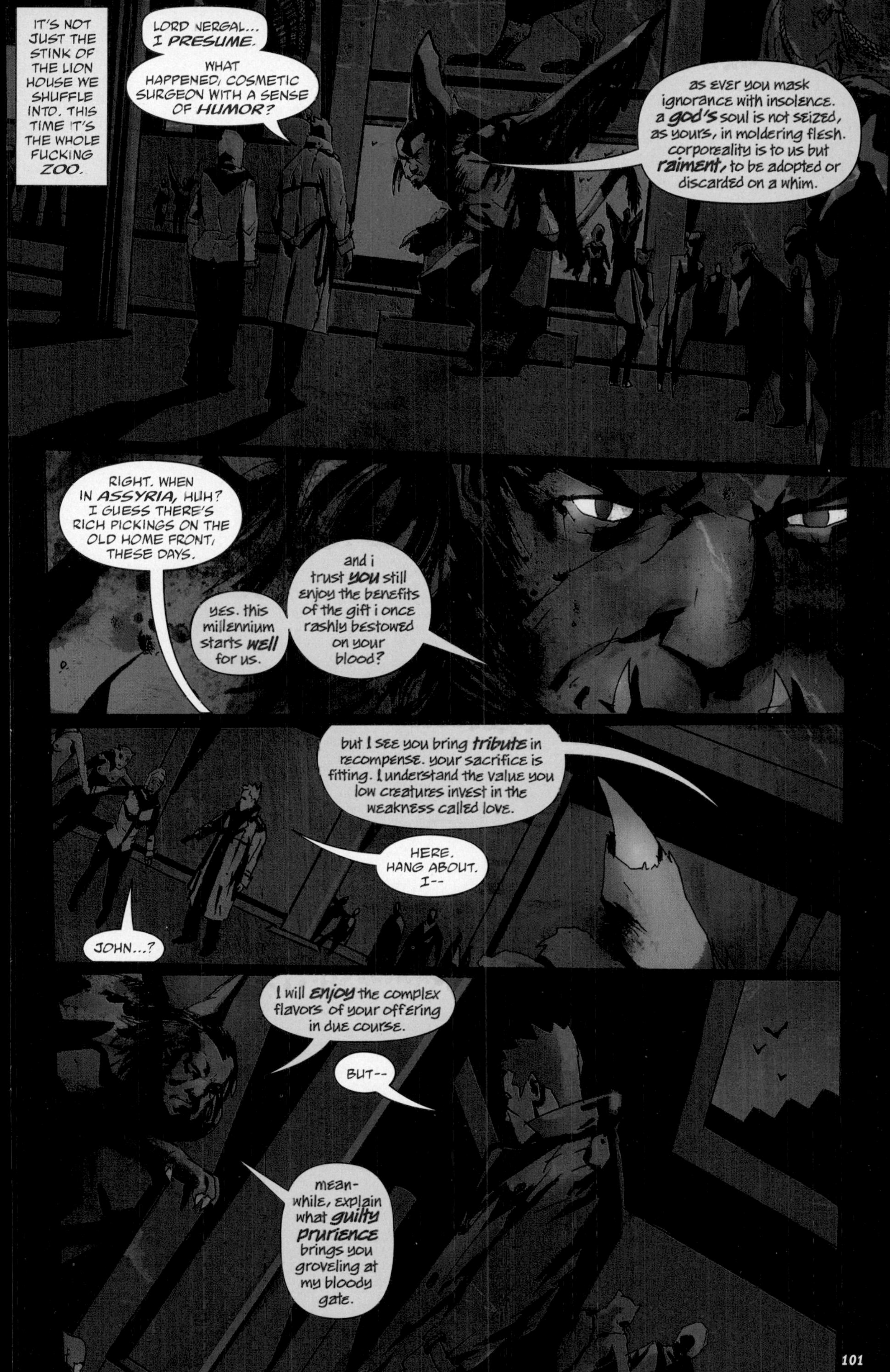
IT'S NOT JUST THE STINK OF THE LION HOUSE WE SHUFFLE INTO. THIS TIME IT'S THE WHOLE FUCKING ZOO.
LORD NERGAL... I PRESUME.
WHAT HAPPENED, COSMETIC SURGEON WITH A SENSE OF HUMOR?
as ever you mask ignorance with insolence. a god's soul is not seized, as yours, in moldering flesh. corporeality is to us but raiment, to be adopted or discarded on a whim.
RIGHT. WHEN IN ASSYRIA, HUH? I GUESS THERE'S RICH PICKINGS ON THE OLD HOME FRONT, THESE DAYS.
yes. this millennium starts well for us.
and i trust you still enjoy the benefits of the gift i once rashly bestowed on your blood?
but I see you bring tribute in recompense. your sacrifice is fitting. I understand the value you low creatures invest in the weakness called love.
HERE. HANG ABOUT. I--
JOHN...?
I will enjoy the complex flavors of your offering in due course.
BUT--
mean-while, explain what guilty prurience brings you groveling at my bloody gate.

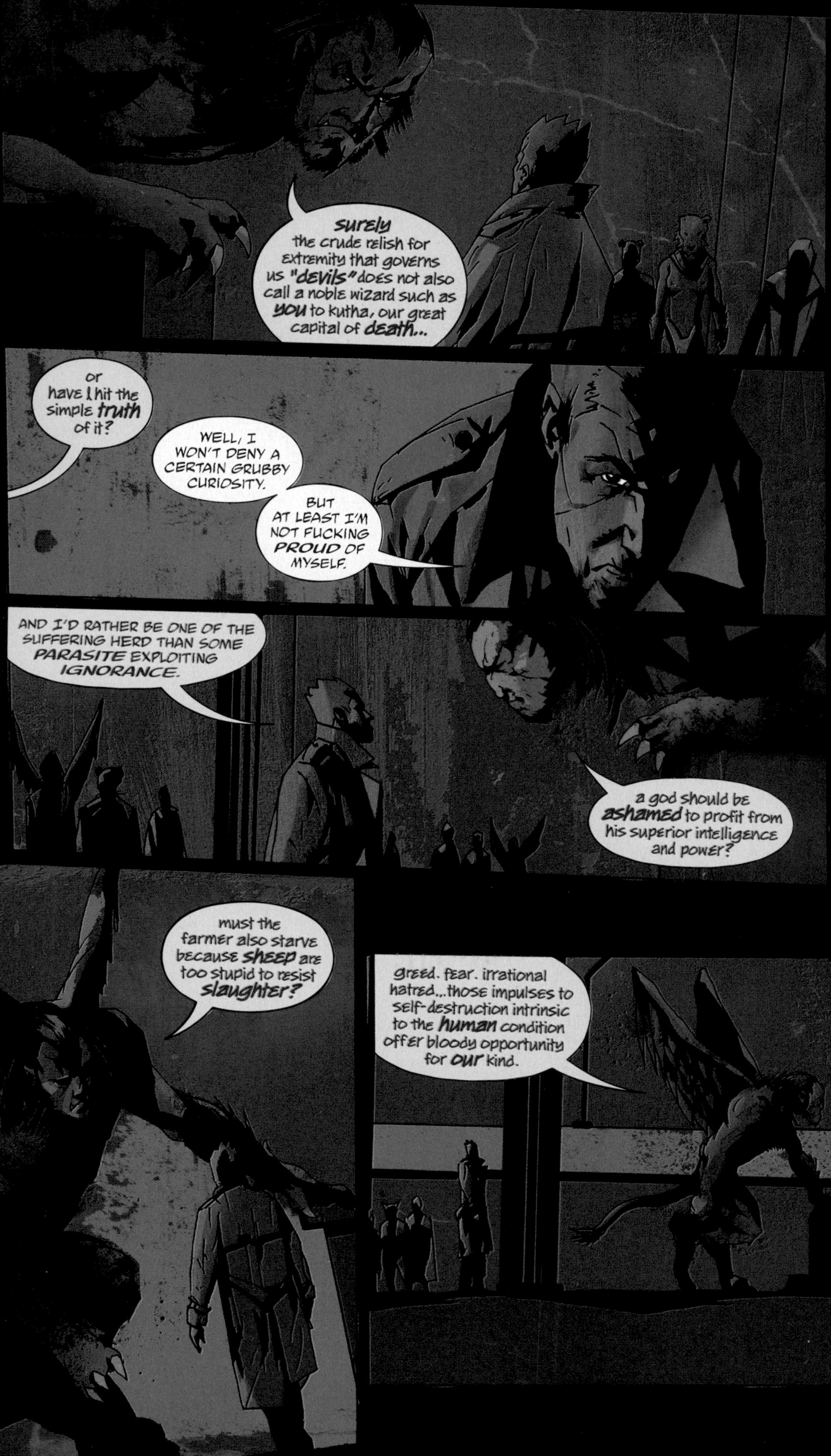
surely the crude relish for extremity that governs us "devils" does not also call a noble wizard such as you to kutha, our great capital of death...
or have I hit the simple truth of it?
WELL, I WON'T DENY A CERTAIN GRUBBY CURIOSITY.
BUT AT LEAST I'M NOT FUCKING PROUD OF MYSELF.
AND I'D RATHER BE ONE OF THE SUFFERING HERD THAN SOME PARASITE EXPLOITING IGNORANCE.
a god should be ashamed to profit from his superior intelligence and power?
must the farmer also starve because sheep are too stupid to resist slaughter?
greed. fear. irrational hatred... those impulses to self-destruction intrinsic to the human condition offer bloody opportunity for our kind.

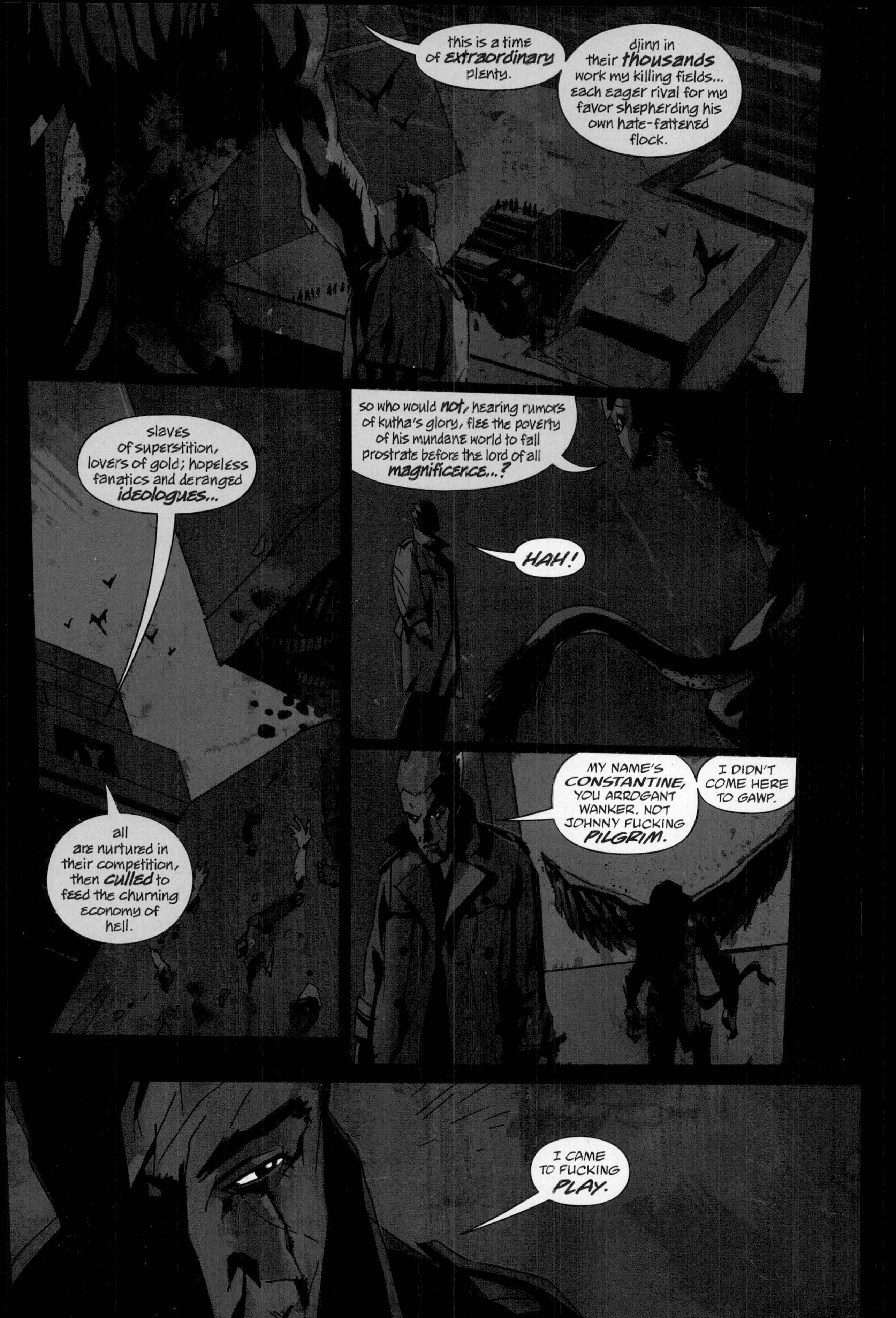

this is a time of extraordinary plenty.
djinn in their thousands work my killing fields... each eager rival for my favor shepherding his own hate-fattened flock.
slaves of superstition, lovers of gold; hopeless fanatics and deranged ideologues...
all are nurtured in their competition, then culled to feed the churning economy of hell.
so who would not, hearing rumors of kutha's glory, flee the poverty of his mundane world to fall prostrate before the lord of all magnificence...?
HAH!
MY NAME'S CONSTANTINE, YOU ARROGANT WANKER. NOT JOHNNY FUCKING PILGRIM.
I DIDN'T COME HERE TO GAWP.
I CAME TO FUCKING PLAY.

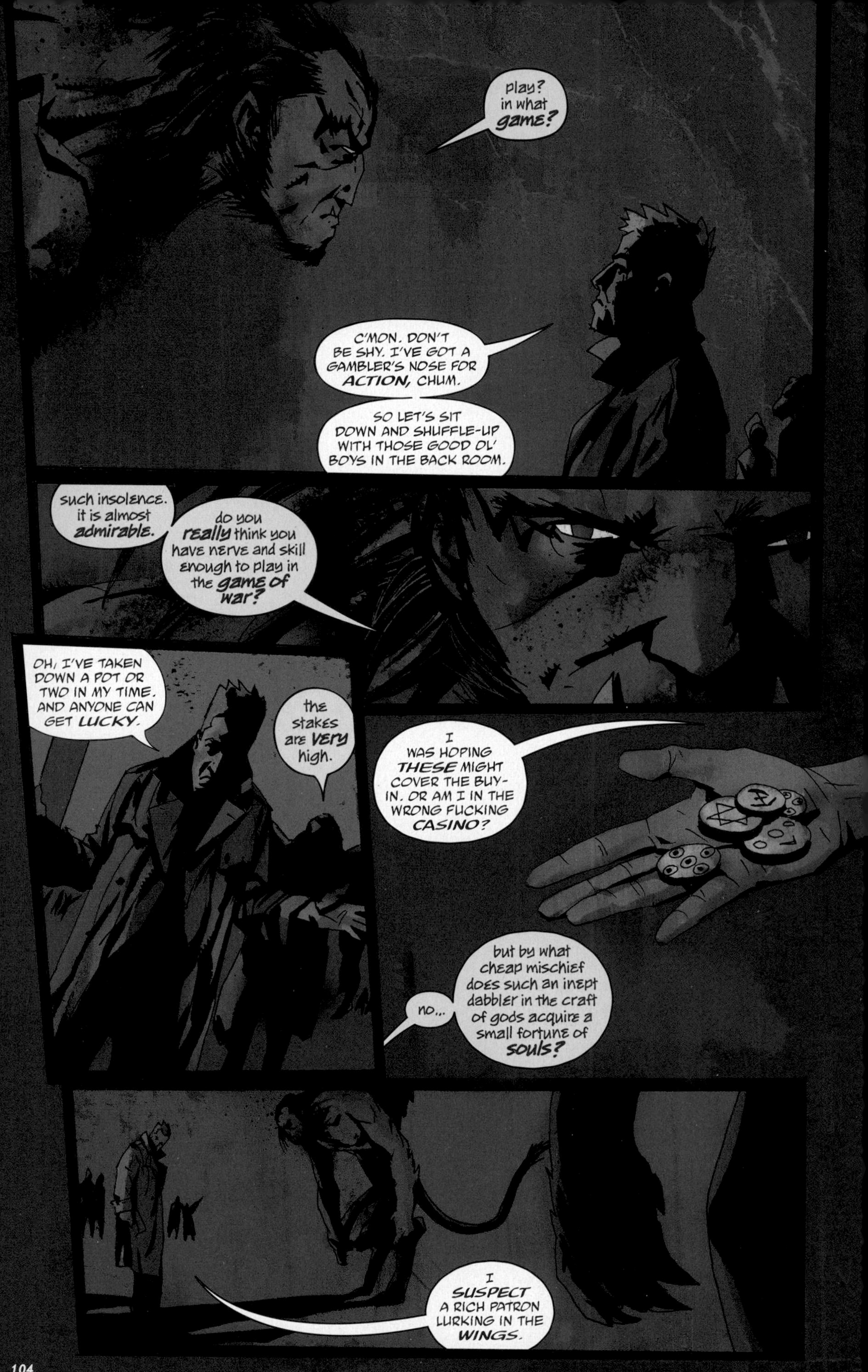
play? in what game?
C'MON. DON'T BE SHY. I'VE GOT A GAMBLER'S NOSE FOR ACTION, CHUM.
SO LET'S SIT DOWN AND SHUFFLE-UP WITH THOSE GOOD OL' BOYS IN THE BACK ROOM.
such insolence. it is almost admirable.
do you really think you have nerve and skill enough to play in the game of war?
OH, I'VE TAKEN DOWN A POT OR TWO IN MY TIME. AND ANYONE CAN GET LUCKY.
the stakes are very high.
I WAS HOPING THESE MIGHT COVER THE BUY-IN. OR AM I IN THE WRONG FUCKING CASINO?
no...
but by what cheap mischief does such an inept dabbler in the craft of gods acquire a small fortune of souls?
I SUSPECT A RICH PATRON LURKING IN THE WINGS.

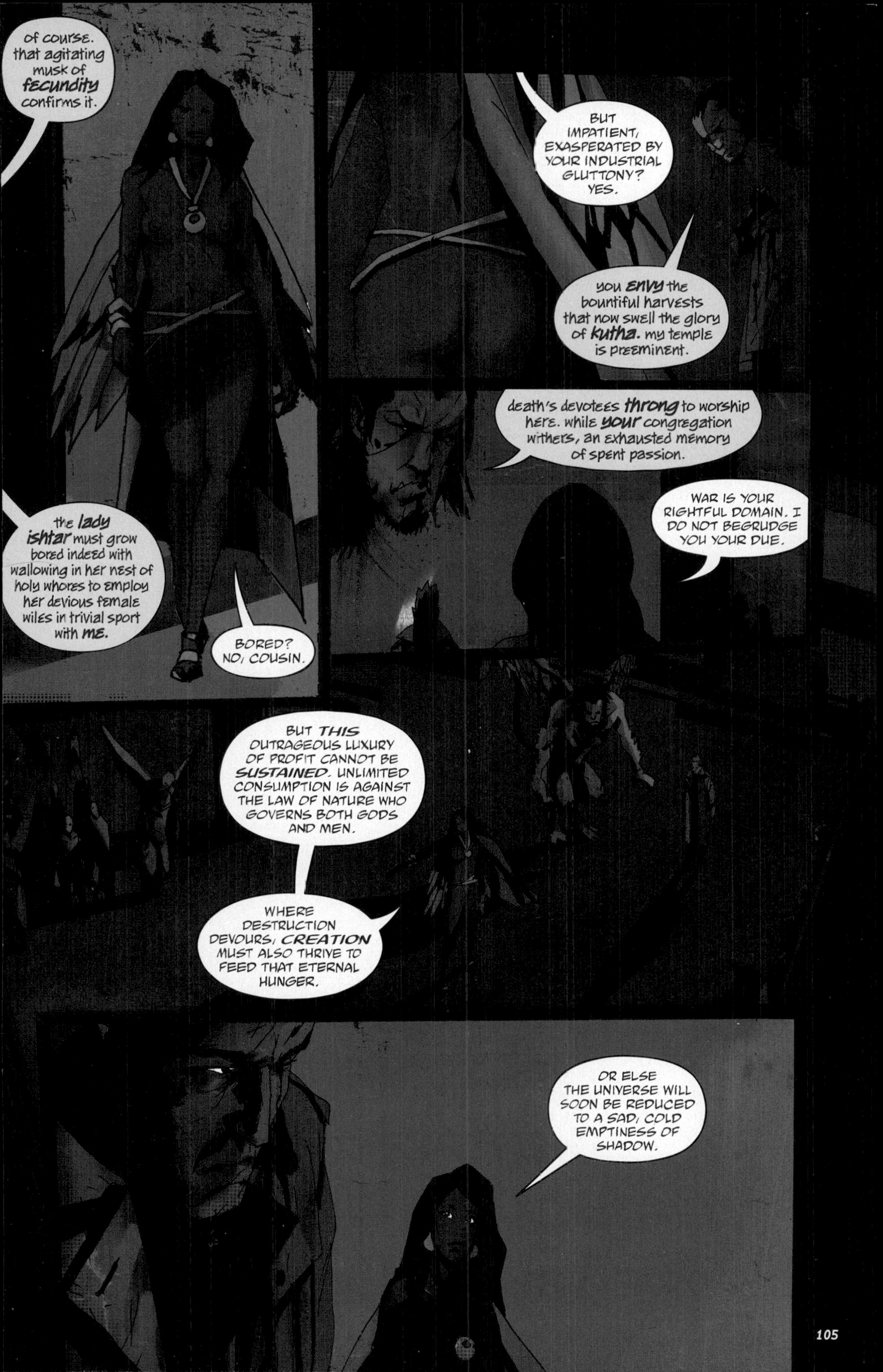
of course. that agitating musk of fecundity confirms it.
BUT IMPATIENT, EXASPERATED BY YOUR INDUSTRIAL GLUTTONY? YES.
you envy the bountiful harvests that now swell the glory of kutha. my temple is preeminent.
death's devotees throng to worship here. while your congregation withers, an exhausted memory of spent passion.
WAR IS YOUR RIGHTFUL DOMAIN. I DO NOT BEGRUDGE YOU YOUR DUE.
the lady ishtar must grow bored indeed with wallowing in her nest of holy whores to employ her devious female wiles in trivial sport with me.
BORED? NO, COUSIN.
BUT THIS OUTRAGEOUS LUXURY OF PROFIT CANNOT BE SUSTAINED. UNLIMITED CONSUMPTION IS AGAINST THE LAW OF NATURE WHO GOVERNS BOTH GODS AND MEN.
WHERE DESTRUCTION DEVOURS, CREATION MUST ALSO THRIVE TO FEED THAT ETERNAL HUNGER.
OR ELSE THE UNIVERSE WILL SOON BE REDUCED TO A SAD, COLD EMPTINESS OF SHADOW.

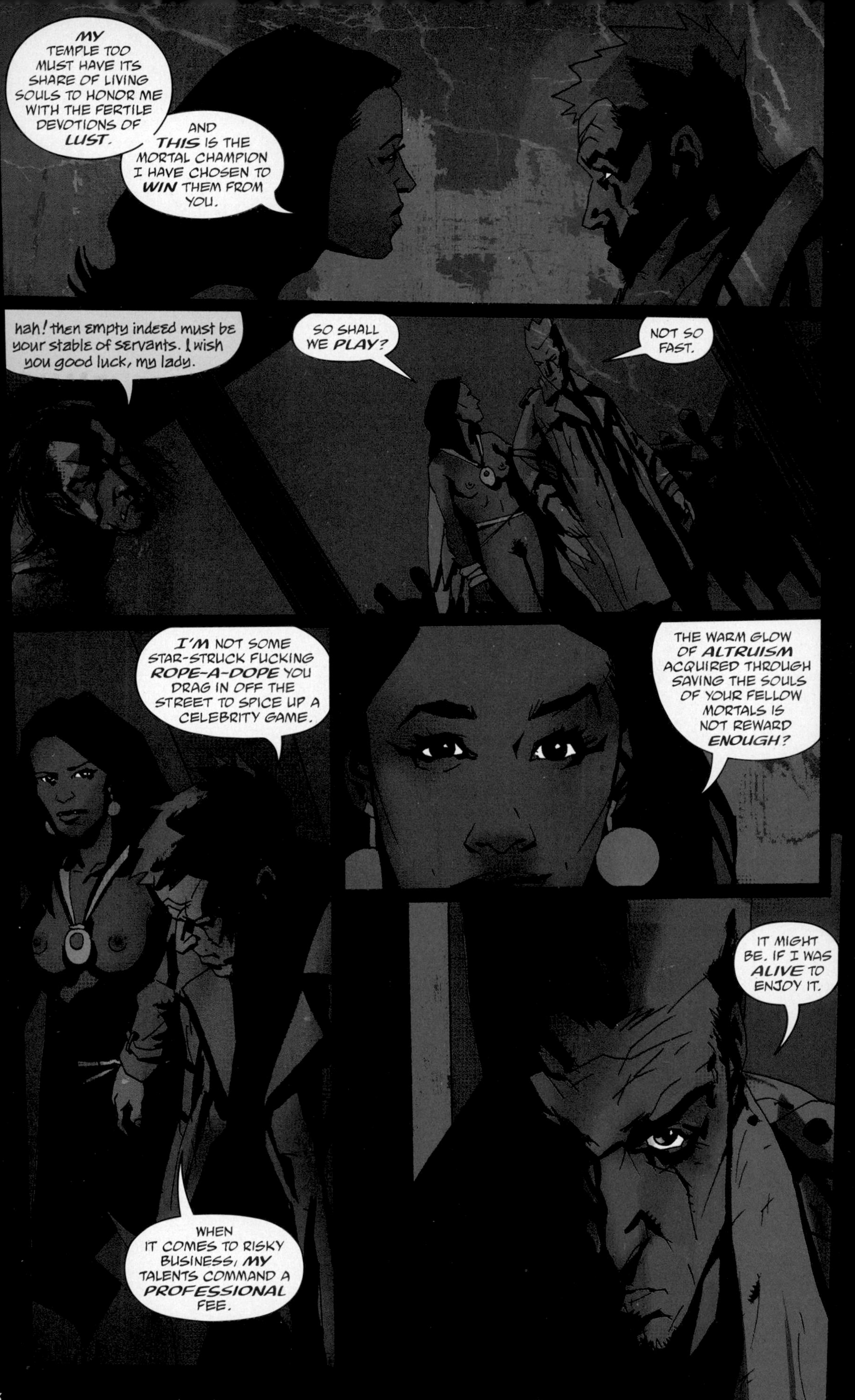
MY TEMPLE TOO MUST HAVE ITS SHARE OF LIVING SOULS TO HONOR ME WITH THE FERTILE DEVOTIONS OF LUST.
AND THIS IS THE MORTAL CHAMPION I HAVE CHOSEN TO WIN THEM FROM YOU.
hah! then empty indeed must be your stable of servants. I wish you good luck, my lady.
SO SHALL WE PLAY?
NOT SO FAST.
I'M NOT SOME STAR-STRUCK FUCKING ROPE-A-DOPE YOU DRAG IN OFF THE STREET TO SPICE UP A CELEBRITY GAME.
WHEN IT COMES TO RISKY BUSINESS, MY TALENTS COMMAND A PROFESSIONAL FEE.
THE WARM GLOW OF ALTRUISM ACQUIRED THROUGH SAVING THE SOULS OF YOUR FELLOW MORTALS IS NOT REWARD ENOUGH?
IT MIGHT BE. IF I WAS ALIVE TO ENJOY IT.

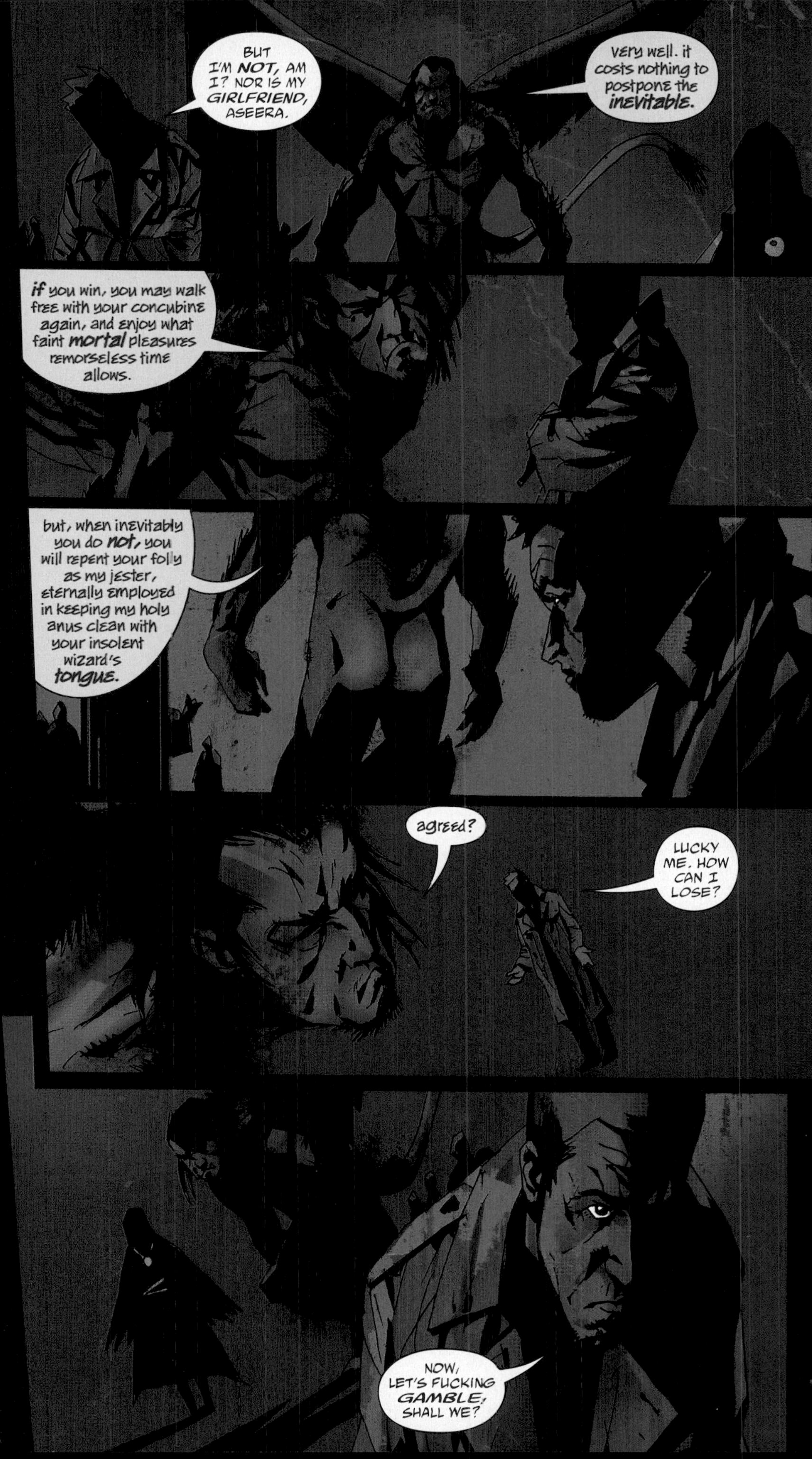
BUT I'M NOT, AM I? NOR IS MY GIRLFRIEND, ASEERA.
very well. it costs nothing to postpone the inevitable.
if you win, you may walk free with your concubine again, and enjoy what faint mortal pleasures remorseless time allows.
but, when inevitably you do not, you will repent your folly as my jester, eternally employed in keeping my holy anus clean with your insolent wizard's tongue.
agreed?
LUCKY ME. HOW CAN I LOSE?
NOW, LET'S FUCKING GAMBLE, SHALL WE?

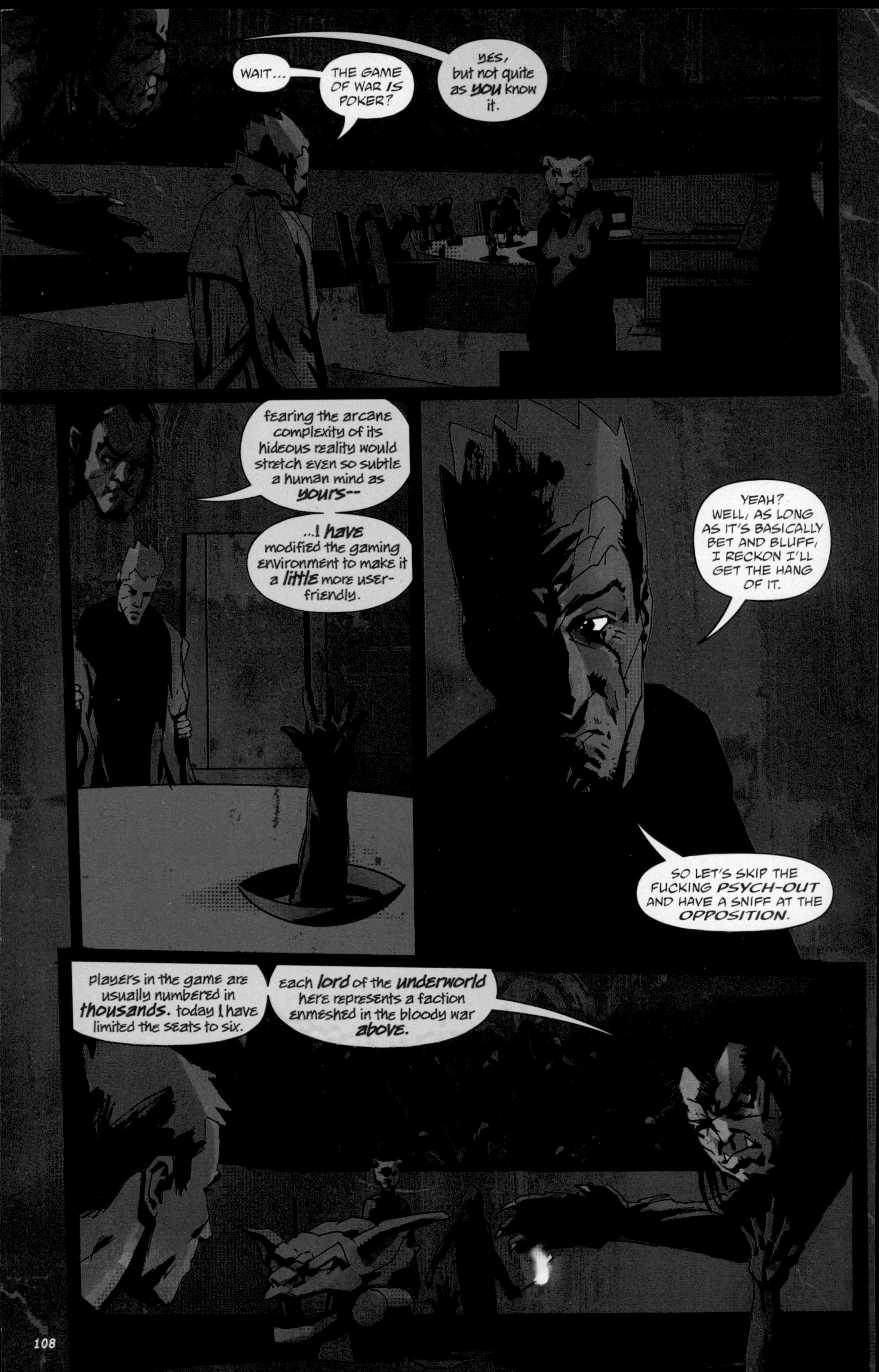
WAIT...
THE GAME OF WAR IS POKER?
yes, but not quite as YOU know it.
fearing the arcane complexity of its hideous reality would stretch even so subtle a human mind as yours--
...I have modified the gaming environment to make it a little more user-friendly.
YEAH? WELL, AS LONG AS IT'S BASICALLY BET AND BLUFF, I RECKON I'LL GET THE HANG OF IT.
SO LET'S SKIP THE FUCKING PSYCH-OUT AND HAVE A SNIFF AT THE OPPOSITION.
players in the game are usually numbered in thousands. today I have limited the seats to six.
each lord of the underworld here represents a faction enmeshed in the bloody war above.

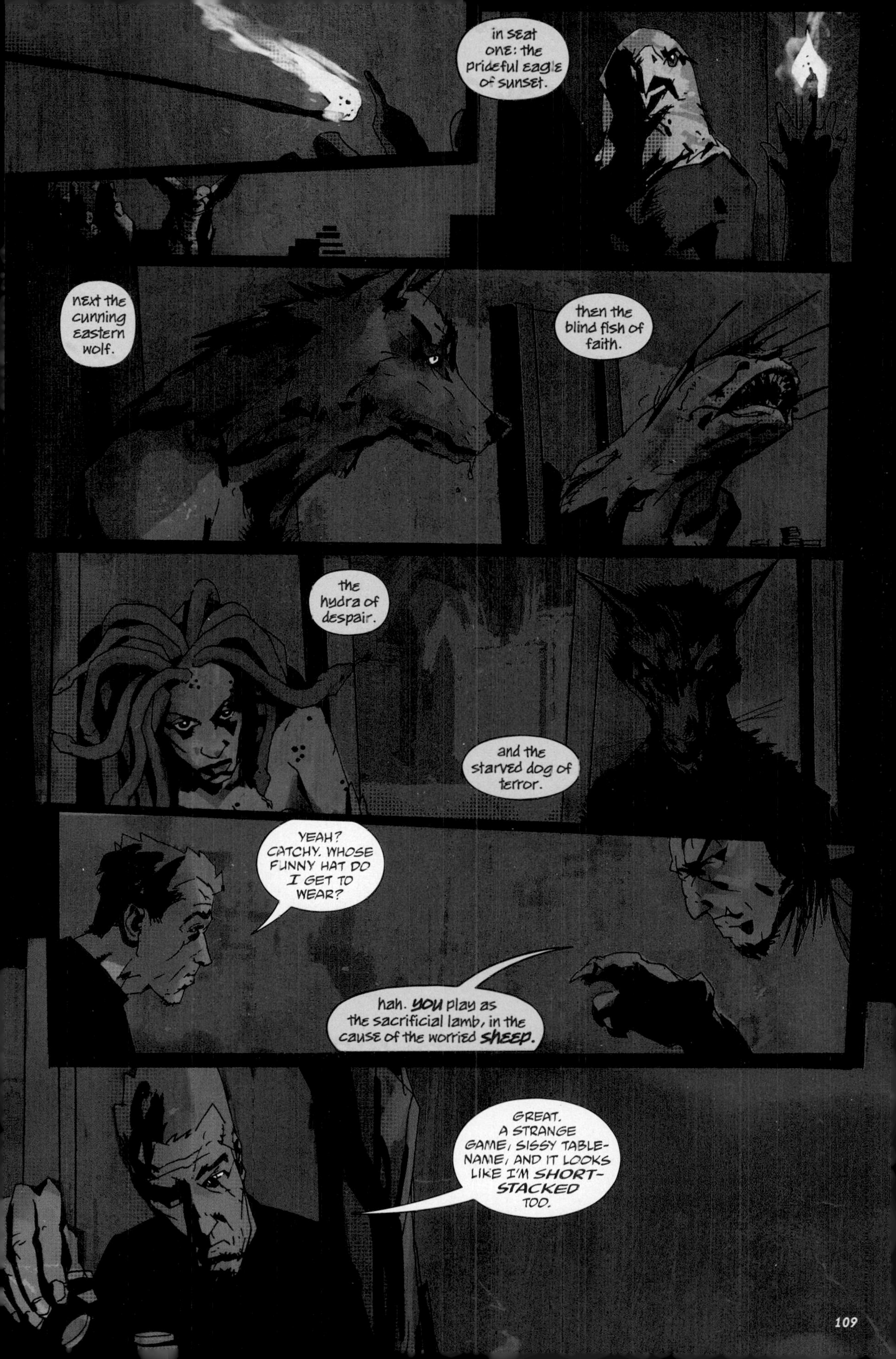
in seat one: the prideful eagle of sunset.
next the cunning eastern wolf.
then the blind fish of faith.
the hydra of despair.
and the starved dog of terror.
YEAH? CATCHY. WHOSE FUNNY HAT DO I GET TO WEAR?
hah. YOU play as the sacrificial lamb, in the cause of the worried SHEEP.
GREAT. A STRANGE GAME, SISSY TABLE-NAME, AND IT LOOKS LIKE I'M SHORT-STACKED TOO.

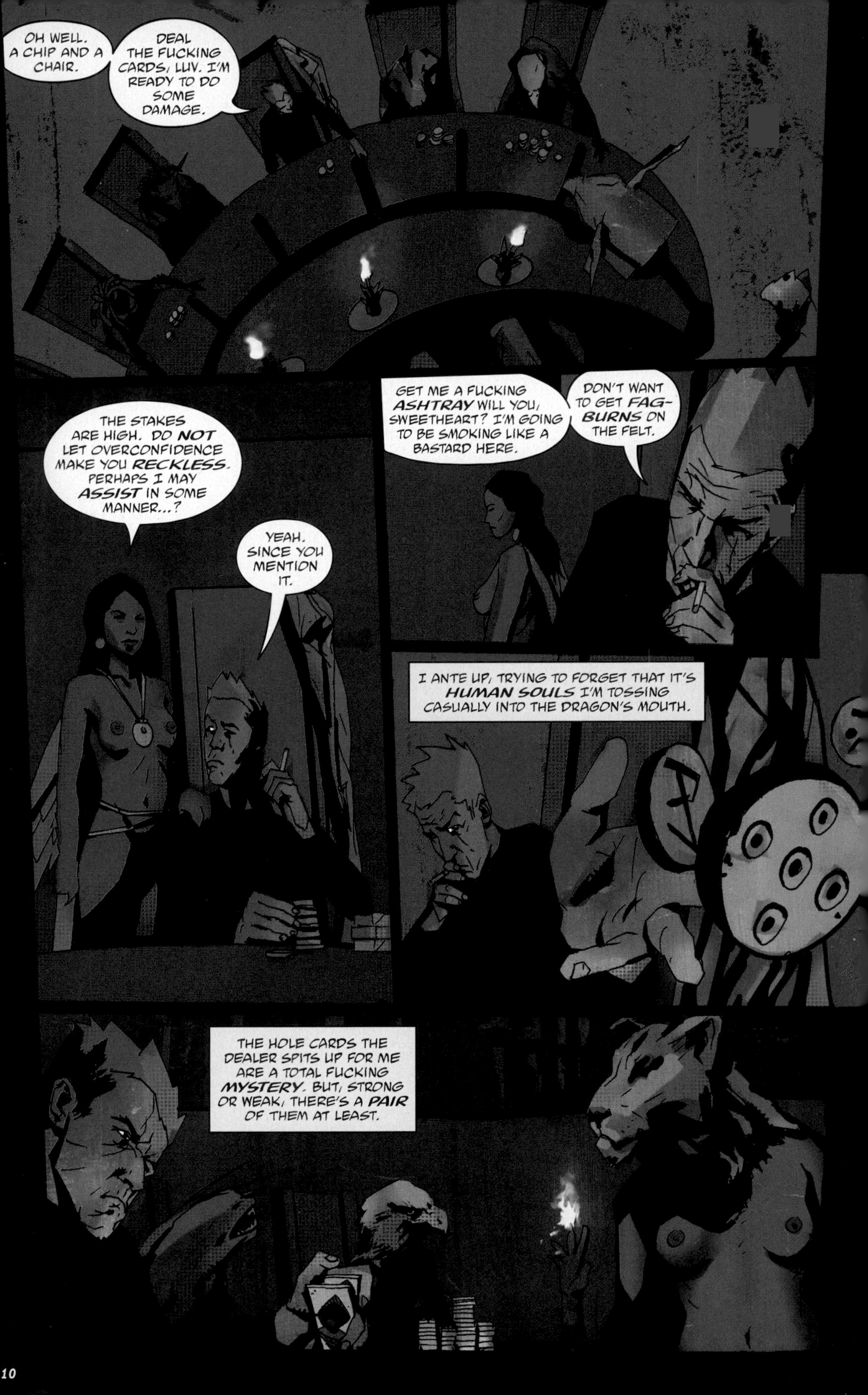

OH WELL. A CHIP AND A CHAIR.
DEAL THE FUCKING CARDS, LUV. I'M READY TO DO SOME DAMAGE.
THE STAKES ARE HIGH. DO NOT LET OVERCONFIDENCE MAKE YOU RECKLESS. PERHAPS I MAY ASSIST IN SOME MANNER...?
YEAH. SINCE YOU MENTION IT.
GET ME A FUCKING ASHTRAY WILL YOU, SWEETHEART? I'M GOING TO BE SMOKING LIKE A BASTARD HERE.
DON'T WANT TO GET FAG-BURNS ON THE FELT.
I ANTE UP, TRYING TO FORGET THAT IT'S HUMAN SOULS I'M TOSSING CASUALLY INTO THE DRAGON'S MOUTH.
THE HOLE CARDS THE DEALER SPITS UP FOR ME ARE A TOTAL FUCKING MYSTERY. BUT, STRONG OR WEAK, THERE'S A PAIR OF THEM AT LEAST.

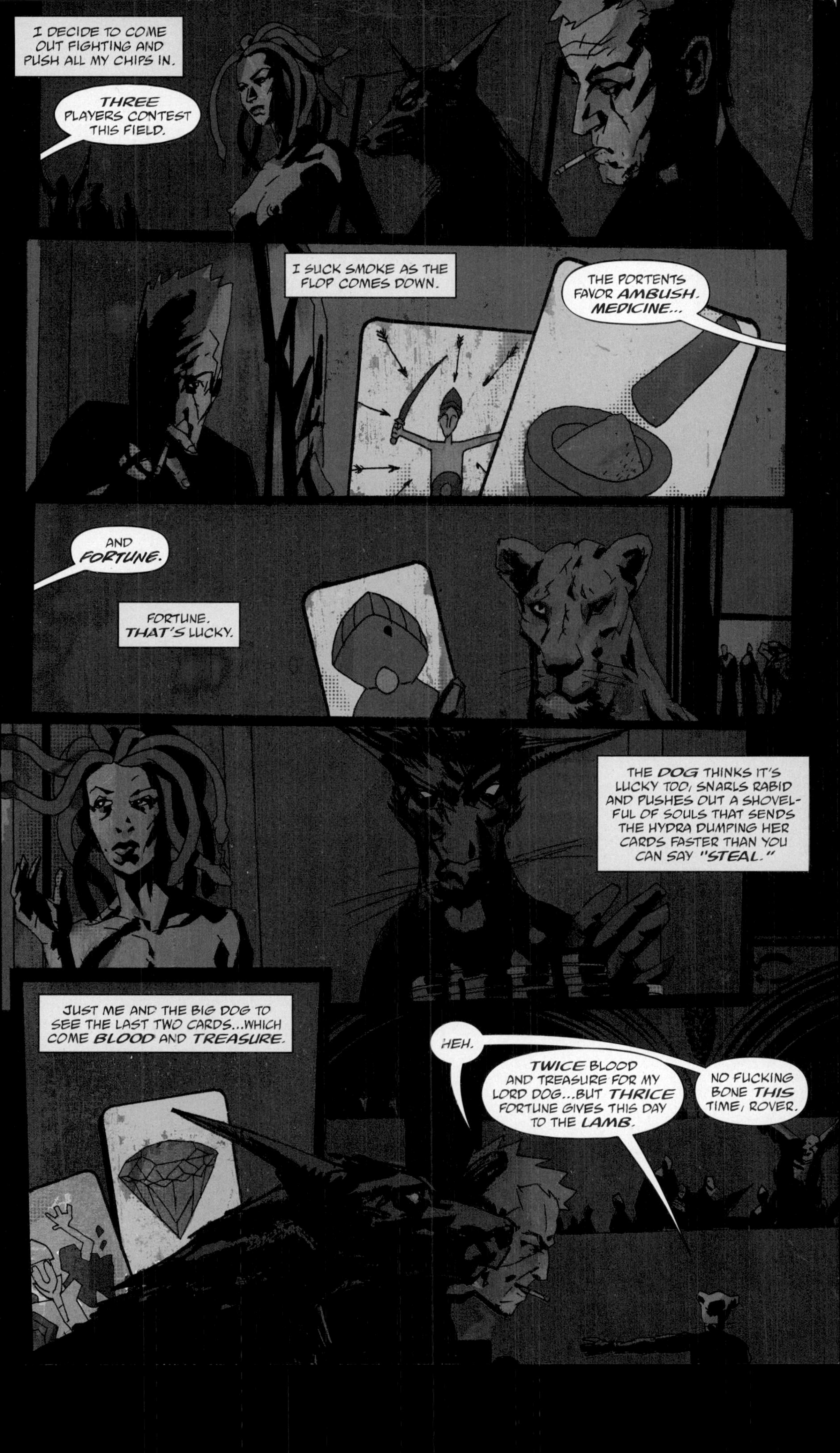
I DECIDE TO COME OUT FIGHTING AND PUSH ALL MY CHIPS IN.
THREE PLAYERS CONTEST THIS FIELD.
I SUCK SMOKE AS THE FLOP COMES DOWN.
THE PORTENTS FAVOR AMBUSH. MEDICINE...
AND FORTUNE.
FORTUNE. THAT'S LUCKY.
THE DOG THINKS IT'S LUCKY TOO; SNARLS RABID AND PUSHES OUT A SHOVELFUL OF SOULS THAT SENDS THE HYDRA DUMPING HER CARDS FASTER THAN YOU CAN SAY "STEAL."
JUST ME AND THE BIG DOG TO SEE THE LAST TWO CARDS...WHICH COME BLOOD AND TREASURE.
HEH.
TWICE BLOOD AND TREASURE FOR MY LORD DOG...BUT THRICE FORTUNE GIVES THIS DAY TO THE LAMB.
NO FUCKING BONE THIS TIME, ROVER.

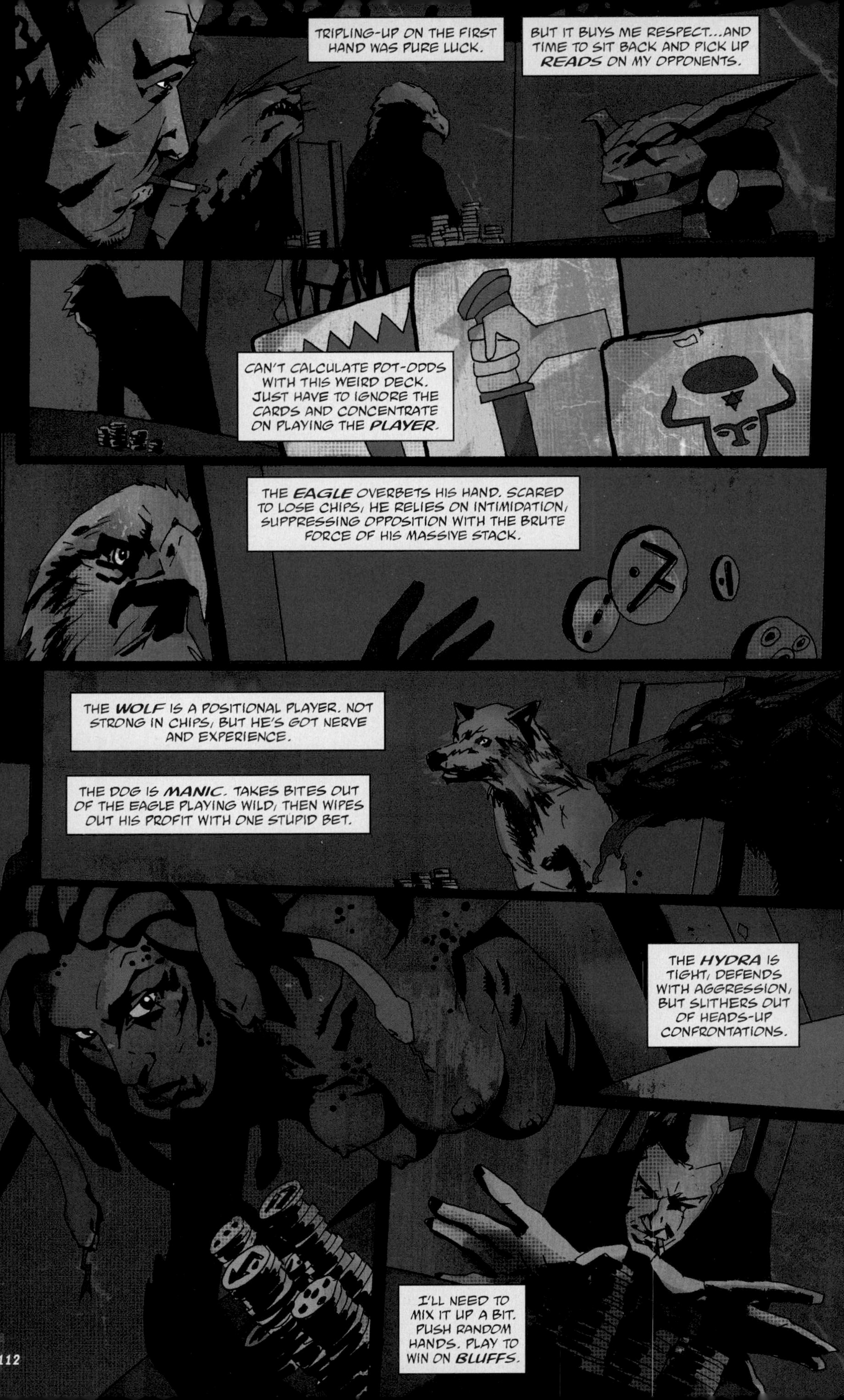
TRIPLING-UP ON THE FIRST HAND WAS PURE LUCK.
BUT IT BUYS ME RESPECT...AND TIME TO SIT BACK AND PICK UP READS ON MY OPPONENTS.
CAN'T CALCULATE POT-ODDS WITH THIS WEIRD DECK. JUST HAVE TO IGNORE THE CARDS AND CONCENTRATE ON PLAYING THE PLAYER.
THE EAGLE OVERBETS HIS HAND. SCARED TO LOSE CHIPS, HE RELIES ON INTIMIDATION, SUPPRESSING OPPOSITION WITH THE BRUTE FORCE OF HIS MASSIVE STACK.
THE WOLF IS A POSITIONAL PLAYER. NOT STRONG IN CHIPS, BUT HE'S GOT NERVE AND EXPERIENCE.
THE DOG IS MANIC. TAKES BITES OUT OF THE EAGLE PLAYING WILD, THEN WIPES OUT HIS PROFIT WITH ONE STUPID BET.
THE HYDRA IS TIGHT, DEFENDS WITH AGGRESSION, BUT SLITHERS OUT OF HEADS-UP CONFRONTATIONS.
I'LL NEED TO MIX IT UP A BIT. PUSH RANDOM HANDS. PLAY TO WIN ON BLUFFS.

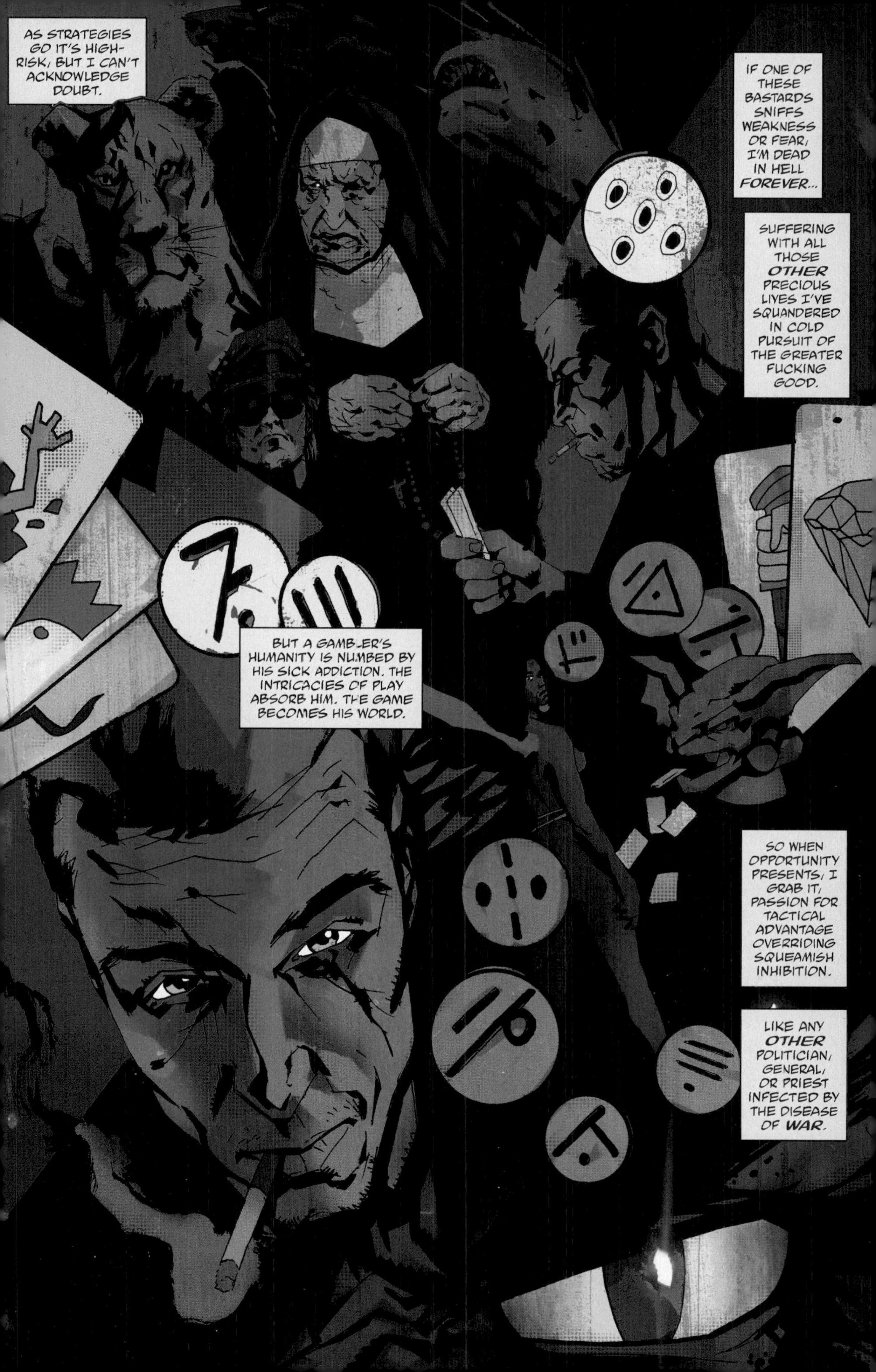
AS STRATEGIES GO IT'S HIGH-RISK, BUT I CAN'T ACKNOWLEDGE DOUBT.
IF ONE OF THESE BASTARDS SNIFFS WEAKNESS OR FEAR, I'M DEAD IN HELL FOREVER...
SUFFERING WITH ALL THOSE OTHER PRECIOUS LIVES I'VE SQUANDERED IN COLD PURSUIT OF THE GREATER FUCKING GOOD.
BUT A GAMBLER'S HUMANITY IS NUMBED BY HIS SICK ADDICTION. THE INTRICACIES OF PLAY ABSORB HIM. THE GAME BECOMES HIS WORLD.
SO WHEN OPPORTUNITY PRESENTS, I GRAB IT, PASSION FOR TACTICAL ADVANTAGE OVERRIDING SQUEAMISH INHIBITION.
LIKE ANY OTHER POLITICIAN, GENERAL, OR PRIEST INFECTED BY THE DISEASE OF WAR.

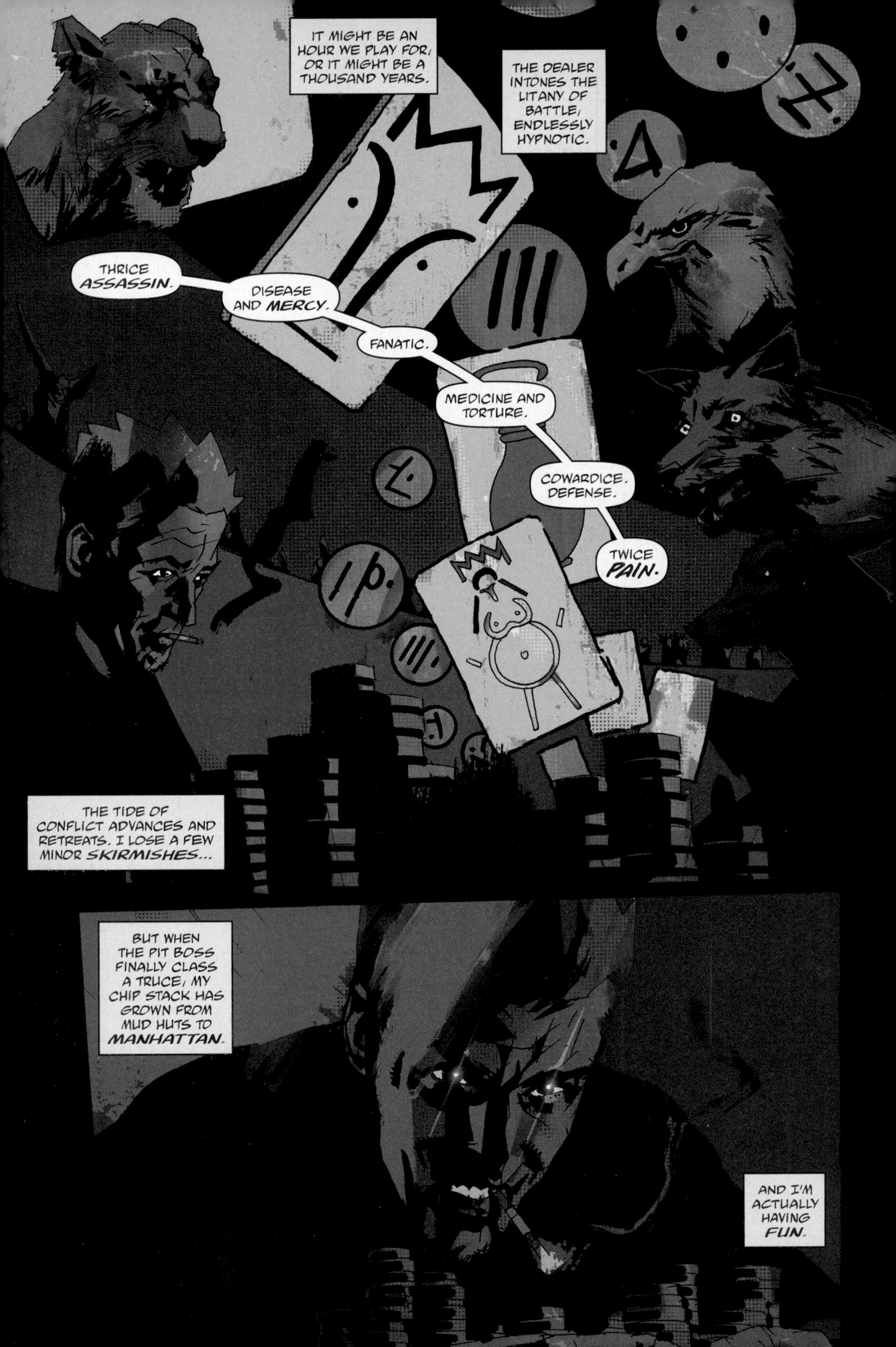
IT MIGHT BE AN HOUR WE PLAY FOR, OR IT MIGHT BE A THOUSAND YEARS.
THE DEALER INTONES THE LITANY OF BATTLE, ENDLESSLY HYPNOTIC.
THRICE *ASSASSIN*.
DISEASE AND *MERCY*.
FANATIC.
MEDICINE AND TORTURE.
COWARDICE. DEFENSE.
TWICE *PAIN*.
THE TIDE OF CONFLICT ADVANCES AND RETREATS. I LOSE A FEW MINOR *SKIRMISHES*...
BUT WHEN THE PIT BOSS FINALLY CLASS A TRUCE, MY CHIP STACK HAS GROWN FROM MUD HUTS TO *MANHATTAN*.
AND I'M ACTUALLY HAVING *FUN*.

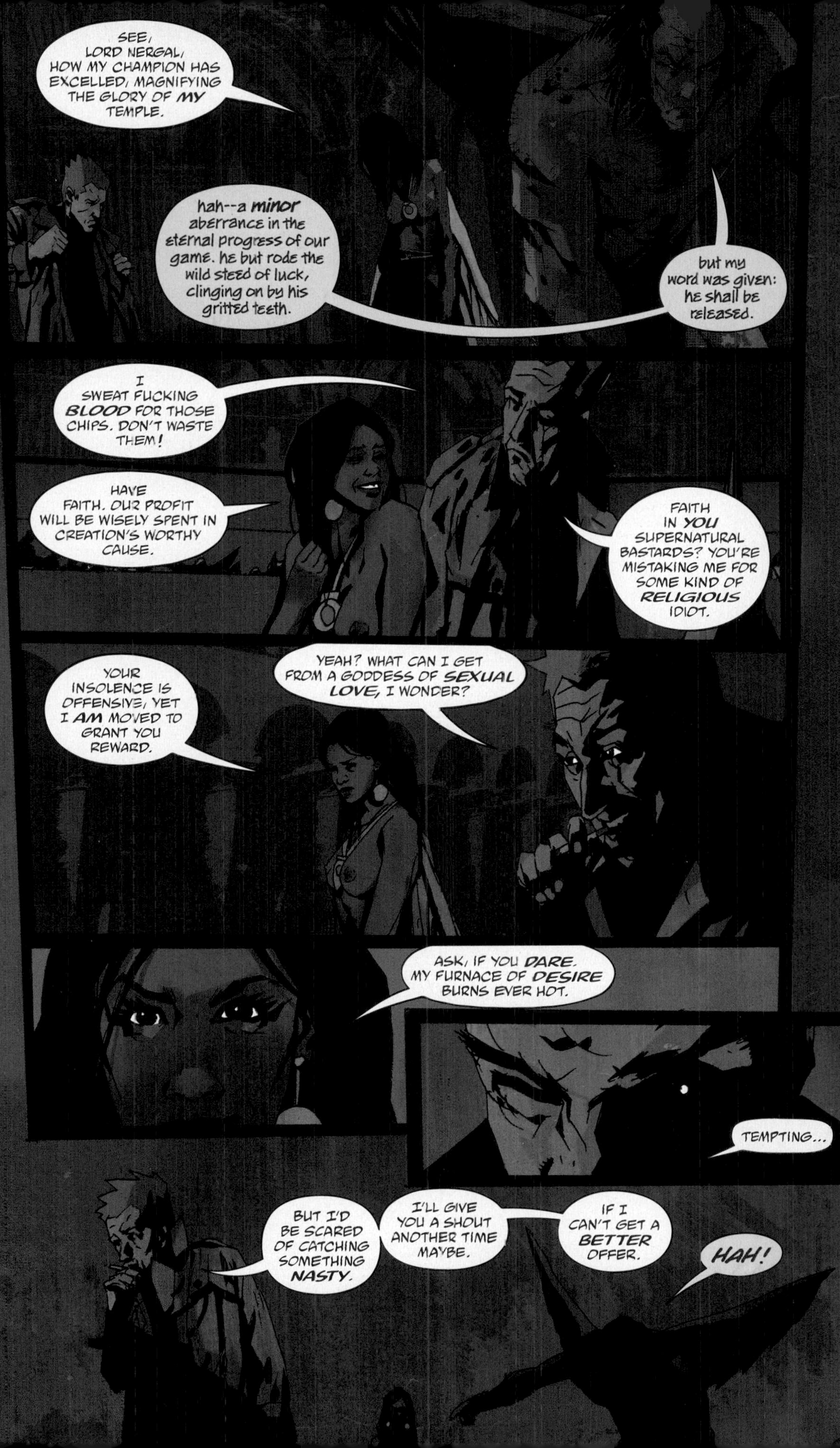
SEE, LORD NERGAL, HOW MY CHAMPION HAS EXCELLED, MAGNIFYING THE GLORY OF MY TEMPLE.
hah--a minor aberrance in the eternal progress of our game. he but rode the wild steed of luck, clinging on by his gritted teeth.
but my word was given: he shall be released.
I SWEAT FUCKING BLOOD FOR THOSE CHIPS. DON'T WASTE THEM!
HAVE FAITH. OUR PROFIT WILL BE WISELY SPENT IN CREATION'S WORTHY CAUSE.
FAITH IN YOU SUPERNATURAL BASTARDS? YOU'RE MISTAKING ME FOR SOME KIND OF RELIGIOUS IDIOT.
YOUR INSOLENCE IS OFFENSIVE, YET I AM MOVED TO GRANT YOU REWARD.
YEAH? WHAT CAN I GET FROM A GODDESS OF SEXUAL LOVE, I WONDER?
ASK, IF YOU DARE. MY FURNACE OF DESIRE BURNS EVER HOT.
TEMPTING...
BUT I'D BE SCARED OF CATCHING SOMETHING NASTY.
I'LL GIVE YOU A SHOUT ANOTHER TIME MAYBE.
IF I CAN'T GET A BETTER OFFER.
HAH!

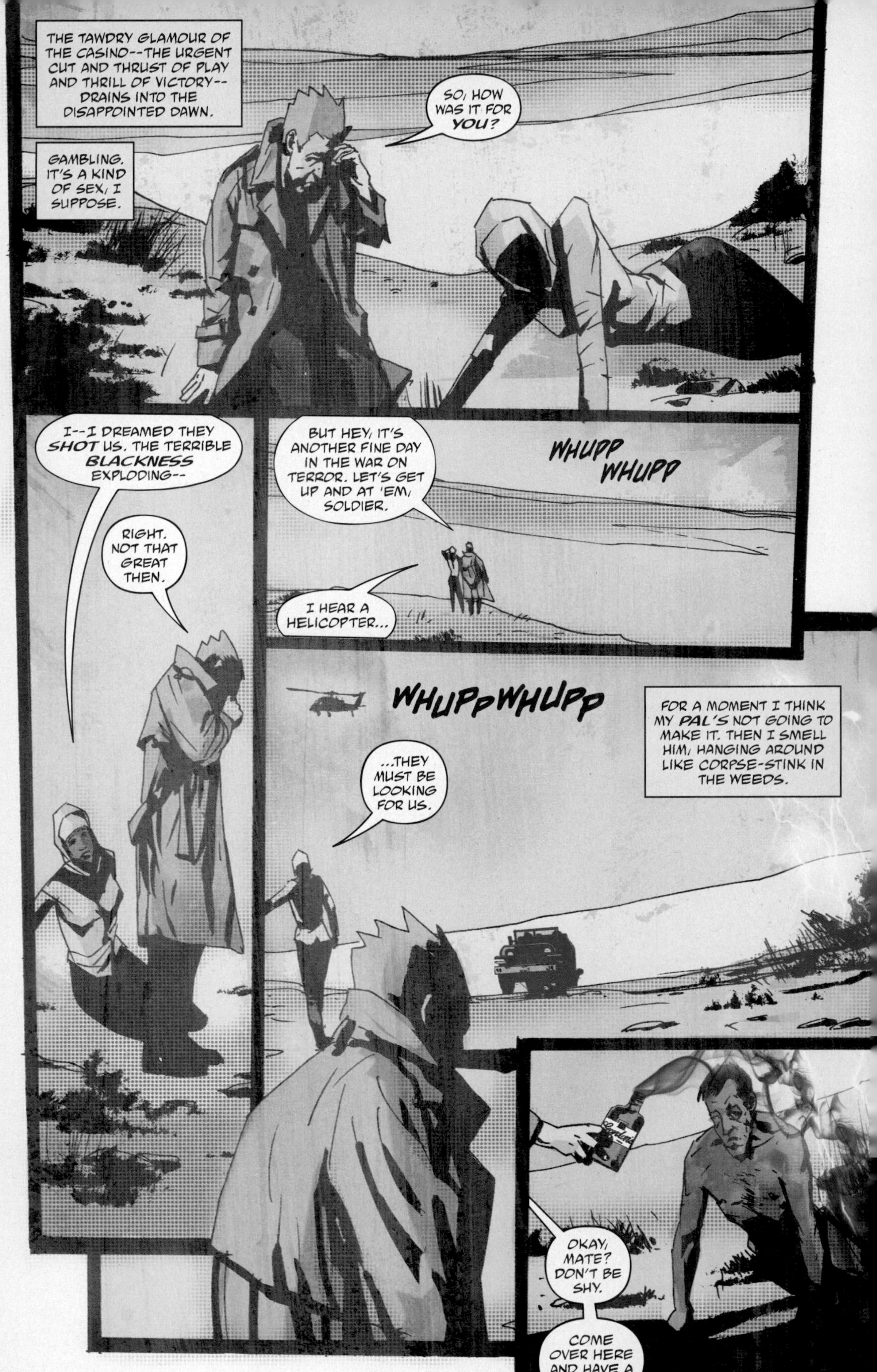
THE TAWDRY GLAMOUR OF THE CASINO--THE URGENT CUT AND THRUST OF PLAY AND THRILL OF VICTORY--DRAINS INTO THE DISAPPOINTED DAWN.
GAMBLING. IT'S A KIND OF SEX, I SUPPOSE.
SO, HOW WAS IT FOR YOU?
I--I DREAMED THEY SHOT US. THE TERRIBLE BLACKNESS EXPLODING--
RIGHT. NOT THAT GREAT THEN.
BUT HEY, IT'S ANOTHER FINE DAY IN THE WAR ON TERROR. LET'S GET UP AND AT 'EM, SOLDIER.
WHUPP WHUPP
I HEAR A HELICOPTER...
WHUPPWHUPP
...THEY MUST BE LOOKING FOR US.
FOR A MOMENT I THINK MY PAL'S NOT GOING TO MAKE IT. THEN I SMELL HIM, HANGING AROUND LIKE CORPSE-STINK IN THE WEEDS.
OKAY, MATE? DON'T BE SHY.
COME OVER HERE AND HAVE A DRINK.

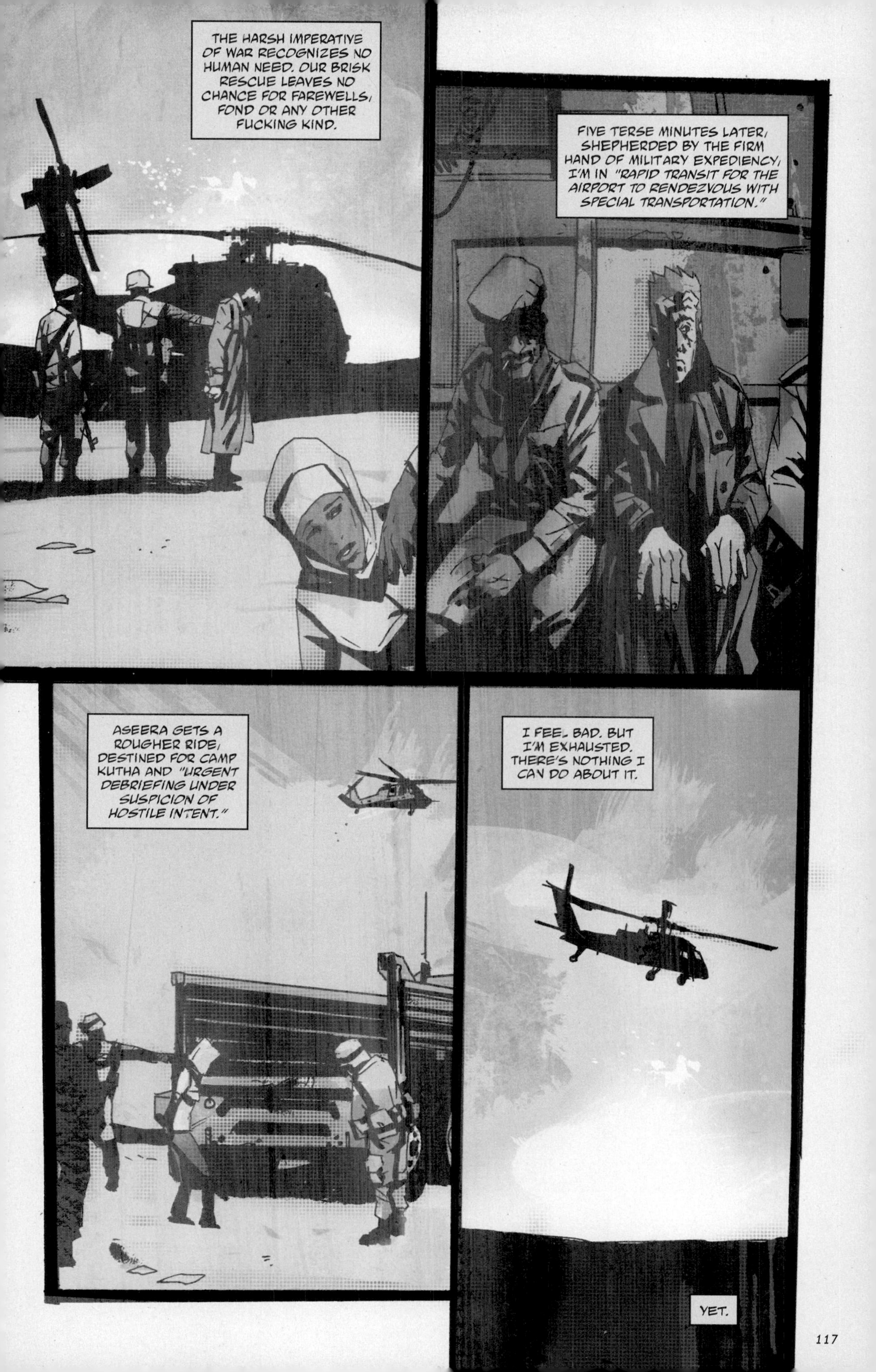
THE HARSH IMPERATIVE OF WAR RECOGNIZES NO HUMAN NEED. OUR BRISK RESCUE LEAVES NO CHANCE FOR FAREWELLS, FOND OR ANY OTHER FUCKING KIND.
FIVE TERSE MINUTES LATER, SHEPHERDED BY THE FIRM HAND OF MILITARY EXPEDIENCY, I'M IN "RAPID TRANSIT FOR THE AIRPORT TO RENDEZVOUS WITH SPECIAL TRANSPORTATION."
ASEERA GETS A ROUGHER RIDE, DESTINED FOR CAMP KUTHA AND "URGENT DEBRIEFING UNDER SUSPICION OF HOSTILE INTENT."
I FEEL BAD. BUT I'M EXHAUSTED. THERE'S NOTHING I CAN DO ABOUT IT.
YET.

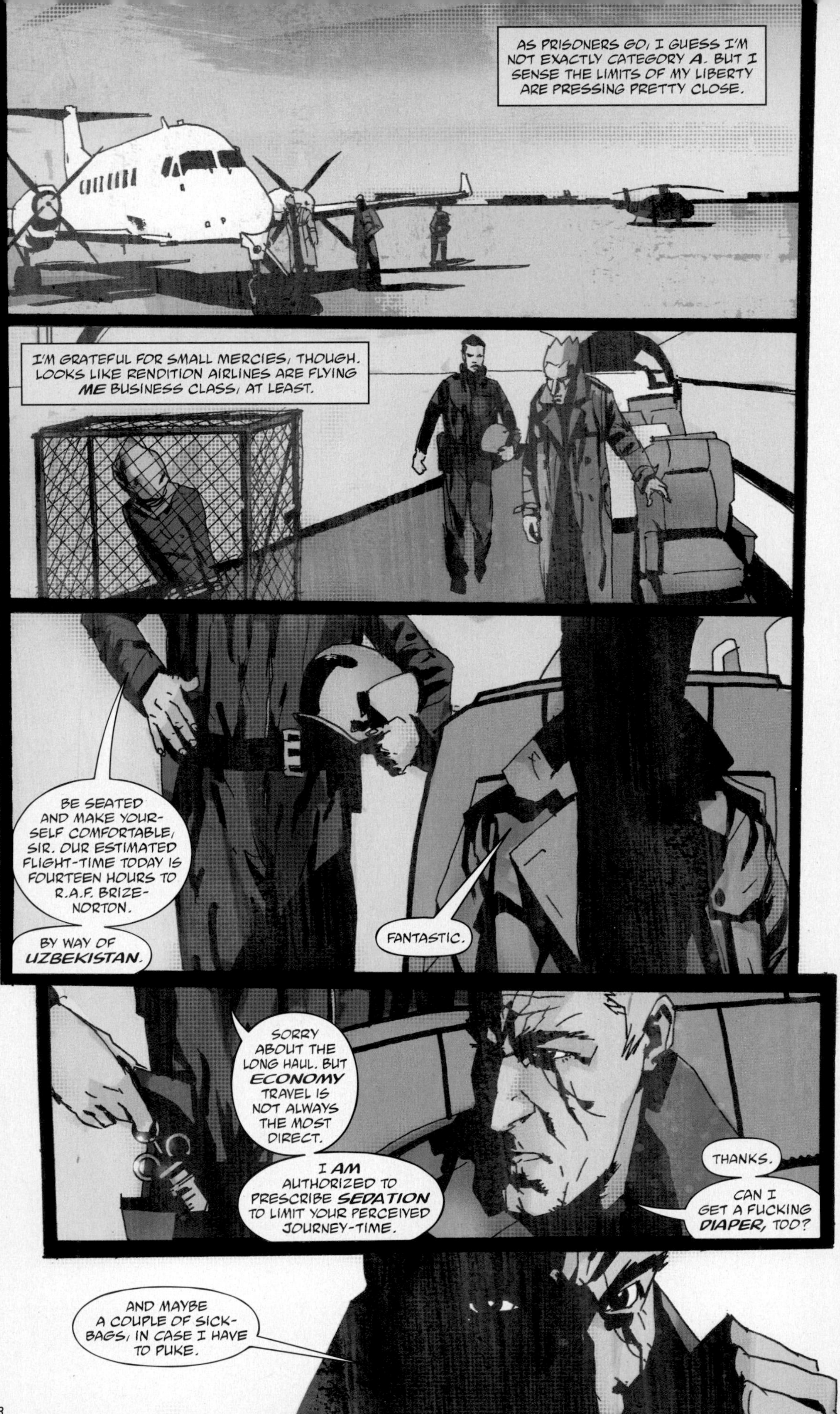
AS PRISONERS GO, I GUESS I'M NOT EXACTLY CATEGORY A. BUT I SENSE THE LIMITS OF MY LIBERTY ARE PRESSING PRETTY CLOSE.
I'M GRATEFUL FOR SMALL MERCIES, THOUGH. LOOKS LIKE RENDITION AIRLINES ARE FLYING ME BUSINESS CLASS, AT LEAST.
BE SEATED AND MAKE YOURSELF COMFORTABLE, SIR. OUR ESTIMATED FLIGHT-TIME TODAY IS FOURTEEN HOURS TO R.A.F. BRIZE-NORTON.
BY WAY OF UZBEKISTAN.
FANTASTIC.
SORRY ABOUT THE LONG HAUL. BUT ECONOMY TRAVEL IS NOT ALWAYS THE MOST DIRECT.
I AM AUTHORIZED TO PRESCRIBE SEDATION TO LIMIT YOUR PERCEIVED JOURNEY-TIME.
THANKS.
CAN I GET A FUCKING DIAPER, TOO?
AND MAYBE A COUPLE OF SICK-BAGS, IN CASE I HAVE TO PUKE.

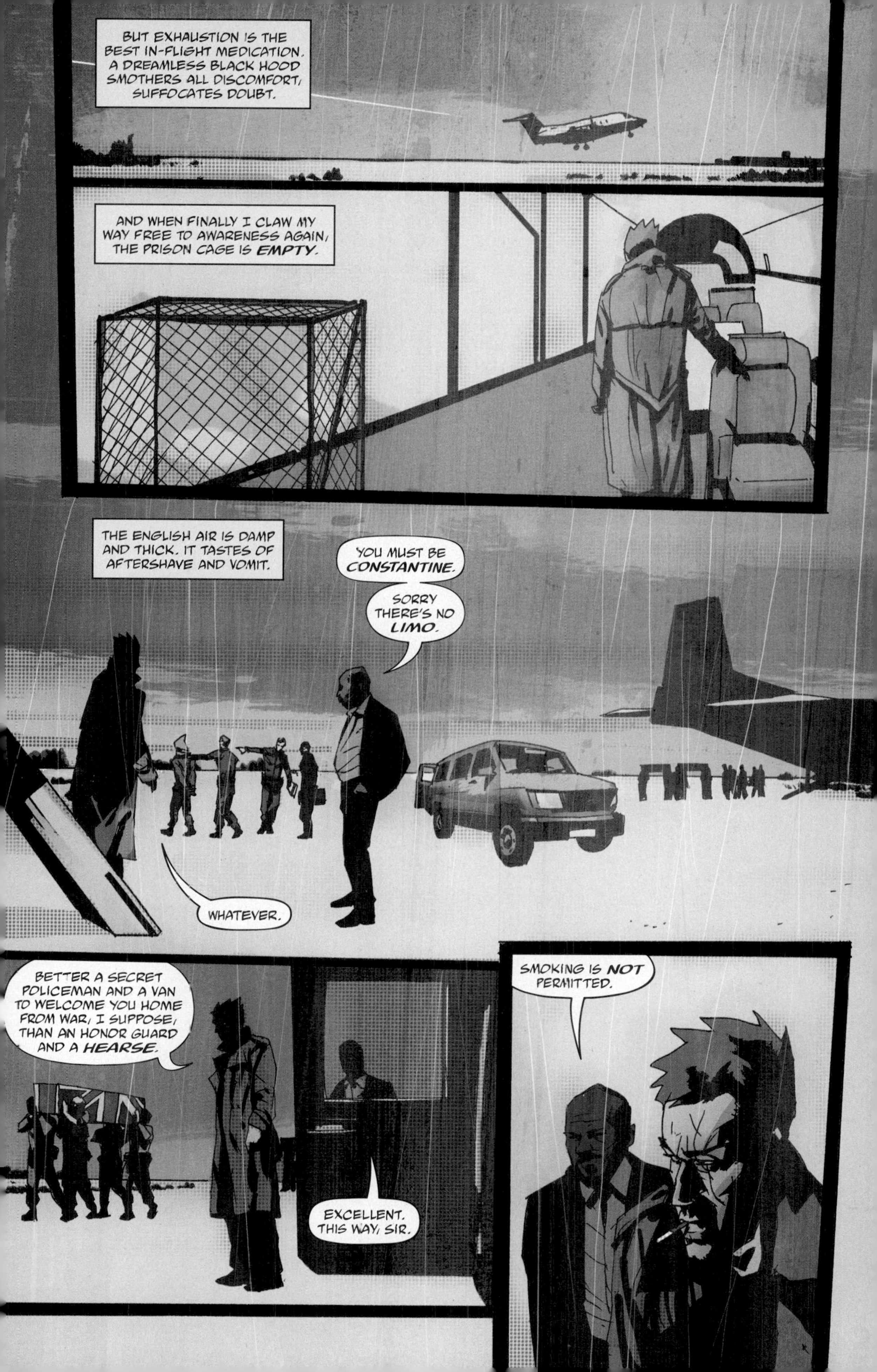
BUT EXHAUSTION IS THE BEST IN-FLIGHT MEDICATION. A DREAMLESS BLACK HOOD SMOTHERS ALL DISCOMFORT, SUFFOCATES DOUBT.
AND WHEN FINALLY I CLAW MY WAY FREE TO AWARENESS AGAIN, THE PRISON CAGE IS *EMPTY*.
THE ENGLISH AIR IS DAMP AND THICK. IT TASTES OF AFTERSHAVE AND VOMIT.
YOU MUST BE **CONSTANTINE**.
SORRY THERE'S NO *LIMO*.
WHATEVER.
BETTER A SECRET POLICEMAN AND A VAN TO WELCOME YOU HOME FROM WAR, I SUPPOSE, THAN AN HONOR GUARD AND A *HEARSE*.
EXCELLENT. THIS WAY, SIR.
SMOKING IS **NOT** PERMITTED.

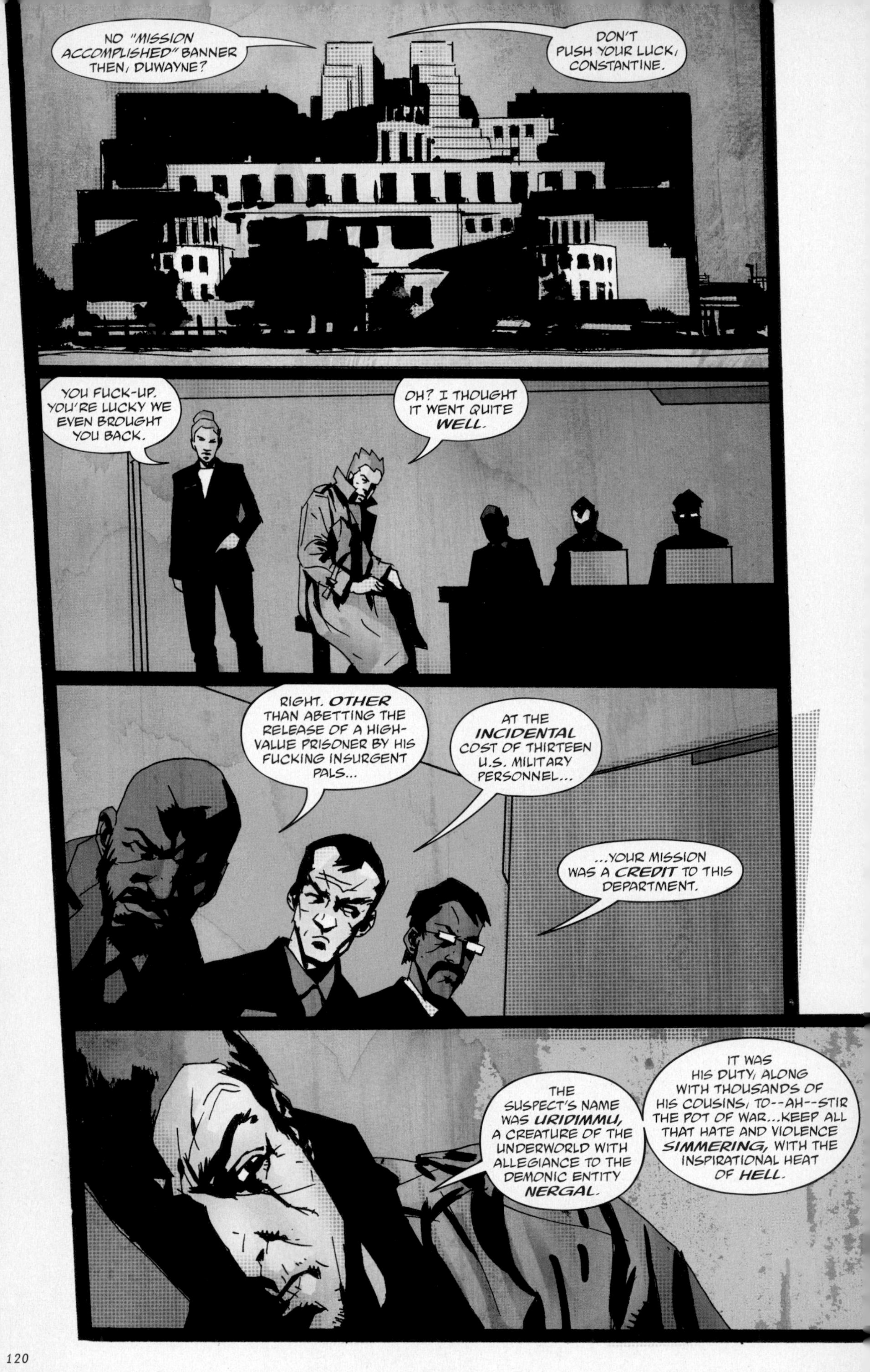
NO "MISSION ACCOMPLISHED" BANNER THEN, DUWAYNE?
DON'T PUSH YOUR LUCK, CONSTANTINE.
YOU FUCK-UP. YOU'RE LUCKY WE EVEN BROUGHT YOU BACK.
OH? I THOUGHT IT WENT QUITE WELL.
RIGHT. OTHER THAN ABETTING THE RELEASE OF A HIGH-VALUE PRISONER BY HIS FUCKING INSURGENT PALS...
AT THE INCIDENTAL COST OF THIRTEEN U.S. MILITARY PERSONNEL...
...YOUR MISSION WAS A CREDIT TO THIS DEPARTMENT.
THE SUSPECT'S NAME WAS URIDIMMU, A CREATURE OF THE UNDERWORLD WITH ALLEGIANCE TO THE DEMONIC ENTITY NERGAL.
IT WAS HIS DUTY, ALONG WITH THOUSANDS OF HIS COUSINS, TO--AH--STIR THE POT OF WAR...KEEP ALL THAT HATE AND VIOLENCE SIMMERING, WITH THE INSPIRATIONAL HEAT OF HELL.

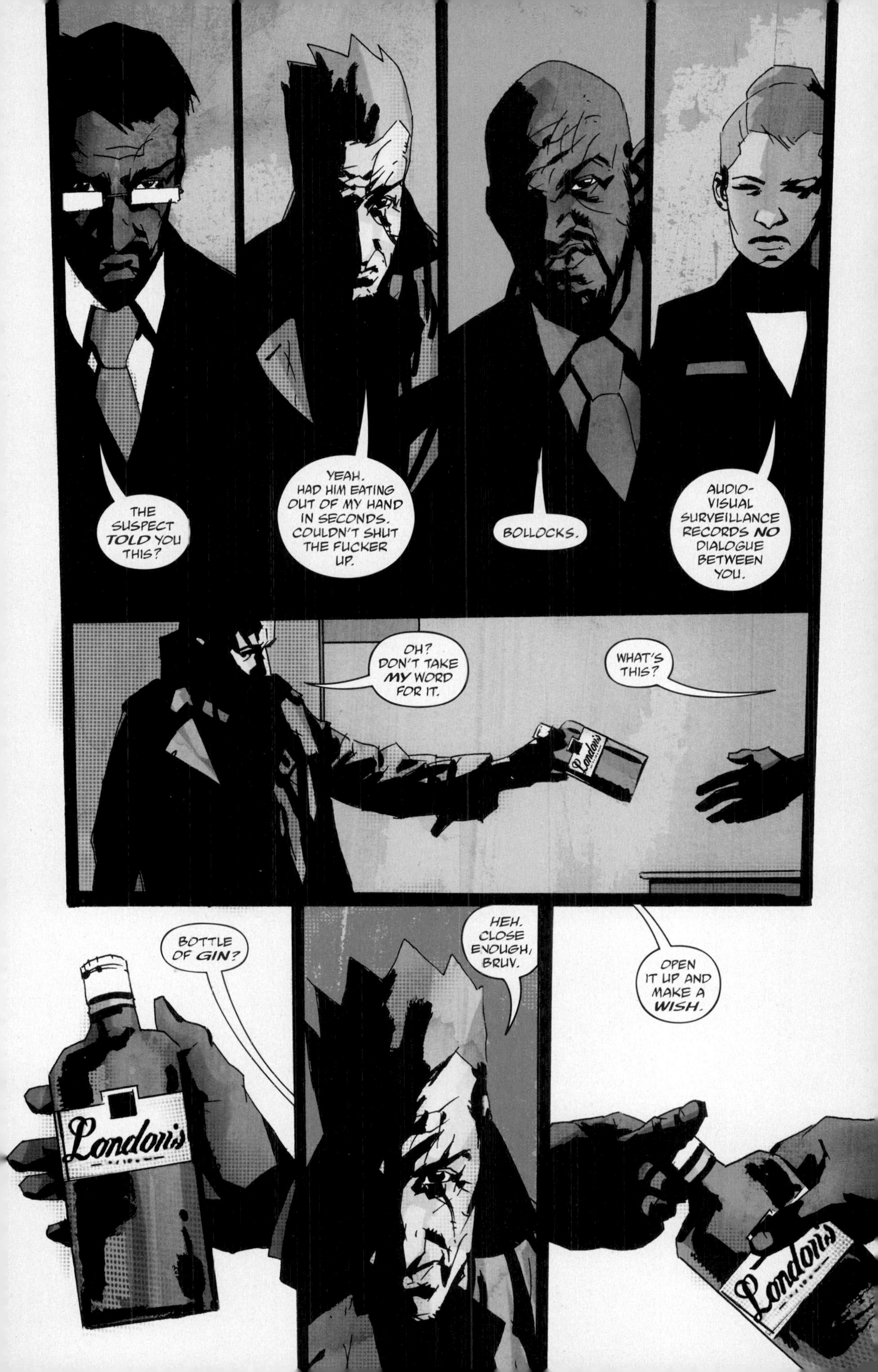
THE SUSPECT TOLD YOU THIS?
YEAH. HAD HIM EATING OUT OF MY HAND IN SECONDS. COULDN'T SHUT THE FUCKER UP.
BOLLOCKS.
AUDIO-VISUAL SURVEILLANCE RECORDS NO DIALOGUE BETWEEN YOU.
OH? DON'T TAKE MY WORD FOR IT.
WHAT'S THIS?
London's
BOTTLE OF GIN?
London's
HEH. CLOSE ENOUGH, BRUV.
OPEN IT UP AND MAKE A WISH.
London's

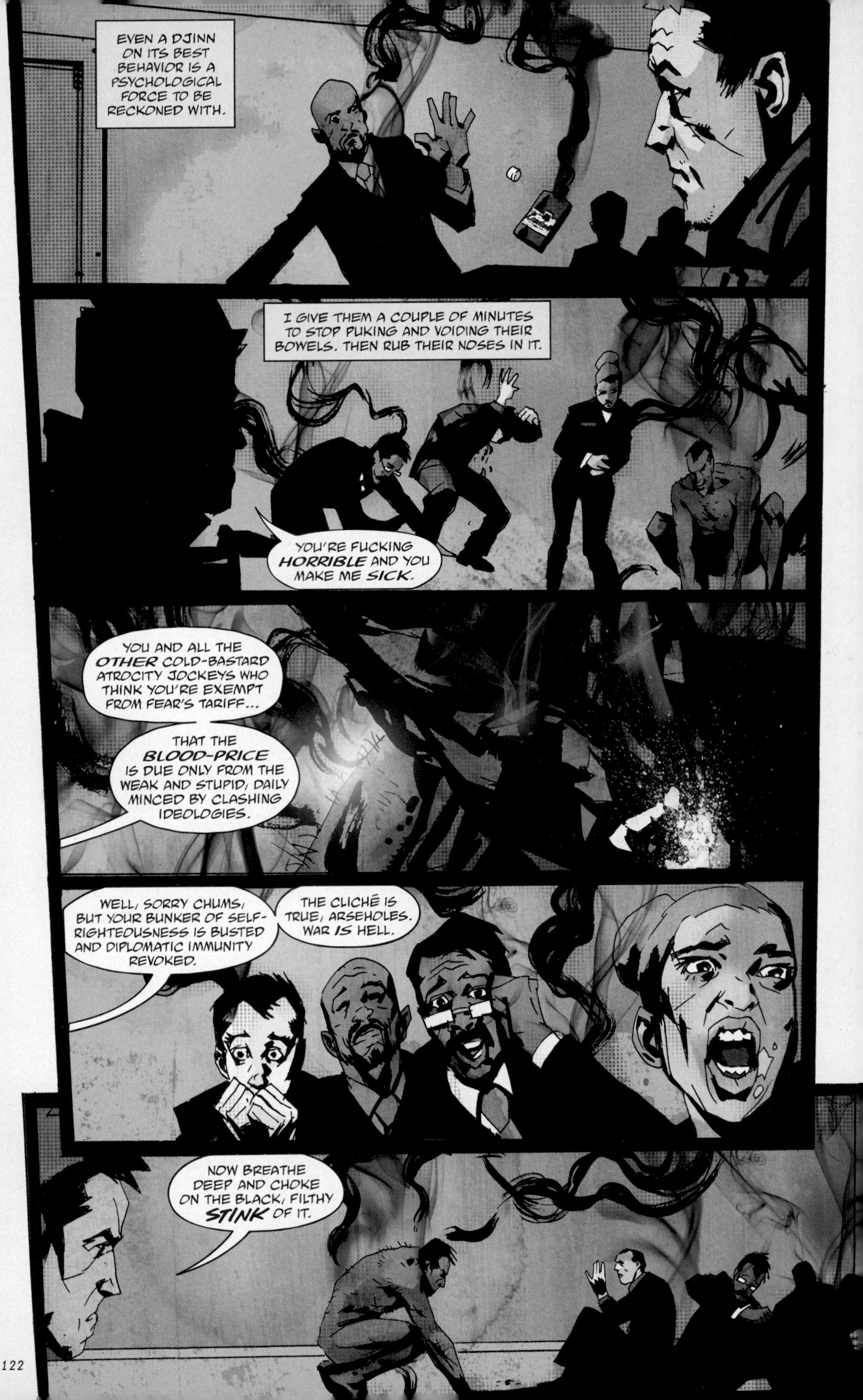
EVEN A DJINN ON ITS BEST BEHAVIOR IS A PSYCHOLOGICAL FORCE TO BE RECKONED WITH.
I GIVE THEM A COUPLE OF MINUTES TO STOP PUKING AND VOIDING THEIR BOWELS. THEN RUB THEIR NOSES IN IT.
YOU'RE FUCKING HORRIBLE AND YOU MAKE ME SICK.
YOU AND ALL THE OTHER COLD-BASTARD ATROCITY JOCKEYS WHO THINK YOU'RE EXEMPT FROM FEAR'S TARIFF...
THAT THE BLOOD-PRICE IS DUE ONLY FROM THE WEAK AND STUPID, DAILY MINCED BY CLASHING IDEOLOGIES.
WELL, SORRY CHUMS, BUT YOUR BUNKER OF SELF-RIGHTEOUSNESS IS BUSTED AND DIPLOMATIC IMMUNITY REVOKED.
THE CLICHÉ IS TRUE, ARSEHOLES. WAR IS HELL.
NOW BREATHE DEEP AND CHOKE ON THE BLACK, FILTHY STINK OF IT.

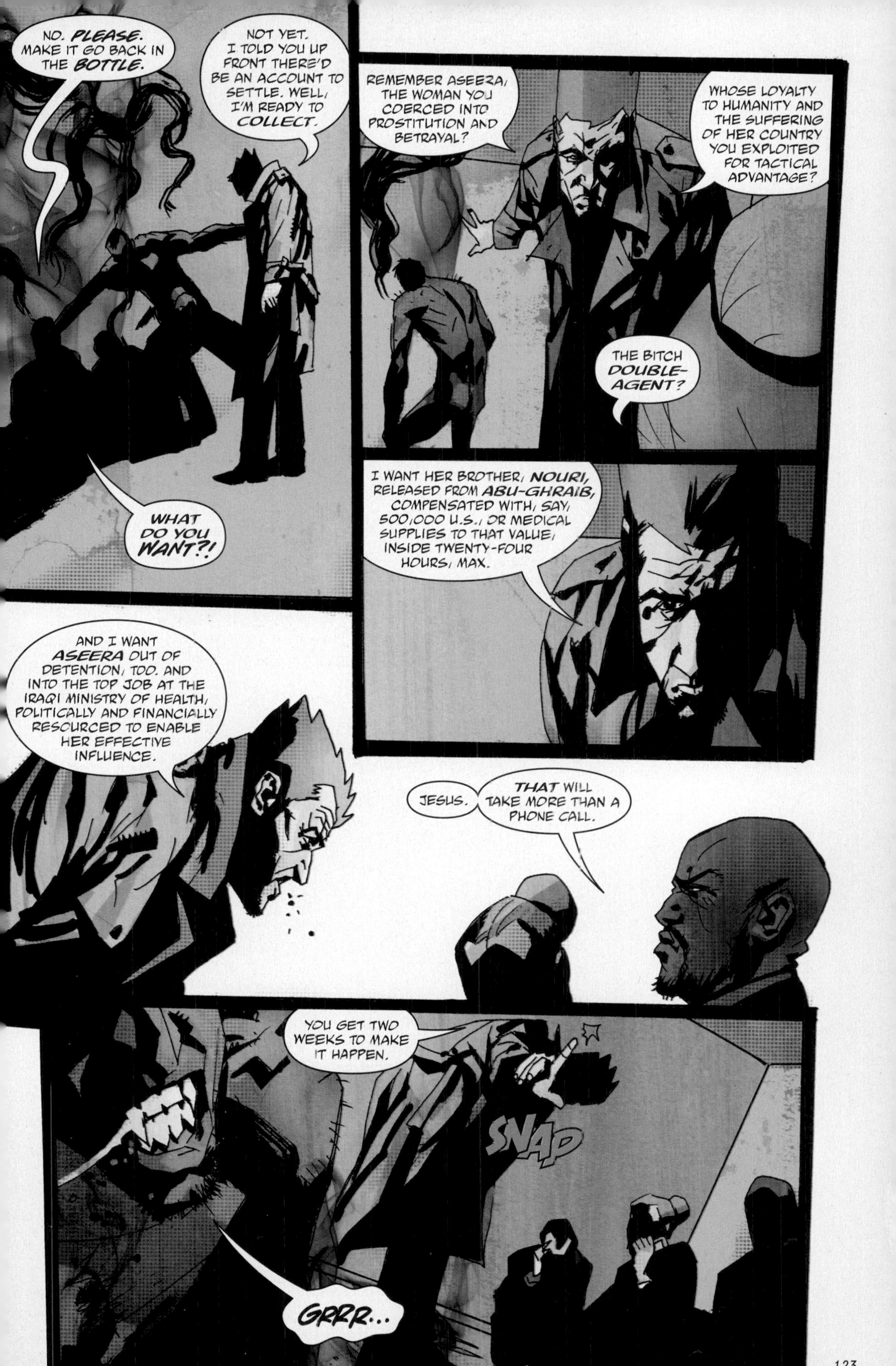
NO. PLEASE. MAKE IT GO BACK IN THE BOTTLE.
NOT YET. I TOLD YOU UP FRONT THERE'D BE AN ACCOUNT TO SETTLE. WELL, I'M READY TO COLLECT.
WHAT DO YOU WANT?!
REMEMBER ASEERA, THE WOMAN YOU COERCED INTO PROSTITUTION AND BETRAYAL?
WHOSE LOYALTY TO HUMANITY AND THE SUFFERING OF HER COUNTRY YOU EXPLOITED FOR TACTICAL ADVANTAGE?
THE BITCH DOUBLE-AGENT?
I WANT HER BROTHER, NOURI, RELEASED FROM ABU-GHRAIB, COMPENSATED WITH, SAY, 500,000 U.S., OR MEDICAL SUPPLIES TO THAT VALUE, INSIDE TWENTY-FOUR HOURS, MAX.
AND I WANT ASEERA OUT OF DETENTION, TOO. AND INTO THE TOP JOB AT THE IRAQI MINISTRY OF HEALTH, POLITICALLY AND FINANCIALLY RESOURCED TO ENABLE HER EFFECTIVE INFLUENCE.
JESUS.
THAT WILL TAKE MORE THAN A PHONE CALL.
YOU GET TWO WEEKS TO MAKE IT HAPPEN.
SNAP
GRRR...

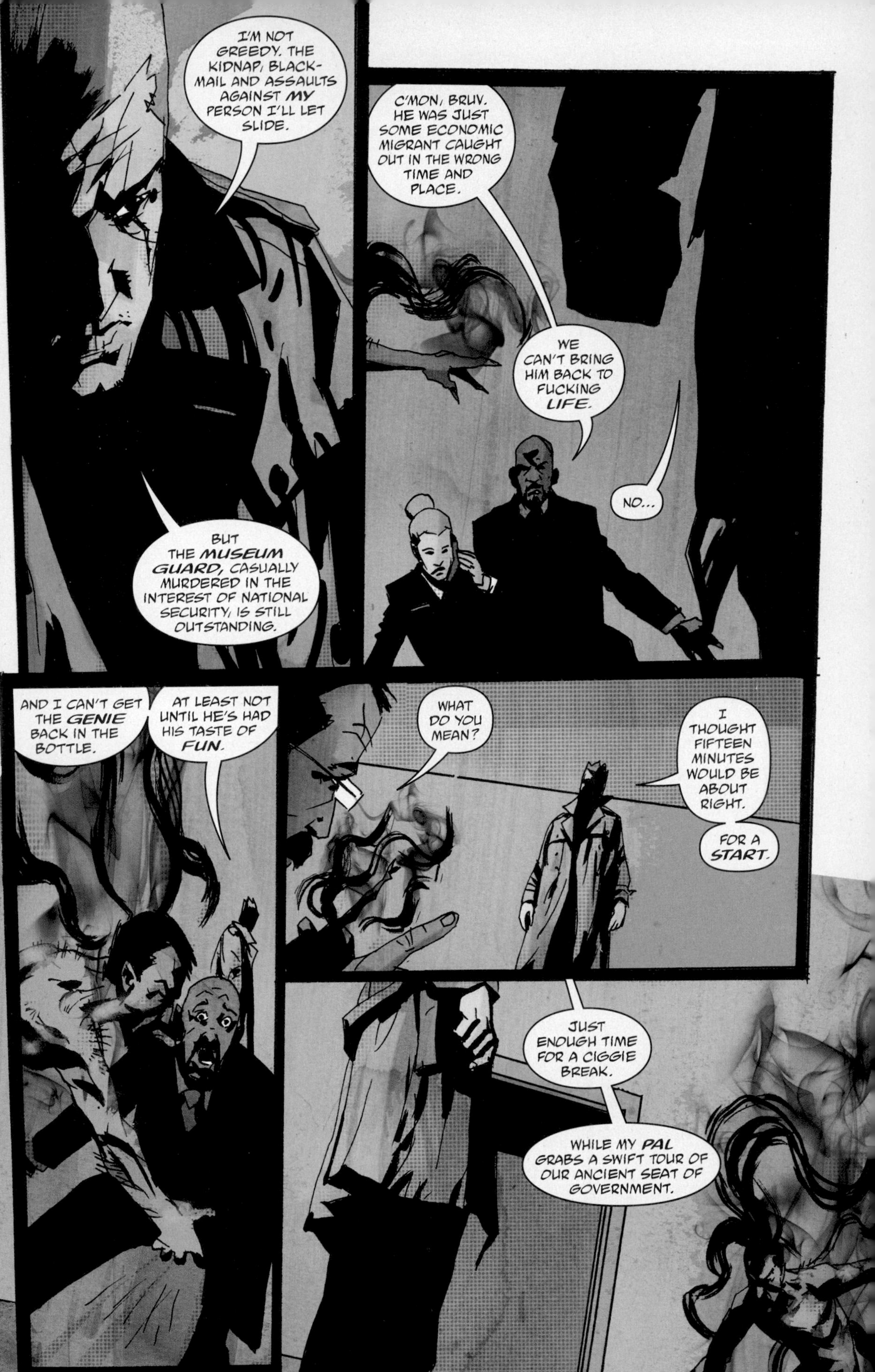
I'M NOT GREEDY. THE KIDNAP, BLACK-MAIL AND ASSAULTS AGAINST MY PERSON I'LL LET SLIDE.
BUT THE MUSEUM GUARD, CASUALLY MURDERED IN THE INTEREST OF NATIONAL SECURITY, IS STILL OUTSTANDING.
C'MON, BRUV. HE WAS JUST SOME ECONOMIC MIGRANT CAUGHT OUT IN THE WRONG TIME AND PLACE.
WE CAN'T BRING HIM BACK TO FUCKING LIFE.
NO...
AND I CAN'T GET THE GENIE BACK IN THE BOTTLE.
AT LEAST NOT UNTIL HE'S HAD HIS TASTE OF FUN.
WHAT DO YOU MEAN?
I THOUGHT FIFTEEN MINUTES WOULD BE ABOUT RIGHT.
FOR A START.
JUST ENOUGH TIME FOR A CIGGIE BREAK.
WHILE MY PAL GRABS A SWIFT TOUR OF OUR ANCIENT SEAT OF GOVERNMENT.

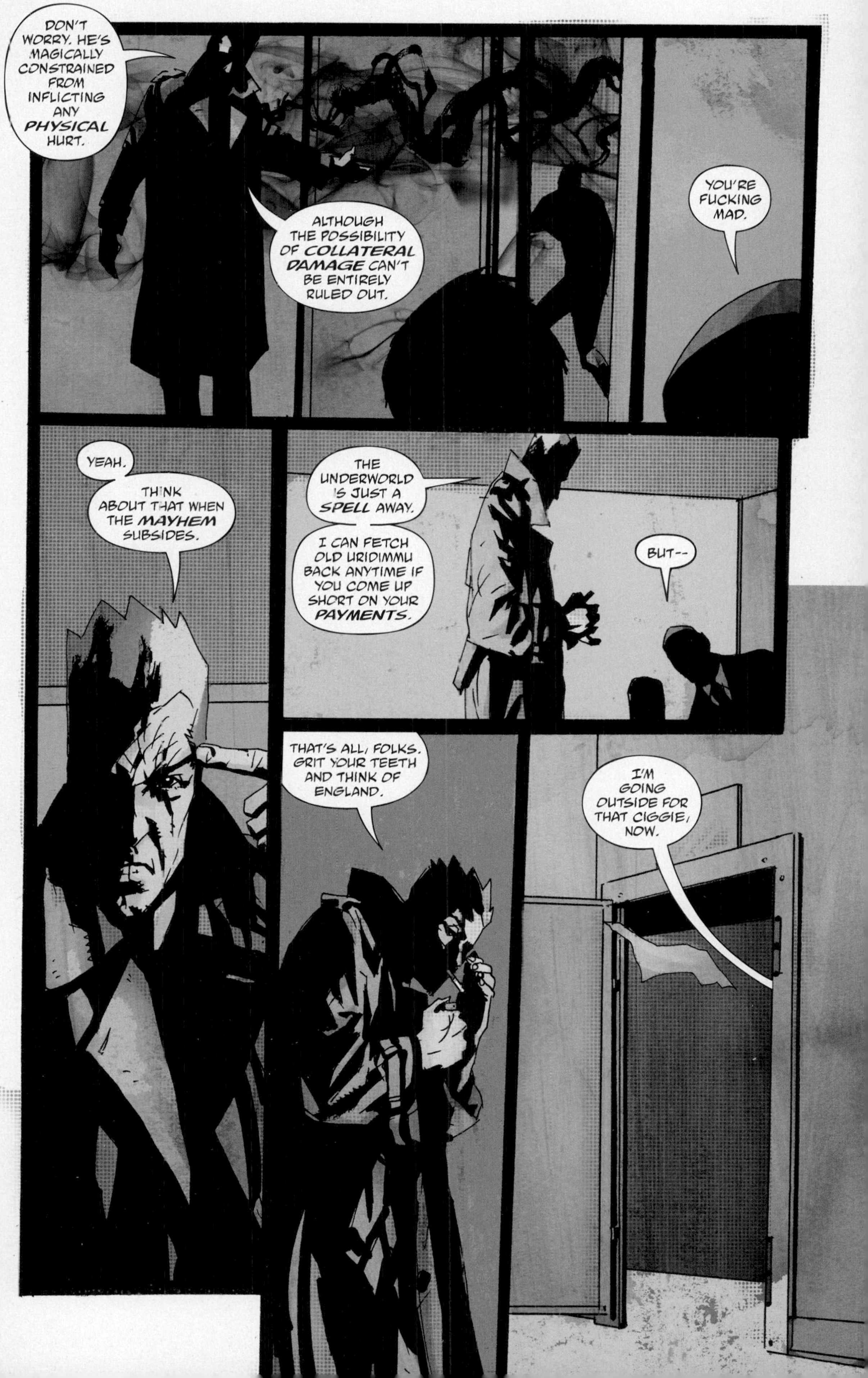
DON'T WORRY. HE'S MAGICALLY CONSTRAINED FROM INFLICTING ANY PHYSICAL HURT.
ALTHOUGH THE POSSIBILITY OF COLLATERAL DAMAGE CAN'T BE ENTIRELY RULED OUT.
YOU'RE FUCKING MAD.
YEAH.
THINK ABOUT THAT WHEN THE MAYHEM SUBSIDES.
THE UNDERWORLD IS JUST A SPELL AWAY.
I CAN FETCH OLD URIDIMMU BACK ANYTIME IF YOU COME UP SHORT ON YOUR PAYMENTS.
BUT--
THAT'S ALL, FOLKS. GRIT YOUR TEETH AND THINK OF ENGLAND.
I'M GOING OUTSIDE FOR THAT CIGGIE, NOW.

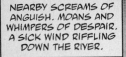

NEARBY SCREAMS OF ANGUISH. MOANS AND WHIMPERS OF DESPAIR. A SICK WIND RIFFLING DOWN THE RIVER.

HELICOPTERS SWARM OVER WESTMINSTER, ALERT TO THE ROTTEN STINK OF EMERGENCY. WHITEHALL HOWLS WITH A PANIC OF SIRENS.

BUT THE SUMMARY EXECUTION OF VICTIMS' ROUGH JUSTICE SEEMS SUDDENLY MORE PETTY THAN POETIC. JUST ANOTHER POINTLESS, SPITEFUL SNARL OF TERROR.

BLAME THE GODS' COLD MACHINATIONS, OR THE FUNDAMENTAL VIOLENCE OF HUMAN NATURE; BUT WHICH OF US WITH THE PRIVILEGE TO VOTE CAN CLAIM INNOCENCE FOR THE FILTHY CRIME OF WAR?

WE HAVE THE *CHOICE* WHO LEADS US, APATHETIC, INTO *PANDEMONIUM*.

BUT WHAT THE FUCKING HELL, EH? SHOULDN'T *JOIN* IF YOU CAN'T TAKE A FUCKING JOKE.

CHAS. WESTMINSTER FUCKING BRIDGE. OUTSIDE FUCKING COUNTY HALL.

AND MAKE IT FUCKING *SNAPPY*, MATE.

I NEED A FUCKING *DRINK*.

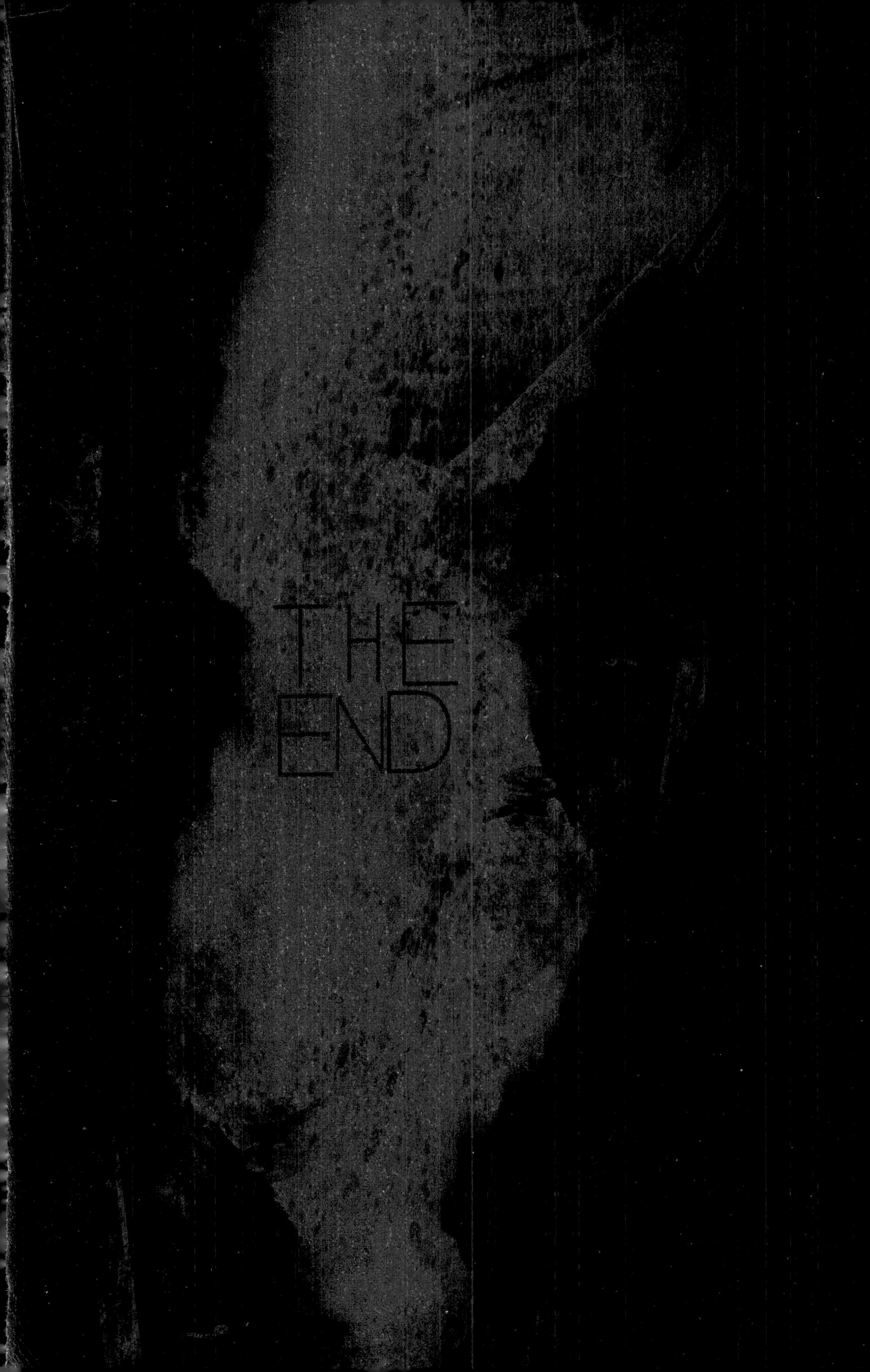
THE
END

THE JOHN CONSTANTINE, HELLBLAZER AUTHOR'S GUIDE

JAMIE DELANO

ORIGINAL SINS
Collecting issues #1-9
Art by John Ridgway
and Alfredo Alcala

THE DEVIL YOU KNOW
Collecting issues #10-13,
Annual #1 and The Horrorist 1-2
Art by Mark Buckingham,
David Lloyd and others

THE FEAR MACHINE
Collecting issues #14-22
Art by Mark Buckingham,
Richard Piers Rayner and others

THE FAMILY MAN
Collecting issues #23-24, 28-33
Art by Ron Tiner, Kevin Walker,
Mark Buckingham, Sean Phillips,
Steve Pugh, Dean Motter
and Mark Pennington

RARE CUTS
Collecting issues #25-26,35,56,84
Written by Jamie Delano,
Grant Morrison and Garth Ennis
Art by Sean Phillips, David
Lloyd, Richard Piers Rayner
and Mark Buckingham

GARTH ENNIS

DANGEROUS HABITS
Collecting issues #41-46
Art by William Simpson
and others

BLOODLINES
Collecting issues #47-50,
52-55, 59-61
Art by Will Simpson,
Steve Dillon, Mike Barreiro
and Kim DeMulder

FEAR AND LOATHING
Collecting issues #62-67
Art by Steve Dillon

TAINTED LOVE
Collecting issues #68-71
Art by Steve Dillon and others

DAMNATION'S FLAME
collecting issues #72-77
Art by Steve Dillon, Peter
Snejbjerg and William Simpson

RAKE AT THE GATES OF HELL
Collecting issues #78-83
Art by Steve Dillon

SON OF MAN
Collecting issues #129-133
Art by John Higgins

WARREN ELLIS

HAUNTED
Collecting issues #134-139
Art by John Higgins

SETTING SUN
Collecting issues #140-143
Art by Frank Teran, Tim
Bradstreet, Marcelo Frusin,
Javier Pulido and James Romberger

BRIAN AZZARELLO

HARD TIME
Collecting issues #146-150
Art by Richard Corben

GOOD INTENTIONS
Collecting issues #151-156
Art by Marcelo Frusin

FREEZES OVER
Collecting issues #157-163
Art by Marcelo Frusin,
Guy Davis, and Steve Dillon

HIGHWATER
Collecting issues #164-174
Art by Marcelo Frusin, Giuseppe
Camuncoli and Cameron Stewart

MIKE CAREY

RED SEPULCHRE
Collecting issues #175-180
Art by Steve Dillon and
Marcelo Frusin

BLACK FLOWERS
Collecting issues #181-186
Art by Jock, Lee Bermejo
and Marcelo Frusin

STARING AT THE WALL
Collecting issues #187-193
Art by Marcelo Frusin and
Doug Alexander Gregory

STATIONS OF THE CROSS
Collecting issues #194-200
Art by Leonardo Manco,
Chris Brunner, Marcelo Frusin
and Steve Dillon

REASONS TO BE CHEERFUL
Collecting issues #201-206
Art by Leonardo Manco,
Giuseppe Camuncoli and others

THE GIFT
Collecting issues #207-215
Art by Leonardo Manco
and Frazer Irving

DENISE MINA

EMPATHY IS THE ENEMY
Collecting issues #216-222
Art by Leonardo Manco

THE RED RIGHT HAND
Collecting issues #223-228
Art by Leonardo Manco

ANDY DIGGLE

JOYRIDE
Collecting issues #230-237
Art by Leonardo Manco

THE LAUGHING MAGICIAN
Collecting issues #238-242
Art by Leonardo Manco and
Danijel Zezelj

THE ROOTS OF COINCIDENCE
Collecting issues #243-244, 247-249
Art by Leonardo Manco and
Giuseppe Camuncoli

PETER MILLIGAN

SCAB
Collecting issues # 250-255
Art by Giuseppe Camuncoli,
Stefano Landini, Goran Sudžuka
and Eddie Campbell

**Look for these other
important HELLBLAZER
collections:**

LADY CONSTANTINE
Written by Andy Diggle
Art by Goran Sudžuka

PAPA MIDNITE
Written by Mat Johnson
Art by Tony Akins and Dan Green

CHAS — THE KNOWLEDGE
Written by Simon Oliver
Art by Goran Sudžuka